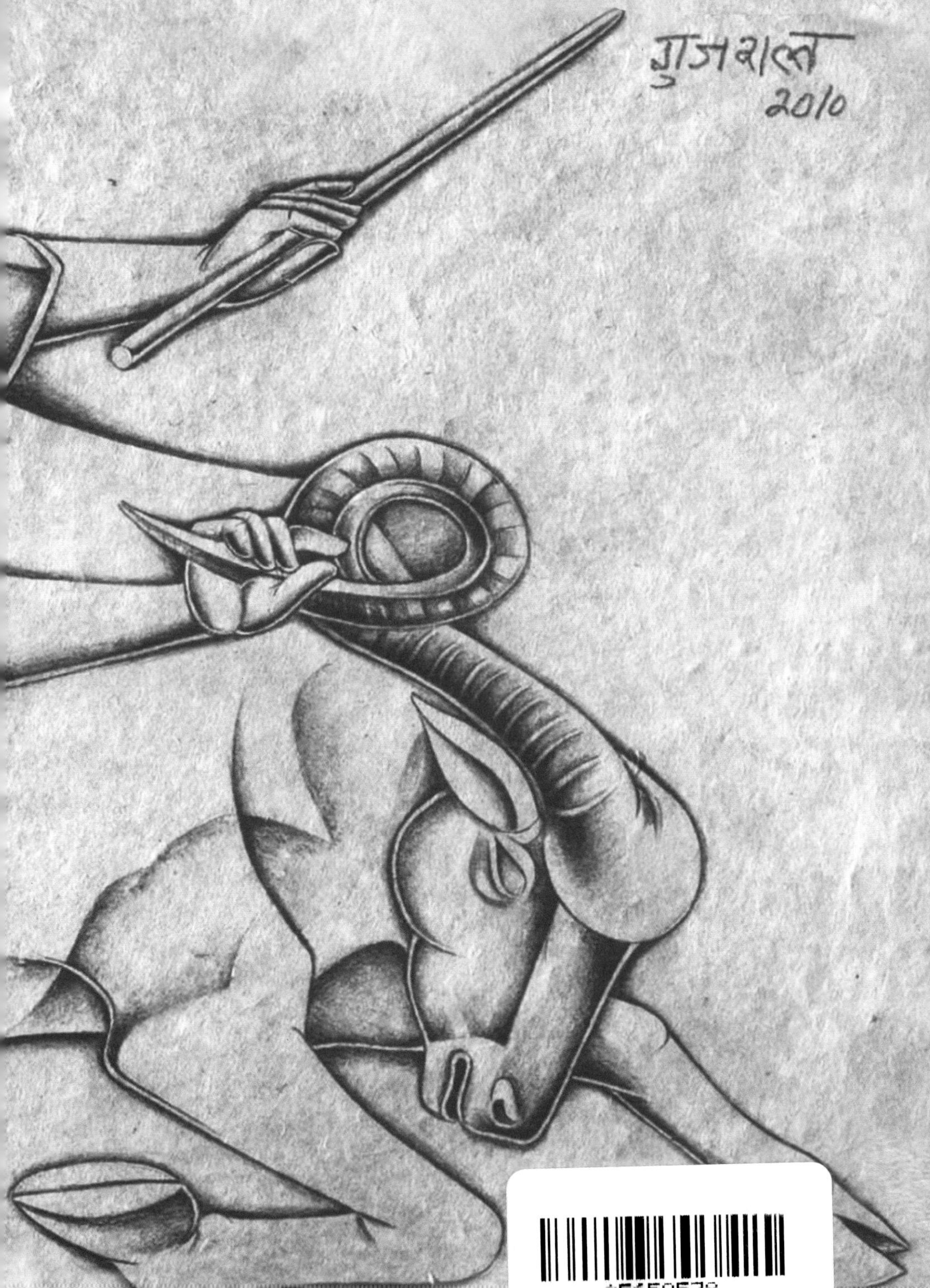
गुजराल
2010

A Brush with Life

A Brush with Life

AN AUTOBIOGRAPHY

SATISH GUJRAL

FOREWORD BY

KHUSHWANT SINGH

HarperCollins *Publishers* India

This edition published in India by HarperCollins *Publishers* 2026
HarperCollins *Publishers* India, Cyber City,
Building 10-A, Gurugram, Haryana – 122002, India
www.harpercollins.co.in

First published in India by Penguin Books India (P) Ltd 1997

2 4 6 8 10 9 7 5 3 1

P-ISBN: 978-93-7307-890-8
E-ISBN: 978-93-7307-756-7

Typeset in 12/16 Adobe Garamond Pro
by HarperCollins *Publishers* India Pvt. Ltd

Printed and bound at
Replika Press Pvt. Ltd.

MIX
Paper | Supporting responsible forestry
FSC™ C016779

This book is produced from independently certified FSC® paper to ensure responsible forest management.

*

HarperCollins *Publishers*, Macken House, 39/40 Mayor Street Upper, Dublin 1, D01 C9W8, Ireland

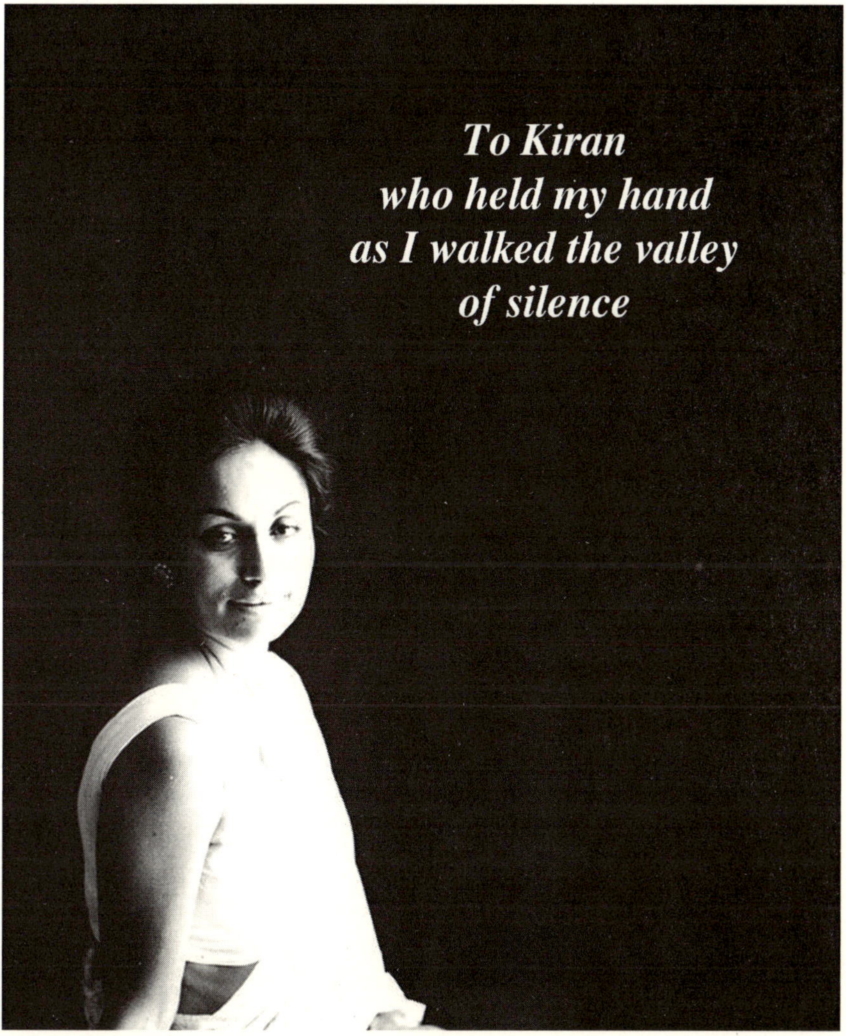
To Kiran
who held my hand
as I walked the valley
of silence

روشنی کا وہی چشمہ تھا
جسے ہر کوئی خوبصورت سمجھتا تھا
اور یہ وہی خواب تھا جو کبھی دماغ تک نہیں پہنچا۔

Wohi chashma-e-baqa tha
Jise sab surab samjhe
Wohii khwab motbir the
Jo khayal tak na pahunche

—Faiz Ahmad Faiz

(What everyone took to be a mirage
Turned out to be a 'perennial spring'
The very dreams we thought were idle
Fantasies turned out to be life realities

—Translated by Khushwant Singh)

روشنی کا وہی چشمہ تھا
جسے ہر کوئی خوبصورت سمجھتا تھا

Contents

FOREWORD TO THE CENTENARY EDITION

Mohit Gujral

WHEN *A BRUSH WITH LIFE* WAS FIRST PUBLISHED THREE DECADES AGO, it offered the world a rare window into the extraordinary journey of my father, Satish Gujral—a man who defied odds, disciplines and definitions. Born into tumult, shaped by silence and driven by an uncompromising creative instinct, he lived a life that was both personal and political, rooted and expansive, Indian and universal.

As his son, and as someone who worked closely with him in the world of architecture for nearly two decades, I had the privilege of seeing dimensions of him that extended far beyond what this book could contain. Yet this autobiography remains a foundational portrait—his own account of a life that was anything but ordinary.

Now, as we mark his centenary, we return to this book not just to remember the man, but to re-engage with the spirit of his time, and to offer new generations a chance to encounter the force that was Satish

Gujral. His legacy today lives not only in canvases and buildings, but in conversations about identity, resilience, expression and the role of an artist in society.

This edition preserves the original text as it was written in his voice, but now includes a newly written foreword and epilogue—my own reflections on the decades that followed, our partnership as father and son and the enduring values that shaped our family.

Time has only sharpened the relevance of his story. His refusal to be boxed into one form or one ideology is, perhaps, his most powerful lesson.

It is with pride, gratitude and deep love that I present this centenary edition of *A Brush with Life*. May it continue to inspire, provoke and illuminate—as his life always did.

New Delhi, August 2025

FOREWORD

Khushwant Singh

THERE ARE MANY REASONS WHY I READILY AGREED TO COLLABORATE with Satish Gujral on the project of writing his autobiography. At first I thought he wanted me to write his life story. I agreed to do so. When he clarified that he wished to write it himself and only wanted me to revise and edit it, I accepted the second alternative with equal alacrity. I did so because Satish Gujral is the most outstanding man I have met in my life. I was eager to be a part of the unfolding of his career from childhood to the present time.

Everyone who is anyone knows that Satish Gujral is stone-deaf and communication with him has to be through writing or with the assistance of his lovely wife, Kiran. But not many people know that he lost his hearing when he was only eight years old. At that time he knew how to read and write Urdu and speak Punjabi. For some years after losing his hearing, he communicated only in these languages. He was sent to the school for the deaf and dumb in Delhi, where he discovered that learning sign language would restrict his world to the deaf and the mute and might impair his power of speech as well. He refused to give in and shifted to the Mayo School of Arts in Lahore. He kept up his knowledge of Urdu by extensive reading of Urdu poetry, novels, biographies and whatever else he could lay his hands on. From Mayo, he went on to the JJ School of Arts in Bombay. There hardly any of his fellow students knew Urdu or Punjabi. He taught himself a smattering of English. Without being able to hear the sounds of English words, he was able to speak and read the language in a matter of months.

Overcoming the handicap of deafness was the least part of Satish Gujral's achievements. A few years after Partition, he won a scholarship to study in Mexico. From the sales of his canvases in Mexico City and New York, he was able to travel through Europe before he returned to India. Recognition came to him by slow steps.

His portrait of Lala Lajpat Rai hangs in the Central Hall of Parliament. His portrait of Pandit Nehru and Indira Gandhi are in Anand Bhavan, the Nehrus' ancestral home in Allahabad. His paintings and sculpture can be seen in private collections and art galleries the world over. It was through him that his elder brother Inder, who acted as his interpreter, got to know Pandit Nehru and Indira Gandhi. He was first inducted into municipal politics, and then made a cabinet minister. He is today India's first Punjabi Prime Minister.

No better example of personal courage and striving for excellence can be found in India and perhaps the world. Satish Gujral is among the highest-rated painters, muralists, sculptors and architects in the country. Without any degree or training in architecture, he has designed many private and public buildings, including the Belgian Embassy in New Delhi.

An equally good reason for my eagerness to collaborate with Satish Gujral is the nature of what he has to say about himself. You will not find a sentence expressing self-pity in this entire narrative. There are many references to how he was hurt by ill-mannered, thoughtless remarks from people around him; he dismisses these people as individuals who knew no better. Far too often he mocks himself, as for example his attempt to increase his height by seeking 'medical' advice from a quack in Ahmedabad who turned out to be as short as himself. His dealings with immigration and customs officials in Britain, the US and Mexico when there was no one around to help him, his being lost in London without a penny in his pocket and without the address of his host, his arrival in Mexico City at night where there was no one to meet him at the railway station, and where he did not know how to go about finding place to sleep—such incidents make the reader's hair stand on end. His incorrigible optimism helped him to overcome every hurdle in his way. And more incredible is the fact that despite his handicap he was able to win the hearts of women he met. Right from the day he boarded that ship which was to take him to England, some young woman or the other was taken up by him: Polynesians, Mexicans and Americans in quick succession, and occasionally, more than one woman at the same time. Finally came his meeting with Kiran, the daughter of Delhi's leading dental surgeon. In the face of strong opposition from her father and stepmother, Kiran eloped with Satish and became his wife when he had little or nothing to offer her by way of material comforts. She bore him three children and became his chief intermediary with the hearing world. From her photograph reproduced in this book you can see yourself that she was probably the loveliest woman to come into his life.

Satish has pronounced views on the architecture of Lutyens' New Delhi and Le Corbusier's Chandigarh, and also on the works of celebrities such as Amrita Sher-Gil and M.F. Husain. They are highly controversial and provocative. I have not read anything as outrageously candid as what he has to say about them.

There is a lot of wit and irony in Satish Gujral's autobiography. It makes very pleasant reading, and at the same time will be a source of inspiration to the younger generation. It is the absorbing story of a man with an indomitable will, who overcame all the handicaps inflicted by nature and made his life a grand success. What faith wills, fate fulfils.

New Delhi, 1997

1

JHELUM: CHILDHOOD YEARS

I WAS BORN IN JHELUM (NOW IN PAKISTAN) ON CHRISTMAS DAY, 1925. My date of birth was registered with the local registrar of births and deaths at the municipal office across the street from our house. Though the official document was lost, the exact hour of my arrival on earth could be worked out from my mother's recollections of the event. Labour pains began before the first holiday when the courts closed for Christmas. She remembered it clearly because it was the first time in the course of her nine deliveries that my father happened to be at home. Mai Khitajan, the midwife, emerged from the darkened bedroom to announce my arrival.

My father Avtar Narain was a lawyer. He was born in a tiny hamlet lost in the ravines encircling Jhelum. The town derived its name from the river which ran by it.

My father was the second of Duni Chand's three sons. My grandfather was Naib Tehsildar in the district of Multan, serving the newly established English government. Multan was more than two hundred kilometres downstream. The river was the chief means of transport of men and material between Jhelum and the towns situated along its banks, down to its junction with the Indus and onwards to the Arabian Sea.

The entire family lived in the same village. Just when he was due to retire, Dada Dhuni Chand lost his wife. Soon after, he himself fell victim to the epidemic of bubonic plague that swept across the region in the first decade of the twentieth century. He was lucky to have died without discovering that in his absence his elder son had squandered all his savings in a foolish business venture, and had disappeared.

It was not clear how my father, then only ten years old, chose to move to Jammu in Kashmir state where a branch of the Gujral clan had settled. He took with him his younger brother Narsingh Narain, then only seven. But the family certainly helped him in one way or another to pursue his studies till his matriculation examination. Then he moved to the DAV College, Lahore. This institution was the hub of the Arya Samaj reformist Hindu movement as well as a hot bed of nationalism. The clan refused to help further, as studies beyond matriculation were not considered necessary, especially when one had no means of supporting oneself. But my father had set his sights beyond the Bachelor of Arts degree. He not only managed to get through his B.A. but joined the Law College and got his LLB. He then set up practice in Jhelum.

The Jhelum was mightiest of the five rivers that gave Punjab its name, deriving from the words *panj* (five) and *aab* (waters). By the time it reached our town, it was an expanse of water stretching more than a mile from one bank to the other.

In the early years of his legal practice my father decided to turn himself into an English country gentleman. He dressed in a black coat and striped trousers. Not content with making himself into a brown sahib, he made my mother follow suit. She gave up wearing *kameez* and *sutthan* (shirt and salwar) for a sari, accompanied her husband to the club, played badminton and did all that fitted with a Westernized lifestyle.

However, during his days in Lahore, the influence of Lala Lajpat Rai, the fiery Arya Samaj nationalist, had taken deep root in my father's psyche. Till then his energy was confined to reforming the Hindu social system. In the mid-1920s Lajpat Rai turned from a religious reformer into a Gandhian nationalist. Following Lajpat Rai's example, my father became a staunch supporter of everything *swadeshi* (indigenous), forsaking all that was *videshi* (foreign) in manufacture or flavour.

These transformations reached us children through our mother. Our house stood as a not-so-mute testimonial to our father's anglicized years. The rooms were not just places to accommodate four charpais to sleep on, but divided according to function: one for receiving visitors; one to eat in; one for the parents and one for the children. We also had a garage which was shared by a car and two buffaloes which my mother had brought in her dowry. The buffaloes kept us supplied with fresh creamy milk morning and evening. The car, which was seldom used, gradually became derelict till only its skeleton remained. My father found many uses for its parts. The chassis was jacked up and the wheels hung on the walls. We took out the tubes to use as life-belts when we went for a swim in the river. My mother made good use of the car seats. Whenever she had guests, she retrieved them from the godown to be used as sofas for the more sophisticated visitors.

The only room which remained inviolate was the *daftar* (office), where my father received his clients. Apart from a large table with its paraphernalia of files, inkpots, pens and pencils, it had rows of almirahs with shelves full of law books. My father made little use of this room as he preferred to sit in the veranda which was airy and lined with potted plants.

The *daftar* soon acquired an elevated status when an electric fan was fitted into the ceiling. It was the first such object in the town and provided the family the coolest room in the house to while away the long, hot summer days.

My mother was a handsome woman. During the brief period that my father aped the lifestyle of the sahibs, she learnt to take care of her looks—a habit that was not viewed favourably in traditional households. Even after she gave up the idea of becoming a *desi* memsahib and took to wearing white *dhotis* of hand-spun *khadi*, she managed to look very elegant. She relished compliments paid to her.

My mother was born in a small village about fifteen kilometres down the river. She was the youngest of the brood of children of the village *sahukar* (moneylender) who was also an *aarhti* (grain trader). She was taught a little Urdu and Gurmukhi.

Pushpa was not the name given to my mother by her parents. My father chose it for her in keeping with Hindu custom by which girls were given a new name by their husbands. It symbolized the acquisition of new property. Her first name was Nido, which was too rustic for my father's taste. So he renamed her Pushpa from the Sanskrit word *pushp* (flower).

My parent's zeal for adopting western lifestyle created a distance between our family and the neighbours. My father accentuated this by making certain alterations in the house he had rented. Originally the house, though it stood in the chowk that was part of the Civil Lines, had no frontal opening; instead its only entrance faced the lane that sliced through the *mohalla* ending at the chowk. By shifting the entrance towards the chowk, my father seemed to have tried to sever what little remained of relations between us and the other families of the *mohalla* and its culture.

My mother, whose conversion to the Civil Lines culture had never been more than skin deep, had her own views on the subject. She ensured that the old entrance which was now in the rear remained intact and kept open from dawn to dusk. This foresight on her part sustained an artery of communication between her and the people of the locality. It facilitated their re-accepting us when my father's conversion to the Swadeshi movement gathered momentum.

Despite his admiration of the British style of living, my father responded enthusiastically to Gandhiji's call for non-cooperation with the government, and boycott of foreign goods. This volte-face took place after long introspection. But once the decision was made, he never looked back. He did not hesitate to make a bonfire of his suits made of imported cloth. Not content with this, he made my mother follow suit. She was utterly bewildered and wept before she gave in to her husband's wishes and consigned her cherished collection of foreign silk sarees, blouses and petticoats to the flames. In due course of time she even developed a sense of pride in having performed this dramatic act of renunciation. All she wanted to prove was that she had a will of her own by first protesting, and after having thought it over, acting of her own accord. But while my father's idealism made him indifferent to the outcome, my mother had strong faith that her sacrifice would not go unrewarded. She spoke with conviction of the imminent collapse of the British empire because so many sacrifices had been made to bring it down.

Our neighbours made snide remarks about our parent's eccentric behaviour. Even as a child I could sense the lofty disdain with which my parents treated what was said about them behind their backs or even in their presence. It only strengthened their resolve. One could not help but marvel at my mother's audacity when she led a *jaloos* (procession) shouting patriotic slogans through the streets. Although barely a dozen women followed her she was not discouraged. And she did not feel let down when her door-to-door appeals for *hartal* (closure of business) in protest of this or that cause received no response. When it came to political conviction both my parents seemed to exist in a sort of a trance where external pressures and realities did not affect them.

Like most Hindu nationalists of his generation, my father's political baptism came through the Arya Samaj. His revulsion for colonial rule was matched by his zeal to undo caste discrimination and religious bigotry prevalent in Hindu society. The townspeople took a tolerant view of his politics, considering him involved in a quixotic battle with the government. However, his crusade against age-old beliefs was not acceptable to them. I am not sure if my mother was opposed to my father's views on the need to reform Hindu society or only wanted to avoid another period of estrangements with her neighbours, but she remained cool towards his reformist zeal. With the family espousing *swadeshi* and the days of the Civil Club behind her, she painstakingly strove to re-establish contact with people of the *mohalla* by keeping the *deoadi* (entrance) open to them.

My mother recalled her husband's obstinate determination to prove that he meant to practise what he preached, when he invited one hundred of the city's *bhangis* (scavengers) to dine in our house to celebrate Diwali. He went further and served them food in my mother's brass *thalis* that she had brought in her dowry. The *biradari* (relations) were outraged and threatened to sever all connections with us. To pacify them, my mother sold the thalis to a *kabariwalla* (junk dealer).

My father was obsessed with patronizing the afflicted and the underprivileged. He would buy things only from the shops that had the least *bikri* (sales), regardless of the quality of their merchandise. This attitude influenced his choice of my first school. It was 'private' establishment, the *dhabha* (wayside eatery) version of a public school. It had two small rooms, one on top of the other and could barely contain its four grades of students. It was in fact the residence of Master Diwan Chand, commonly known as 'Diwan Chand Jhalla (Crazy)'. However crazy he may have been, he was not crazy enough to believe that so many boys could be packed into such small rooms and still be effectively instructed.

The rooms which otherwise accommodated Master Jhalla, his wife and three grown-up children, were temporarily used for students during school hours. The overflow had to squat on jute mattresses spread out on the road in front of the 'school'.

The arrangement was washed out during the monsoons. It did not matter very much because when the rains came books were the last things on our minds.

Master Diwan Chand knew this, as every teacher should. As soon as he noticed dark clouds gathering in the sky, he proclaimed that Raja Inder, the rain god, was about to bless us. It was declared a holiday.

Sitting on the road was great fun. We could partake in the activities of the bazaar and even make quick sorties to our home without invoking the ire of Masterji. Master Diwan Chand's wife treated us as members of her extended family by asking us to give her a hand in running household errands. At her bidding we went to fetch onions from the greengrocer, or helped her peel potatoes or shell peas.

Twice a year the Inspector of Schools came to inspect Master Diwan Chand's establishment. Two days prior to his arrival, the boys were ordered to scrub floors, dust the jute mattresses and help move Masterji's household goods to a neighbour's shop for temporary safekeeping. My father was well aware of all this but he also knew that Master Diwan Chand had a family to feed.

Come July and Master Diwan Chand's Sanatan Dharam School would close for the long summer vacations. That suited my father's temperament very well. He had cultivated a passion for mountain scenery, a passion enthusiastically shared by the entire family.

Each July, a few weeks before our yearly exodus to Kashmir, my mother would start preparing for impending migration. The first hint was the extended sunning of woollens smelling of the naphthalene that had preserved them from depredation by rats.

My mother was in the habit of stockpiling vast quantities of baggage; my father considered it prudent to hire a truck which could accommodate all of us and our trucks and bedding rolls.

Heera Singh, who lived a few houses behind ours, was used for this annual exercise as he transported us from the plains to the hills every summer. Though the part of the journey his lorry was meant to cover was no more than a hundred-odd kilometres, his preparations made it appear as if we were going to spend the entire vacation on his vehicle. He was not fully to blame, as it took him nearly twelve hours to get us from Jhelum to Jammu. Having run on *kuchcha* (unpaved) roads and over trackless sand dunes for many years, the truck was battered and worn down.

Heera Singh's passengers were reconciled to the idea that in addition to paying their fare they were expected to push the truck when it broke down, which was often. The journey was enlivened by Heera Singh's repertoire of folk songs.

He had a melodious voice. My mother liked his singing. He could tune his voice to the drone of his engine and keep time by thumping on the dashboard as if it were a tabla. With so much to keep us occupied we never bothered about the time it took to get to Jammu. During the journey, my mother showed concern for Heera Singh's truck as if it were made of bones and flesh and not wood and steel.

Due to her concern for the truck, Heera Singh was never asked to drive beyond Jammu. The steep, tortuous climb through the Banihal Pass might prove too much for his truck.

At Jammu we were joined by the families from Lahore. From that point onwards, the topics my mother discussed underwent a complete change. Most of these families originally belonged to Jhelum and had prospered in Lahore. She thought if her husband had done the same, he too would have done better for himself and his family.

As a young and upcoming lawyer, my father had caught the eye of Lala Harkrishan Lal Gauba. He was a giant among Punjabi industrialists. In a short time he had built an empire out of nothing. It covered all kinds of corporate enterprises: banking, insurance, trading and the generation of electricity. He had made my father a director of his bank and offered him the post of managing director. At that time quite a few of my father's friends and colleagues had opted out of the legal profession to enter the corporate world, and moved to Lahore. Before my father could make up his mind, the crash of the New York Stock Exchange had its impact on Indian industry. It knocked the bottom out of Harkrishan Lal's industrial empire. Amongst others, the People's Bank Collapsed and reduced a few multimillionaires to paupers overnight. Those associated with the bank's management likewise suffered heavy losses. My father was one of them.

The echoes of this catastrophe were heard in our home for years to come. It was like a ghost who refused to be exorcised and resumed haunting our home whenever we were in the company of families from Lahore.

Those days Pahalgam had few visitors. That was precisely the reason why my father and his friends preferred it to other scenic spots in the Kashmir valley. The men stayed back in the scorching plains and only joined us in September when the law courts were closed. This routine was maintained for three summer months every year except when my father or mother, or both, were in prison.

During our sojourn in the mountains, my mother would make us a breakfast of tea, toast, eggs, butter and jam. We were deprived of our usual tumblers of *lassi* (buttermilk) and fresh homemade butter spread over the previous night's leftover chapatis. This made it hard for us to swallow English-style breakfasts. But once we got used to it, it was even harder for us to return to our old *desi* diet when we returned to Jhelum.

It took us some days to get used to life in Pahalgam. For the first few nights our sleep was disturbed by the unrelenting roar of the hill stream, the Ludder, as it coursed down over rocks and boulders. But by the time we returned to Jhelum we missed the background roar as much we missed our breakfasts of toasts and jam.

The roaring echoed in our ears like notes of a melody coming from a long distance. We looked forward to returning to Pahalgam the following year. The scenic beauty of Pahalgam is unrivalled. Besides the range of high mountains covered with evergreen forests, it has several hill torrents which run into the Ludder at different points. All are rapid and violent, foaming over rocks, dashing against boulders and hissing like angry snakes. There was only one spot close to where we camped, where a tributary made a large calm pool while joining the Ludder. This stretch of water was our favourite rendezvous. The old and the young bathed in this pool during the sunny morning hours under blue skies.

Our open-air pool posed quite a challenge to the bathers. Its snow -fed waters were too cold to stay in for too long. Only the foolhardy would venture to swim across it. It had many boulders separated by a few feet from each other at the crucial point where the pool joined the seething torrent. These partly-submerged and partly-exposed boulders formed a sort of a dam. One needed audacity and perseverance to leap from one boulder to the other to make it to the other side. Much as we kids wanted to try, we had to bide our time till the elders left to take their afternoon siesta. It was on one such fated afternoon that I was foolhardy enough to try and cross the river. This one action changed the course of my life.

2

THE DESCENT OF SILENCE

I VIVIDLY REMEMBER MY ATTEMPT AT CROSSING OVER TO THE OTHER side of the Ludder. As I leapt from the first boulder to the next the boys watching from the bank cheered me. Emboldened by the applause, I jumped on to the next boulder. And the next. But on the fourth leap I missed the flat top of the boulder, was hurled against the side and swept away by the icy swirling waters. It was only after regaining consciousness a few days later that I learnt how foolish I had been.

Apparently what had happened, as my mother described it, was that as soon as I had fallen into the raging torrent I was washed downstream. One of my legs got caught in the cleft of a rock near one of the banks and the boys who were running alongside the stream succeeded in pulling me out. The impact of crashing into the rocks and the exposure to the icy water took their toll. I had bruises all over my body and was running a high fever. My mother put poultice made of the pulp of *kwar gandal* (a variety of cactus) over the swellings. The pain and temperature did not subside. I was taken to a hospital in

Srinagar. The X-ray was not reassuring. The doctors diagnosed it as a case of osteomyelitis, an infection of the bone for which no cure was known. My father accepted the surgeon's advice that my femur had to be cut to prevent the infection spreading further.

But he rejected the doctor's verdict that it was incurable.

A few weeks later he took me to Lahore to get a second opinion. By that time infection had spread to three-fourths of the femur. The best the doctors could do was to make many more cuts to try to salvage whatever remained of the healthy bone. They confirmed that the diagnosis made by the doctors in Srinagar was correct. The further the infection spread the more surgeries it would entail. The more they cut my bone, the more vehement was the condemnation of Western medicine by the people of our locality: they denigrated it as *angrezi dawabazi* (English medical jugglery). My father was not spared; it was his aping of the sahib's ways by going to the hills every summer that had brought this calamity upon our family, according to neighbours.

At his wit's end, my father gave in to my mother's suggestion that vaids and hakims be consulted. A hakim of Milot—a hamlet not far from Jhelum—was known for his miraculous cures. He specialized in curing *nasoor* (interminable bleeding). The cure-all was *bati,* a small tube rolled out of herbal material and inserted into the wound. The application of this felt worse than chili powder on a cut or on raw tissue. It made me scream. The effect of the hakim's treatment was traumatic. I howled and beat my forehead as I writhed in agony. By the end of the week my senses became numb, initiating a gradual loss of hearing. That frightened my mother and she decided to stop the treatment for a while. But the faith in quackery had taken its toll. The worst was yet to come.

I have a hazy recollection of the fateful day that changed my life. Had I overslept? I did not hear the familiar sounds of the morning: the cawing of crows, chirping of sparrows, the creaking of the handpump in the courtyard, the chatter of servants. Not till my mother shook me by my shoulder did I realize that it was morning and the sun shone brightly in the courtyard. I opened my eyes to a silent world. Was it a dream or a nightmare in broad daylight? The intensity of my mother's grip as she shook me was real enough to destroy the delusion that I might be dreaming. Something had gone seriously wrong but I could not fathom what it was. My mother also noticed that there was something very odd about my behaviour.

My fears were confirmed when I opened my mouth and tried to speak, I could not hear myself. My responses to my mother's question made no sense to her. She shook me again and shouted with all the strength in her lungs. I could only see her open and shut her mouth with increasing frenzy. Others in the courtyard joined her in yelling what was perhaps my name. I could not hear a word.

At last my father arrived on the scene. He was his usual calm and composed self. I could not trace any sign of anxiety on his face. He ignored my mother's agonized questions and sat down beside me. It was only after he had shouted into my ears once, twice, thrice and got no response that the truth dawned on him. He leaned back, still very much in control of himself. I could see that he realized that my mother had reason to be perturbed. He kept his cool till the doctor arrived and confirmed that I had lost my hearing, perhaps forever. My father accepted the diagnosis without betraying any emotion. But I noticed that he had to make an effort to get to his feet. As he walked away, I could see that he had lost his jaunty gait. A few minutes of suppressed and controlled grief had added a few years to his age.

For my father, suffering was a strictly private affair which he was loath to share with anyone. This trait was in sharp contrast to my mother's—she wanted everyone to share her sorrows as they shared her joys. Initially he had disapproved of his wife's openness about everything, but gradually understood her need to express her feelings in order to maintain her emotional equilibrium. She continued instinctively to involve herself in the culture of the *mohalla* into which she had been born and in which she had her roots.

This culture provided little room for privacy. My father had distanced himself from it when he had begun his law practice and assumed a Westernized lifestyle. It also suited his temperament. And even though he had renounced the brown sahib culture of the Civil Club and became a *khadi*-wearing Gandhian, his somewhat solitary nature prevented his reintegration into the *mohalla*'s way of life. The *mohallawalas* continued to hold him in awe and regarded his reserve as a remnant of his anglicization. It was not the same with my mother. She had a strongly local orientation.

She wept and wailed while staring into my face. This went on day after day. Although I could not hear her voice, I could see her tears.

I lay in the courtyard wrapped in a shroud of silence. No sound could penetrate the invisible wall that had risen between me and the rest of the world. Hallucinatory hours passed, during which I felt I was watching a movie without a soundtrack. As with silent movies I had to strain my vision and force my imagination to substitute or invent what others could hear. As time passed, my vision seemed to get stronger. It began to serve a dual function.

Besides my two elder brothers, Inder and Raj, I had a cousin Onkar, the son of my father's elder brother, whom my father had adopted at his brother's request. Onkar's mother had died during childbirth. Onkar had been adopted before my mother had any of her own children. I felt the closest to Raj, who was three years older than I was. Unlike Inder and I, he did not resemble our father either in features or complexion. He took much more after our mother. My mother was darker than us and our two sisters Uma and Niti who came after me. My mother had lost four other children either at birth or in early infancy.

Raj, like our mother, had well-proportioned features. Even at that early age he was very particular about his looks. His concern with his appearance further intensified because of the taunts he was subjected to about his swarthy complexion. Nevertheless, like Inder, Raj inherited my father's consummate flair for dominating others around him. From the very beginning I accepted Raj as my elder brother, guide and philosopher.

Raj's likeness to our mother gave him certain advantages. She pampered him more than was his due. Apart from physical similarities, they shared many other traits. Both loved to sing, and both made up for their lack of musical talent by singing with great gusto.

My closeness to Raj grew with my increasing isolation. No one else seemed to realize my predicament as fully as he did. Other people would shout into my unreceptive ears or scribble on a slate that was kept beside my pillow. The more I struggled to make sense of what they were trying to say, the more derisive laughter I evoked. Each guffaw sank like a knife into my heart. As a result of constantly being ridiculed, I began to lose my self-esteem.

The slate I kept at my side was of no use. Children of my age hardly knew how to compose a full sentence in Urdu, which was not their spoken language. Adults who knew the Urdu script had different problems. They could not be bothered to write casual conversation on my slate or communicate with me through the language of gestures.

As I sank deeper into the silence, I began to realize how insidiously the absence of sound erodes one's sense of being. Sound provides the necessary and consoling reassurance of one's existence, of tangible space and the passage of literal time. Without sound a person loses his or her equilibrium. This excruciating perception dawned upon me very slowly. The failure to hear my own voice made me feel as if I was living in a phantasmagoric and surreal cocoon. At times I doubted my own sanity.

My father was aware of this. The doctors had told him all they knew about the physical and psychological implications of the total absence of sound. The first concrete symptom was gradual loss of coherent speech.

When a person experiences sustained, absolute unbroken silence, his or her ability to efficiently reproduce remembered sound rapidly diminishes. Sending me to an institution for the deaf and dumb was one alternative considered by the family. Perhaps lip-reading would open up a channel of communication and provide me a semblance of awareness of the world around me.

Though himself still a boy, Raj was quick to realize the importance that communication held for me. Within a few days, he learnt how to reach me with a mixture of speech, scribbling on my slate, and gestures. We grew closer to each other.

As the pain in my leg lessened, I developed enough strength to hobble around the house. The combination of a limp and loss of hearing provoked the ill-mannered to make unkind remarks about my handicaps. I was unable to hit back. Raj always retaliated on my behalf. The fights that ensued from his sensitivity became an additional source of worry to my mother and she was consistently on the watch for our straying out of the house together.

A popular activity among the locals was swimming in the river, especially in the summer. It was equally popular among those who could swim and those who could not, as it provided much-desired relief from the heat of summer.

One day Raj and some friends of my brother Inder decided to go for a swim in the river. The river jamboree turned into tragedy. My mother was then away to Amritsar to attend a wedding. That absence was to haunt her for the rest of her life.

In spite of my father being a good swimmer, as was my mother, none of their children had learnt the art of keeping afloat in water. We were happy bobbing up and down in the shallows. As I watched my two elder brothers jump and frolic close to the bank, an older boy who wanted to show off his prowess in swimming grabbed Raj, who at fourteen was a slender lad, and jumped into the fast-moving stream.

That was the last I saw of Raj. When the older boy surfaced, he was alone. The swift current took Raj to his watery grave. It all happened so suddenly that it took the rest of us a long time to realize what had transpired.

I limped downstream after the others, hoping against hope to see Raj come up. I spotted my father standing at the main *ghat*. The news had reached him. He had got some divers to go midstream to look for Raj. He was calm but his eyes had a glazed look. The expression on his face was to stay in my memory for days, months and years to come.

Raj's body was found four days later, fifteen kilometres downstream, entangled under a raft of logs. My father chose to stay at home and let my uncle Narsingh Narain and a few others go to fetch it.

With Raj's death the shroud of silence that enveloped me became thicker. To make matter worse, my leg started giving me more trouble. The infection spread from the left femur to the right hip. I was bed-ridden again and subjected to another round of surgical operations. Luckily this time my bone was not infected, but my hip muscles were ravaged for more than a year.

My parents had no respite from these calamities. They began to look for solace and atonement in their own different ways. My mother was convinced that it was due to a curse for some unknown deed which had brought the family to its present predicament. To atone for it she sought out everyone who could suggest the right kind of penance to purge her of her past sins. The *deodhi* in the rear of the house became conclave of sadhus and sayeens belonging to different castes, creed and religions. Some offered *jaaps* (reciting mantras); others advised making offerings to deities, yet others simply sang hymns in praise of their gods and invoked their help to rid the house of the curse which had fallen on it. The one who best exemplified this was a *sayeen* who sang of the glory of Hazrat Jilani. No one knew who Saint Jilani was except that he was buried in distant Iraq near a place called Karbala.

The *sayeen*'s appearance was awe-inspiring. He was tall, his eyes bloodshot, his long hair wildly scattered about his shoulders. He was invariably clad in a black gown that came down to his ankles. Round his neck he wore strings of beads of different colours. He gave the impression that he had come more to bless or console the family than to seek alms, which he would accept only as his due.

When he sang, he closed his eyes, covered his left ear with the palm of his left hand and raised the right skyward towards the heavens. He looked like one possessed. His praise of Hazrat Jilani was adapted to the needs of the house where he was invited to intone. His usual litany was as follows:

Tera uncha mahal makan Mian
Tera jhuman laal nishan Mian
Tera khadam ek jahan Mian
Ya ghaus-ul-azam Jilani

(May the palace you live in touch the sky
May the red flag of your regime flutter high
May the world pay obedience to you
Praise be to the glory of Jilani)

Since a curse had been placed on our house, the Sayeen Sahib made suitable changes in his litany.

Bara sal hua beda ghark hua
Tha tu lutf apne par laga
Na wasal-e-sanam na khuda hi mila
Ya gussa-ul-azam Jilani

(It is ages since luck forsook you
Happiness ceased to come your way
You got neither your beloved nor found God
Praise be to the glory of Jilani)

As the *sayeen* sang this morbid version in our *deodhi,* day after day, my mother sobbed and wept as if repenting for past sins. She seemed as much in a trance as the *sayeen* himself.

I had no difficulty in following what the *sayeen* sang as I had heard him many times in the past. His wild gesturing made it easier for me to translate his words in graphic forms.

My father found solace in tending his garden. His preoccupation seemed odd, as the only other place in Jhelum that had any horticultural pretensions was the Company Bagh, a small plot of green which was only an extension of the Civil Club. The Bagh was a legacy of the East India Company in whose times it had been laid out.

Since there was not enough space for a lawn, my father bought a lot of earthen flowerpots and put them wherever he could find space for them. His devotion to his plants became an obsession. He knew every leaf, bud and blossom. If he discovered any missing, there was a hell to pay. His outbursts of temper, which had become a thing of past, returned with, redoubled fury.

The hours he spent reading grew longer. But instead of literature he turned to reading religious texts such as Bhagavad Gita and the Upanishads.

With Raj gone and elder brother in college at Lahore, I felt more isolated than ever before. However my father, despite the many shocks he had received, convinced himself that he could salvage something from the wreck I had become. He would sit with me for hours, slate in hand, to provide the company which children of my age no longer did. But adults cannot talk like children; at best they can make children think like adults. Perhaps because of being constantly in my father's company, I matured faster than others my age.

Without going through childhood I became an adolescent. It may have been my father's subconscious wish that I should live my life in a condensed form and thus be spared prolonged physical and emotional suffering.

At the time there was either no children's literature in Urdu; or perhaps my father was not aware of it. The books he dumped on my *charpai* were more suited to boys at least ten years older than I. However, he was selective in the choice of what he brought. The earliest among those were biographies his mentor Lala Lajpat Rai had written or translated during his detention in the Andamans. They told the stories of heroes who had fought for freedom of their respective countries. Among them were Garibaldi, Mazzini and Abraham Lincoln. One day my father found me reading Urdu version of Sherlock Holmes which a cousin had given me. It alarmed him, because he regarded such fiction as addictive trash detrimental to serious thinking. He thought over the matter and instead of biographies, began bringing me works of fiction of which he approved.

To start with, there were short stories by Munshi Premchand which had been published in *Chowbisee* and *Battisee.* They were followed by novels: *Godaan, Chowgan Hasti* and others. For a while he also gave me collections of short stories by Sarat Chandra Chatterji but soon stopped doing so when he found that reading them only increased my forebodings about the world. These stories often described the lot of the afflicted and the wretched sections of humanity.

My first confrontation with him on what made suitable reading came after he quietly removed a volume of *Atif Laila* (*The Arabian*

Nights). I had picked up at the shop of our neighbourhood tailor, Fazal Hussain. I had begun to while away a few hours each day watching him and his assistants cut and stitch clothes.

I learnt of my father's disapproval after I visited Fazal Hussain's shop the next day and asked for another part of *Atif Laila.* Fazal Hussain refused to comply. Through crude gestures he made me understand that my father thought I was too young to read sexually explicit material.

I was taken aback as I had never before been told that there were different kinds of literature for different age groups. Later I learnt that what made *Atif Laila* off limits for me were the frequent references to copulation. Though the Urdu descriptions were fairly euphemistic, my father became anxious about how I would interpret them. He did not realize that by transporting me into an age beyond my years he had aggravated the confusion in my mind, which neither of us would be able to resolve.

Later, when my father found me reading Maupassant's short stories, he decided to confront me. Having read them himself, he could not very well denounce Maupassant. His objection was that I could not possibly be mature enough to understand or assimilate the contents of the stories. The exchange between us was brief but frank and vehement. He realized the futility of arguing with me. He quickly sensed that the boy he was talking to was no longer a child but an adult with a nascent erotic sensibility.

Though I was still far from having any carnal desires, the concept of sexual attraction was no longer a mystery to me.

In the years that followed, the family went through a series of shocks.

First, my adopted brother Onkar Narain was arrested. As I have said earlier, Onkar was son of my Uncle Ram Narain. My uncle's wife had died while she was delivering her second child, a girl, and he had promptly left the first child Onkar, then a toddler of five, in my mother's lap while she was still a newly-married bride. His excuse for doing so was that he was taking a second wife and did not want to expose his children to a stepmother.

He left his other child with her maternal grandparents. Having got rid of his children, he took up the job of a clerk in a government department in Jhelum. By the time my father had got into the thick of politics, uncle Ram Narain had been promoted to the post of Jailer in Quetta (Baluchistan). Even from that distance he wrote to my father instructing him to keep the parental identity of Onkar Narain a secret. After all he was happily married, well settled and had to take care of the children he had with his second wife. He kept his distance from my father particularly after my father's disloyalty to the English became evident.

Uncle Ram Narain had learnt his lesson the hard way. This was during the martial law regime in 1922. He was then a petty clerk. Tough he was loyal enough to join a cheering crowd that lined-up along the route of the visiting British Commander-in chief, he unwittingly found himself in an absurd but problematic situation. It was entirely the fault of his funny moustache. Though the appendage was real enough, an English corporal scrutinizing faces in the crowd for possible troublemakers assumed it was false, and had been deliberately put on to mock the army chief. He caught my uncle by the scruff of his neck and had him put behind bars. My father eventually managed to get his brother out. Tayaji, as we called him, was not a man to take further chances and to ruin his career.

To prove his loyalty to the British, he filed an affidavit swearing undying loyalty to the Crown and announced that he had severed relations with his brother (my father) and his own son Onkar. Notwithstanding this callous behaviour, my mother gave Onkar as much care and affection as she gave the children she had carried in her own womb. She showered so much love on Onkar that I did not realize till I was six or seven years old that Onkar was not my blood brother but a cousin adopted by my parents.

Onkar was only ten years younger to my mother. Strong emotional bonds sustained them, generated by the closeness in their ages as well as the fact of his coming into my mother's life much before the birth of her first surviving child. Onkar had my father's temperament; he was as withdrawn and had little rapport with his adoptive father. My mother knew how to ease tensions and was better able to understand Onkar's waywardness. She made Onkar play the roles of a son, a brother and a friend all rolled in one.

No one in the family was unduly perturbed when the police suddenly swooped into our house one day and took Onkar away. Police raids and arbitrary arrests had ceased to hold any surprise or fear for us. What mortified my parents was the charge they heard in court, where Onkar was produced a few days later. Unknown to both, Onkar had been actively involved with revolutionary anarchists led by Bhagat Singh and Chandra Shekhar Azad.

My parent's reactions to this discovery were very different to each other's. My mother was unnerved by forebodings of the consequences for Onkar. My father was not as concerned with the legal outcome of Onkar's underground activities as their moral ramifications. He was Gandhian with unshakeable faith in the principles of non-violence. And yet he could not suppress the sense of pride that surged within him on discovering that his adopted son had dared to risk his life for the sake of his country.

The two men who had been dominant in my father's life were Mahatma Gandhi and Lala Lajpat Rai. He had unreservedly accepted the Gandhian creed of non-violence and its stand against British imperialism. He also accepted Lajpat Rai's zeal for reforming Hindu society and ridding it of its meaningless rituals and caste taboos. He considered Lalaji, as he reverently referred to Lajpat Rai, to be the epitome of patriotic virtues. He had come close to Lalaji personally and was an ardent member of his Servants of the People Society.

In 1929 a mammoth rally was organized by Lajpat Rai outside Lahore Railway Station to protest against the visit of the Simon Commission appointed by the Crown to introduce unpopular political reforms. A huge agitated crowd carrying black flags tirelessly shouted: 'Simon go back!' An Englishman named Scott, the local superintendent of Police, hit Lalaji on the head with his baton. My father was witness to his unprovoked assault which ended Lalaji's life a few weeks later. He attended on Lalaji during his last days.

Lalaji Lajpat Rai was popularly known Punjab Kesri (Lion) and was treated as the uncrowned king of the Punjab. What hurt the people most was the fact that a mere inspector of police could raise his hands against a man of Lalaji's stature. Like others, my father was deeply angered and disturbed. He burned with desire to avenge the insult to the man he worshipped.

A few days later, Bhagat Singh and Rajguru, two revolutionary terrorists of the Hindustan Socialist Republican Association shot dead a police officer they took to be Scott, along with his clerk Charan Singh in broad daylight. The Englishman, however, was identified as Sergeant J.P. Saunders. My father was torn between his conviction that violence was evil and his sense of relief that policeman deserved what he got. Bhagat Singh escaped, and was later arrested when he and his colleagues detonated a bomb in the Central Hall of Parliament. During the investigations that followed, Onkar was named among the conspirators.

My father sat in the court impassively listening to the charges of conspiracy, treason and murder against the accused, including his adopted son. All the charges carried the sentence of death.

It was different with my mother. After she got over the initial shock of Onkar's arrest, she heard the charges without betraying any emotions. She was a woman reborn, unrepentant and defiant. With tears streaming down her eyes she sang:

Hathkadyaan jinhaan da gehnen mein
Unhaan phaansiaan jhooley lainey mein

(Those for whom handcuffs are bracelets
Will treat the gallows as if they are swings)

As night fell and the visitors departed, the spirit of bravado suddenly evaporated and she broke down. She wept and sobbed. My father went up to the terrace and sat there by himself, lost in his thoughts. Onkar was sentenced to eight years' imprisonment with hard labour.

The case of Chacha Narsingh Narain was as enigmatic as Onkar's as far my father was concerned. Chacha Narsingh Narain, three years younger than my father, was lame. The slight limp as he walked was enough to make him the butt of ridicule. He had a year or two of schooling before his father Dada Duni Chand died. But once in Jammu where elders of the local *biradari* sat holding the purse-strings of the clan's savings, any further schooling for a *langra* (lame) was considered stretching the *biradari*'s generosity beyond limits. They had not reckoned with my father. He managed to get his *langra* brother admitted to school and to take his higher secondary examination. He could not do more. Chachaji never overcame the psychological complexes he had developed because of his physical deformity.

After getting through his higher secondary examination, he decided to give up further studies and settle for whatever was expected of a man with a limp. My father reconciled himself to this unwillingness to study any further and set Chacha up with a shop that sold bicycles and gramophones. But he was outraged when Chachaji expressed a wish to get married, to just about any woman who was willing to settle for a lame man. He accepted the very first offer of marriage that came his way. This was from the parents of a girl who was a deaf-mute and unlettered. To my father, this amounted to accepting the orthodox notion that those with physical deformities were a caste apart from others, and that the handicapped were condemned to live, marry and procreate as an isolated community.

Chacha Narsingh Narain shared none of his brother's views. Tortured by years of ridicule, he had lost the will to fight. He did not have the vision to see that the marriage he was looking forward to like a thirsty man seeking an oasis in a desert, would be no more than a mirage of his own making. Unfortunately, mirages do not turn into an oasis simply because one yearns for them to do so. It was not Chachaji who paid the price for his foolishness but the generations that followed him.

Though none of his children were born lame or deaf-mutes, they inherited some eccentricities from their parents. Two of his three daughters took their own lives, as if this was the only way to escape from the stigma of having been sired by handicapped parents.

A year after Raj drowned in 1936, my father overcame his reluctance to have me admitted to an institution for the deaf and dumb. I am not sure how and why he took this decision. He was either disappointed with the slow pace of progress I was making under his tutelage, or had simply run out of patience. He set high store on academic learning and insisted that each member of his family had to go to college regardless of the clan's economic situation or the individual's physical and mental aptitude.

The excitement over the prospect of my going to a school in Delhi, the capital of the country, made me brush aside any anxieties about problems I would have to face in a strange environment. I refused to think about such matters.

The school for the deaf and dumb to which I was admitted was enclosed within the walls of Kotla Feroze Shah, one of the ancient cities of Delhi. It was a short distance from the walled city called Shahjahanabad, which had been founded during the Mughal era. Its inmates appeared to be a different species of human being.

The warden of the school sensed how lost I was in the alien environment and did her best to make me feel more at home. According to her theory, in medieval Europe the deaf and the mute were treated the same way as women caught in adultery—they were stoned to death. It was decreed that an adulteress had to be destroyed because Satan had entered her body. A deaf-mute had also to be destroyed because he or she was unable to imbibe the Gospel and therefore unable to resist satanic influences. What she meant to convey through this gratuitous information was that I should thank my lucky stars that I found a place in her institution that provided shelter to the rejects of the hearing world!

Father Vincent, the patron saint of deaf-mutes, devised a sign language enabling those devoid of hearing and speech to communicate with the use of fingers. Thus he was partly successful in breaking through the walls of silence that enveloped their world. Lady Noyce, daughter of the then Viceroy Lord Linlithgow, introduced sign language to India. The institution was named after her—Lady Noyce School for the Deaf and the Dumb. The great drawback of this sign language was that it could only be used between deaf-mutes and not with others who were not similarly affected. Few among those who could hear bothered to learn it. No one could invent the magic formula—Open Sesame—to enable deaf-mutes to enter a world in which there were vaults full of riches available to those who could hear and speak 'normally'.

My misgivings did not please the warden. She felt I had exaggerated expectations which my condition did not warrant. All said and done, she did not think that the pupils of the deaf and dumb school should expect to be treated as equals by 'normal' people. She could not make an exception in my case. Her candour, however sharp its edge, was also tinged with sympathy. Strangely enough, this touched my rawest nerve.

The warden was a Christian missionary from Rawalpindi. She had volunteered to work in this institution as self-inflicted penance to atone for this suffering her mother, a deaf-mute, had undergone.

She did not tell me more about her mother. Nor did I have the curiosity to probe into her unhappy childhood, as I had more than my fair share of unfortunate people in my own family.

The school had no day scholars. I was surprised to discover that most of my fellow students had their homes and families in the city. The warden impressed on me that both the parents of deaf-mutes and the handicapped themselves found life at school easier than life at home. Blood alone, she told me, does not bind a family together. More important is communication, the sharing of ideas. It is the power to communicate that distinguishes humans from animals to quickly detach from their offsprings. She insisted that by providing means of communication the school helped inmates to interact with their own kind, something they had not been able to do with their blood relatives. Therefore they preferred to stay in the school hostel rather than return home for the night. What she did not tell me was that not admitting day students was not school policy but a choice made by parents themselves. Whether parents had really agonized over the effects it would have on their problem children, or had simply wanted them out of sight, was not a question the warden debated. She simply considered this immaterial.

My being unlettered in sign language, and the warden being the only one who could communicate in written Urdu, created a special bond between us. My questions made her wonder what had prompted my father to send me to this school.

Doctors had warned my father that since I was totally deaf, there was a strong likelihood of my losing my power of speech as well unless some means of communication was kept going. But confining me to a world where speech was absent was by no means a solution to my predicament.

The warden agreed that if I began to use sign language I would soon forget how to activate my vocal chords. It took me sessions to make her agree that my staying on in the institution would do me more harm than good. I did not know to which world I belonged. I felt like one drifting in a vacuum, a kind of amorphous weightlessness which would not anchor me to anything or anybody. I slid into a deep depression.

Finally, the warden wrote to my father. She did not tell me what she had written, but when I got back home a few weeks later, my father showed me her letter.

She had concluded her letter by quoting an Urdu couplet that I had once recited to her:

Wo aur hain, duniya jinhein maidan-e-amal hai
Wo aur hain, duniya jinhein ishrat ka mahal hai
Main wasl-e-gardab hun, kishti mein khalal hai,
Keh paband-e-salasal hun, main azad nahin hun.

(They are others for whom the world is full of action
They are others for whom the world is a pleasure palace
I am in a boat caught in a storm and have sprung a leak
I am caught in a vice, I am not free)

My father was more relieved than anxious or dejected on seeing me back home. Undaunted, he began to look for other alternatives.

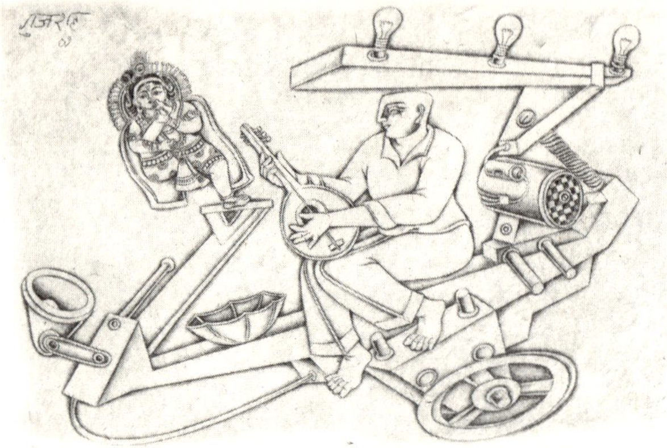

3

LAHORE

HAVING NOTICED ME DOODLING ON MY SLATE WHILE I LAY ON MY sickbed, my father began to consider a new idea. He wondered whether it was possible for me to develop the vocabulary of the medium that did not involve sound. Without telling my mother, he wrote to Inder asking him to find out if there was an institution in Lahore to train students who were artistically or graphically inclined.

With my father's indifference towards the household the authority to make decisions had passed on to my eldest brother, Inder. Though he was still in his teens, he was recognized as the heir-apparent. He was not the first-born child of our parents but the first to survive; my father doted on him. Inder had inherited many of his traits. This affinity of temperament drew them close to one another.

In his student days my father had been very fond of horse riding. In Jammu he had attended riding classes and attained considerable proficiency. His love for horses became a passion when he was in his brown sahib incarnation. After he married and settled in Jhelum, he acquired a majestic black stallion and a syce to look after it.

The horse and the syce were the first to occupy the garage; the car which came later shared this space.

With the arrival of buffaloes in my mother's dowry the horse was moved out into the open. Although there was enough room in the garage to accommodate the car and the animals, Nani Paro advised my mother against keeping a horse in close proximity with milk-yielding buffaloes. According to Nani's wisdom, horse urine had an adverse effect on the fertility and milk-yielding potential of buffaloes.

Though Bishan Dass, the veterinary sub-inspector, tried his best to dispel Nani Paro's superstition, Nani and her daughter remained unconvinced and the horse had to be kept apart from the buffaloes.

Kala Ghora, as the *mohalla* urchins called my father's stallion, did not have to stay alone in the open. It was soon given a companion, a white pony that my father got for Inder when he was five years old.

My mother described how father and son rode out early every morning towards the open grounds in the cantonment area. There my father taught Inder the art of horsemanship. They would canter, gallop and jump over ditches without any fear. I never witnessed these intense hours, as riding also was among the many luxuries my father gave up when he took the Gandhian path.

The riding sessions created closer bonds between father and son, and left a permanent imprint on Inder's later career. The audacity of spirit which Inder demonstrated when he took to politics was undoubtedly inherited from our father. Inder was only ten years old when, like our parents, he courted arrest. Although he was kept in the police station only for a night, his actions reassured my father that his son was following in his footsteps.

Inder found an art school in Lahore where I could learn drawing, painting, sculpting and much else. My mother was dismayed to hear of the profession my father had chosen for me. To her, it was somehow the final confirmation that I would never recover my hearing and she was not willing to accept this fact. She was equally unhappy at the choice of vocation. She looked upon drawing and painting as an activity that was the equivalent of making cane chairs, which was usually done by the blind or mentally handicapped. She felt terribly let down by the husband in whom she had reposed so much faith and confidence. It was easier for her to bear the loss of a child—and she had lost more than one—but to see one of her children fade slowly away from her sight was beyond her endurance.

Her despair was compounded by the location of the school chosen by my father. It was a hundred miles away from Jhelum and I would have to live in a hostel. At the age of thirteen I would be exposed to ridicule because of my inability to communicate with other students. Visions of this nightmarish possibility began to haunt her. She was relieved to hear that the school was reluctant to admit anyone with my handicap. Her relief was short-lived.

Never one to accept any verdict as final, my father took me to see his friend Sir Sikander Hayat Khan, then Chief Minister of Punjab. Sir Sikander gave my father a patient hearing. Then he put his arm around my shoulder and told my father he could not order the principal to admit me—rules were rules—but he would request him to take me as a personal favour.

Principal Suminder Nath Gupta, a well-known artist of his times, to whom we returned after Sir Sikander had telephoned him, told my father he would allow me to sit through regular classes for one year without registering me as a student. Then he would see what progress I had made before deciding whether or not I should be added to the rolls.

Despite the knowledge that I had been accepted on these conditions, admission to the prestigious Mayo School of Arts filled me with a pride and self-confidence I had not known before. It was the first time I was being treated as a 'normal' human being. My father boosted my newfound self-esteem by coming over from Jhelum to spend every weekend with me. Though it entailed a journey of four hours each way, and neglect of his professional work, he never let me down till Inder took over from him.

Inder was six years older than me. We had not been particularly close to each other as long as our brother Raj was alive. When I shifted to Lahore, the emotional distance between us began to narrow at an astounding pace.

Apart from the initial euphoria on being accepted to the Mayo School, I was excited for various other reasons. Till then the only school I had attended was Master Diwan Chand Jhalla's Sanatan Dharam School, and institution for the deaf and dumb in Delhi which I did not deign to call a school but a sort of asylum. The Mayo school was in Lahore—a city held in much esteem and awe in the provincial world of Jhelum. Those few individuals fortunate enough to study in Lahore acquired a halo of privilege, and were looked upon with envy. Among these were the Ghai brothers, Iqbal and Krishan, twin sons of our immediate neighbour Lala Lekh Raj. Our mother was a childhood friend of Masi Ishro, his wife. We boys were in awe of the Ghai twins, but in a certain way we resented them. This feeling was accentuated by the fact that though our father could afford to send his sons to schools even better than those in Lahore, he was unable to do so because of his political activities. We had been refused admission to private schools set up in hill resorts under English patronage. It was surprising that despite his fierce commitment to the Gandhian way of life, my father hankered after having his sons educated in British-type public schools.

Masi Ishro and my mother were born in the same village, grew up together and settled in the same town after their respective marriages. But while my mother started her married life as the wife of an upcoming lawyer who had the added gloss of being a brown sahib, Masi Ishro had married a man who was a gateman at a railway level-crossing. Though Lekh Raj later acquired a significant amount of real estate in the town and became prosperous, my mother never forgot his humble origins and felt doubly humiliated by Masi Ishro's sons having overtaken her own in getting their schooling at Lahore.

The fact that the Ghai brothers were Inder's age added to the tension. When they came to Jhelum during their vacation, our rivalry with them and the relations between my mother and Masi Ishro would reach a breaking point. Though my mother never regretted joining the freedom movement with her husband and making a bonfire of the foreign clothes she owned, there were moments when she was acutely aware that this was precisely why her children had been deprived of getting as good a schooling as the sons of Masi Ishro.

Though education at Lahore had nothing to do with the later success of Iqbal Ghai and his brother-in-law Pashwari Lamba in becoming the ice cream kings of India, my mother ascribed their success to their early years in Lahore.

There were other examples of Lahore being the miraculous economic node that made kings out of commoners. The most notable was Mohan Singh Oberoi who, though not strictly a native of Jhelum but of a hamlet close to my father's ancestral village Pari Darwaza, became a legend in Jhelum. He was orphaned at an early age and had risen from abject poverty to become India's greatest hotelier, owning a chain of five-star hotels across the Indian subcontinent, Egypt, Europe and United States. In Jhelum we believed that he owed his success to his mother's foresight in sending him to college in Lahore.

Since my mother herself narrated these exciting success stories of men who had been educated in Lahore, I found her misgivings over my joining the Mayo School rather baffling. Also, I could not accept her low opinion of painting as a profession. What was to her no better than weaving cane chairs was to me closer to poetry and a nobler vocation than any other. I had read enough about artists to acquire enormous respect for them. I did not feel I would be like a lost soul in an alien environment, as my mother feared. My father had spared no effort to build up my self-confidence ever since the possibility of my going to Lahore became a reality.

My first few months at the school were not very promising and I feared my father's efforts to help me stand on my feet might prove to be in vain. The euphoria he had inculcated began to diminish at a disheartening pace. The feeling that my mother's fears were not as exaggerated as I had thought before leaving home, enveloped me like a black shroud.

The Mayo School of Arts did indeed have all that my father had said. It was housed in an impressive building designed in the 'Indo Gothic' style of the nineteenth century. Its location enhanced its magnificence. Its spacious courtyards were laid with emerald green lawns and flowering shrubs. It had broad corridors and large classrooms lined with pictures and examples of the disciplines taught there.

What had impressed my father most was the list of illustrious men who had been principals of the school, including John Lockwood Kipling, father of Rudyard Kipling. In front of the school ran the Mall—known to the locals as Thandi Sarak (Cool Road). Facing the entrance was a traffic island on which was mounted an ancient cannon known to the English as the Kim's gun, and to the Punjabis as Bhangianwali Tope, the cannon of the opium-eating Sardars. The prestigious institution and its historic environment had lost some of their glory. The cannon had lost its lustre. Signs of decay were visible on the peeling plaster of the walls and corridors.

John Lockwood Kipling belonged to that breed of empire-builders who, while conscious of the benefits of colonial administration, rejected Lord Macaulay's verdict that Indian culture was worthless. Kipling and other Englishmen who shared his vision believed that it was their duty as rulers to preserve Indian arts and crafts.

Their attitude was patronizing. They believed that a colonized people should be encouraged to develop according to their own cultural and aesthetic and religious traditions. Unlike Macaulay, they did not subscribe to the belief that Indian notions of art were inferior to the European. They saw them as different, and capable of yielding equal if not better results.

Lockwood Kipling did not have much success in Bombay, where he was first posted as the Principal of JJ School of Arts, founded by the Parsi millionaire Sir Jameshedji Jeejibhoy who had made his money by trading in opium. He fared better in Lahore, where he was destined to spend the rest of his years in India.

The curriculum he presented for the Mayo School of Arts envisaged training master-craftsman or *mistris* by including in the syllabus diverse techniques such as stone and wood carving, metal work, clay moulding, drawing and design. To these subjects he added scale drawing and copying of old building plans.

Lockwood Kipling was convinced that the *mistri* was not simply a skilled labourer to be hired as a mason or a carpenter, but a creator and coordinator, well-versed in techniques of construction. It was this total involvement that made it unnecessary for him to prepare more than a few rough notes and drawings and see the work in hand to its completion. By contrast, the specialized training of a Western architect distanced him from his projects, hence the need to prepare meticulous and detailed plans.

The school had not deviated from the curricula drawn up by Kipling. In fact nothing had changed since his days; even the school garden and choice of shrubs surrounding its lawns were the same as the ones he had chosen. At the time I enrolled, everything had a dilapidated look and bore a very faded resemblance to what Kipling had visualized for its future.

Trainees put through Kipling's curriculum were being drawn from sections which were totally different from those that Kipling had aimed to preserve. Traditional craftsmen had long since either given up their professions or were scattered in different parts of the country doing the very kind of menial work that Kipling feared they would be reduced to doing.

No one had any illusions about what the future had in store for the students. The castes from which the majority of students came had no concept of the skills the curriculum meant to embellish. In fact, the talents and abilities Kipling strove to save from extinction were already extinct. What the school had were boys from poor families who sought to acquire skills that could ensure them a livelihood in an urban society; boys for whom the job of a sign painter or draftsman were attractive propositions. Most of them were either unlettered or had just a smattering of Urdu, Hindi or Gurumukhi.

In the hostel where I shared a room with another boy and spent my after school hours, the atmosphere was like that of an orphanage. This was not very surprising as quite a few of the boys were in fact orphans. The harsh impact of this close brush with deprivation might have been softened if some of the students had shared a modicum of cultural or intellectual affinity with me.

There was not one who remotely understood my ideas or concerns.

However their poverty gave me an advantage I would not otherwise have enjoyed. My handicap usually made me the butt of ridicule; I was treated either as a vegetable without feelings or intelligence, or jeered at and mimicked. Though such cruelty was not entirely absent at Mayo, my comparative affluence made the other boys a little more deferential towards me. The disparity between us could at times become perverse. Their pent-up hatred towards those more fortunate than themselves found in me an easy target. They spat venom upon me and often succeeded in hitting my rawest nerve.

In my naive initial euphoria, I had anticipated making friends quickly, with students interested in artistic concepts, personalities, symbols, techniques. Instead, I found impoverished souls who spent their evenings mouthing obscenities, washing their soiled clothes or cooking food.

However strong my revulsion at the time, I have to admit that it was the artisan's abilities the curriculum at Mayo forced on me, that later became my assets. They were foundation of my skills as a painter, sculptor and architect in later life. I was able to assimilate and fuse diverse techniques and disciplines. This would not have been possible but for the vision of John Lockwood Kipling.

Hardly any of my contemporaries made good in later years. One who deserves mention is Inderjit. Inderjit was a year junior to me. He was shy, somewhat rustic and very withdrawn. He would have remained unnoticed but for his strange clothes. Other boys though no better dressed, found his striped pyjamas outlandish enough to subject him to merciless taunts. In contrast to his indifference towards his garments, Inderjit was obsessed with his hair. He applied generous quantities of oil on his scalp and was forever combing his hair in class and the hostel.

Inderjit re-emerged later in life as the partner of the Punjabi poet Amrita Pritam who was many years older than him. She gave him a new name, Imroz. I recognized him as a character in one her novelettes in which the hero is in the habit of sleeping at night in his trousers and spending the day in striped pyjamas.

I run into Inderjit, alias Imroz off and on in Delhi with his lady friend. They make an odd couple. He has retained some of his earlier simplicity. He experimented in many fields—painting, batik, film—but did not achieve much success. His only claim to fame was his status as the lover of the most beloved poet of the Punjabi language, Amrita Pritam. Her one poem invoking the spirit of Warris Shah (composer of the epic ballad *Heer Ranjha*) to rise from his grave and witness the havoc caused to his beloved Punjab has had an enormous emotional impact upon me. About the only thing I envy about Inderjit alias Imroz is Amrita's affection for him.

The one thing I could not stomach in Mayo's hostel was the tasteless and badly served food. My father, who knew how fussy I was about food, arranged for me to eat in Inder's hostel, which was only half a kilometre away.

Joining my brother every day for meals brought us closer to each other. Besides eating with him, I learnt a great deal from him about literature and poetry, and above all, how personality was moulded by social commitments. He also sensed that my resentment and frustration at being handicapped was building up to a climatic rage which, unless channelled into creative pursuits, would be my undoing. It was Inder who infused in me a fervour for social revolution. He felt that this would ease my burden and instil in me the hope of a better world.

I began to mix with Inder's friends. Because of his involvement in leftist politics most of his friends were socialist intellectuals. They included quite a few destined to become eminent writers and poets of the Urdu language. Among them were Faiz Ahmad Faiz, Ali Sardar Jafri and Krishan Chander. Though I could not converse much with them, just being acquainted with them boosted my morale.

The spirit of the times is accurately defined in a couplet of Israr-ul-Haq-Majaz:

Dekh shamsheer hai yeh, saaz hai yeh, jam hai yeh
Tu jo uttha le shamsheer, bada kaam hai yeh

(See here I the sabre, here the lute, here the goblet of wine;
If you are a man of courage, choose the sword as thine)

Such was the enthusiasm created by 'progressive' writers that eminent romantic poets like Hafees Jalandhari, who had enchanted a whole generation with lyrics like *Abhi to main jawan hun* (I am still young), were branded decadent and banished to *adabi Siberia* (literary exile).

Following Hitler's attack on the Soviet Union on 2 September 1939, the ban on the Communist Party was lifted. There was a corresponding change in the attitude of the self-styled progressives towards earlier as well as modern writers. Poets like Ghalib and Mir Taqi Mir were resurrected, and Western classics were given new orientations. No one questioned their greatness, but contemporary writers were either lauded for being committed to revolutionary change or condemned for being insular romantics. This may not have bothered the intellectuals of the Party but left the rank and file very confused.

For me it was a time of great enrichment. What had been beyond my reach because of my inability to read English now came within my grasp through translations available in Urdu. Western classics fell into my lap like the apple which the law of gravity had caused to drop on Newton's head. I discovered worlds I had not even dreamt of. I was reassured by the words of Will Durrant: 'There is no reason to feel lonely when through books one can walk with Napoleon and talk to Shakespeare'.

My gradual conversion to socialism did not surprise my father. Whatever his reservations about Communism, he did not come in the way of Inder or me accepting its ideology. Following the Nazi attack on the Soviet Union, the Communist Party of India found itself opposing Gandhiji and the Indian National Congress. The Communist Party chose to put the demand for Independence on the shelf till the Axis powers were defeated, and came out in support of the British and their allies, while Gandhi continued to press for immediate independence as the price for cooperation with the government. He continued to exhort his followers to 'do or die' in their fight against foreign rule. Our parents were among the first to be arrested in the 1942 Quit India movement. They remained in prison for some years.

As I look back I find my father's tolerance of his son's politics quite amazing. He let Inder speak his mind at public meetings organized by the Congress Party over which he presided. This continued throughout the war years, during which the Indian National Congress, the party to which my parents belonged, and the Communist Party of India to which Inder and I belonged, were at loggerheads with each other.

That was the kind of man my father was. He let his children think for themselves and act independently. Nothing exemplified this better than his attitude towards religion. He was a deeply religious man. He prayed thrice a day, once at dawn and once before each meal. His devotion to the Arya Samaj was as strong as his commitment to the freedom struggle. Yet he never made any attempt to influence our ways of thinking. Neither Inder nor I had much use for religious ritual: we sensed God in the physical presence of labouring humanity in general. Both of us also refused to tread the Gandhian path and preferred to follow Karl Marx. But as time passed we came to recognize the validity of Gandhian concepts in the Indian context. Our father lived long enough to see this transformation in us.

Let me return to the Mayo School of Arts. Next to Lockwood Kipling, the man who became a living legend for us was a handsome young Bengali, Bhubesh Sanyal. He added a touch of romance and poetry to the otherwise prosaic philosophy of the school, with its dull altruism. Lockwood Kipling and Sanyal had little in common. The Englishman was a reformer who had been laid in his grave a long time ago. The Bengali babu was still in the prime of his youth and very much a part of the Lahore scene. Two other characters in the Sanyal saga were the principal of the school and his beautiful daughter Kalyani who was the most sought-after girl in Lahore's upper-class circles. She fell in love with Bhubesh Sanyal and eloped with him. The affair became the hot topic of discussion in the city's elite circles and inevitably caused an explosion in the area around Bhangianwali Tope. It earned Bhubesh a permanent place in the annals of the school.

Though not yet eighteen, I became increasingly conscious of sexual impulses and my body began to show signs of approaching manhood.

There was as yet nothing specifically carnal about my desires but my adolescence was suffused with sensuality. In this frame of mind, the Bhubesh Sanyal–Kalyani Gupta drama assumed larger-than-life proportions, and I let my fervent imagination paint their romance in vivid splashes of colour.

Principal Suminder Gupta succeeded in retrieving his daughter. Bhupesh Sanyal was fired from his job. After leaving Mayo, Bhupesh founded his own arts school where wives, sisters and daughters of Lahore's prestigious families came to learn painting and sculpture. For me, he became the textbook image of an artist, someone who possessed all that I did not have. He was a remarkably handsome man of slender build, fine facial features and a mischievously seductive gait. He also had irresistible charm. It was not surprising that Kalyani Gupta fell head over heels in love with him. She was by no means the first nor the last woman to succumb to Sanyal's charisma.

I was tempted to leave Mayo and join Sanyal's studio. My senior teacher, Sardari Lall Parasher, who had succeeded Bhupesh Sanyal at Mayo, persuaded me not to defect.

Prasher was the odd man out at the school and quite the opposite of Bhupesh Sanyal both in physical attributes and intellectual bent. He had not been to an art school nor served as an apprentice to a guru. He was a self-taught painter and had a Master's degree in literature. He was erudite and had amassed vast knowledge of art history. However, these attributes proved more of a handicap than an advantage in the school's prevailing atmosphere. His seniors despised him because his intellectualism gave them a feeling of inadequacy, while his juniors dismissed him as a pretentious snob. Teachers in the lower grades were hired from the ranks of past students. Prasher's lack of training in techniques of craftsmanship lowered him in their eyes. They dismissed his university degree as bookish baggage which was of no consequence in a school of applied arts.

The *ustad shagird* (teacher-student) relationship was basic to this type of training. The *ustad* expected his *shagird* to be like a slave attending to all his needs. The most cherished of these errands was preparing the *chillum* (smoking bow) for the *hookah* (pipe); next was the privilege of serving *chai-pani* (tea and water) to which the *ustads* were equally addicted. Students who graduated with distinction had first to master these arts.

I hated doing these menial errands. To my relief I was soon disqualified for the one I found the most distasteful—preparing the *chillum.* I simply could not master the art of filling the earthen bowl with glowing embers and raw tobacco. However, Master Ata Mohammmed, our design teacher, had other things in mind as far as I was concerned: he was a homosexual.

In the beginning he showered favours on me by teaching me with extra attention, and overlooking my clumsiness in preparing his *chillum.*

Seeing my growing closeness to Prasher, he became very jealous. He suspected that Prasher had succeeded where he had failed. Once Master Ata Mohammed came to this conclusion, he behaved like a woman spurned, and went about finding ways to humiliate me. Serving him *chai-pani* was no longer good enough. He ordered me to wash and polish his bicycle every evening before he left school for his home.

In those days a bicycle was a status symbol in the way an automobile is today. It had to be scrubbed and polished regularly. A lackey had to hold it ready for the master to mount just as a car door is held open for an honoured guest. Since this job was usually performed by orderlies, my being pressed into service gave Master Ata Mohammed sadistic pleasure. Classmates who resented my exemption from other menial errands were also pleased to see my being treated like a chaprasi.

My new assignment only provoked me to mischief. After having stood with the bicycle at the gate for a few evenings, I struck on a diabolical plan to put an end to my servitude. I bought a tin of glue and smeared it on the masterji's bicycle seat. I took care to give the bike frame a thorough wash and a rub with a duster. Things went as planned. Master Ata Mohammed mounted his machine and rode off.

The time for reckoning came next morning. My classmate and friend Hanif, who lived in Master Ata Mohammed's neighbourhood and usually accompanied him to the school and back every day, came running to the hostel. He was full of foreboding regarding my future in Mayo. Master Ata Mohammed, he told us, could not dismount from his bike as his salwar was stuck to the seat. Hanif had to help him enter the house with his bicycle attached to his posterior and help him take off his salwar to free him from the machine.

Master Ata Mohammed was in a terrifying rage. He was determined to teach me a lesson. The only way to assuage his temper was for me to fall at his feet and beg his pardon.

Before I could heed Hanif's advice, Master Ata Mohammed cycled into the hostel. He went straight to Principal Gupta's residence which was on the ground floor. It took the principal a few minutes to emerge from his house and pronounce my expulsion from the school. However, in the evening Hanif took me to Master Ata Mohammed where I prostrated myself at his feet as Hanif had advised me to do.

Ata Mohammed forgave me. He patted my cheeks and kissed me. He told me to return to his class next morning, but never again asked me to clean his bicycle, bring him tea or fill his *chillum* bowl. He stopped making passes at me.

The unhealthy atmosphere in Mayo forced Prasher to keep aloof from his colleagues and students. If it had not been for a few chance encounters outside the school I would probably never have gained entry into his close circle of friends.

I often skipped classes and whiled away the time at Rama Krishna's bookstore close to the school. Prasher was a frequent visitor to the bookshop. He did not spend much time browsing but strode through the store to visit his friends, the artist Roop Krishna and his English wife Mary who lived on the floor above and whose family owned the premises.

Fortunately for me, the links I forged with Prasher during these brief encounters in the bookstore turned out to be abiding. As I grew closer to him, I realized that he had much in common with Roop Krishna and Mary, who was also an artist like her husband. Prasher, Roop and Mary formed a threesome bound by common interests and perspectives. After a while, I began to accompany Prasher upstairs and listen to the conversation.

Roop Krishna was an angry man. Also scrupulously honest and outrageously frank. He had no time for the second-rate and little patience with charlatans who assumed the airs of masters-painters. He was particularly aggravated by the position of self-styled progressives. He looked down upon them as intellectually dishonest propagandists. For Roop, art had nothing to do with social or political beliefs, only with aesthetics. He considered the brain to be an organic repository of memories rather than a source of aesthetic inspiration.

Roop Krishna's *bête noire* was Charles Fabri, a Hungarian émigré who was curator of the Lahore Museum. Fabri was a man of many talents: a linguist, art historian, painter, critic, and above all, a man who knew, understood and loved India and Indians. This last trait made him defend those artists who had earned Roop Krishna's ire and vituperative scorn.

For Roop, aesthetic truth had to be absolute. He could not tolerate half-truths. Fabri, on the other hand, subscribed to the view that contemporary Indian artists needed encouragement so that they might eventually arrive at the complete truth. This patronizing attitude disturbed Roop Krishna.

Their confrontation reached epic proportions when Amrita Sher-Gil arrived in Lahore. She was only in her mid-twenties when she had her first ever exhibition in the city. Fabri hailed her as the only genius colonial India had produced. Roop Krishna, who had spent years in Paris meeting and seeing great artists at work, had scant respect for Amrita's talent. He considered it *passé,* dated by more than half a century, and a poor imitation of past European masters. When Amrita brought some of her canvases to him, Roop Krishna unceremoniously tossed them out of his balcony onto the street below.

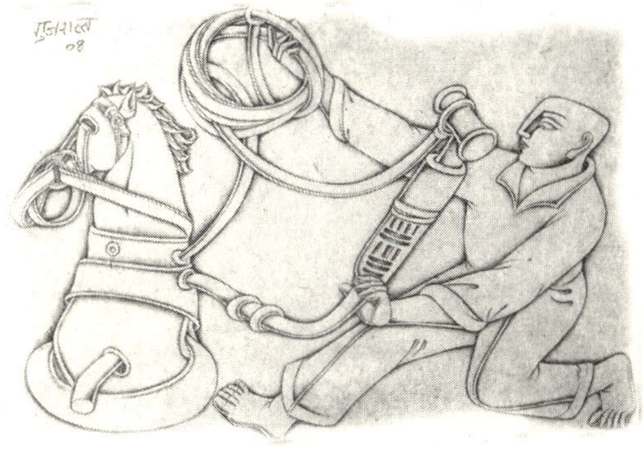

4
BOMBAY

As MY TIME AT THE MAYO SCHOOL CAME TO AN END, MY FATHER, INDER and I made an assessment of what I had gained and what I should do next.

The five years of going through the curriculum designed by Lockwood Kipling did not make an artist of me in the accepted sense of the term. I was reconciled to the fact that I was no more than a glorified *mistri* (craftsman) in the sense that Kipling meant it. I could draw, mould, cast, design and plan reasonably well. My father thought I was good enough for the post of a draftsman in the office of a civil engineer-cum-architect. Since this was the vocation chosen by so many other graduates of Mayo with qualifications identical to mine, there was nothing particularly unusual in my father's vision of my future. The other alternative was to become a graphic artist with an advertising agency, or paint cinema hoardings. However I felt that the curriculum had broadened my horizons enough for me to try to be an artist as well as an artisan.

For many years Shanti Niketan, the university founded by Rabindranath Tagore, had held a strange fascination for me. It seemed to me to be not an institution but a way of life.

With my physical impediment I had developed a certain utopian view of distant places. I fantasized about cities and societies where an individual's handicaps were not obstacles to self-development.

Shanti Niketan with its renowned arts department, Kala Bhavan, and the cultural aura created by the galaxy of poets, painters and composers of dance and music, was one such place I dreamed about. My enthusiasm for it refused to be dampened by what Prasher and Roop Krishna had to say about it. Both viewed it as an institution that was trying to turn back the wheel of artistic evolution in India. For them, Gaganendra Nath Tagore and Ramkinkar Baij were sole exceptions. The rest, including Nand Lal Bose and his associates, were no more than revivalists of the Bengal School which had influenced Shantiniketan since the early twenties. Prasher and Roop Krishna unequivocally criticized this movement. What finally destroyed my illusions about Shanti Niketan was neither my disenchantment with A.R. Chughtai—he was a revivalist based in Lahore whose work had initially attracted me—nor Roop Krishna's passionate denunciation of revivalism, but the forthright manner in which Prasher criticized the general style of living in Shanti Niketan.

A handicap, he assured me, would be a handicap wherever I went. He advised me to opt for a place which offered me scope to evolve as an artist.

Prasher's relentless logic, though unpalatable to me at that time, made good sense. I gave up dreaming about Shantiniketan.

This option having been put aside, Prasher and Inder agreed that I should join the JJ School of Arts in Bombay. However, they naively assumed that by simply weighing the pros and cons of different institutions they could effectively decide the future course of my education. They did not consider the problems I would have to face.

They thought that since I had adjusted to life in Lahore, I would just as easily adjust to Bombay. Their reasoning was very simplistic.

My mother, ever the realist, brought everyone down to earth by asking how, with my limitations, I could be expected to cope with living in another state where I did not know the local language. A person who could hear might manage to get along with some sort of pidgin, but the only people who would be able to communicate with me would be those who could read and write Urdu. She rightly concluded that the only way to solve my dilemma was for me to learn English.

It was a task for which I was totally unequipped. I had failed before, and would fail again. Since I could not hear the sounds of the English language, I was unable to organize them in any coherent sequence to form correct words or assimilate the phonetics. Had I known a little English before I lost my hearing, my progress would have been smoother.

Pronouncing English was for me like a blind man groping about in the dark with faltering steps. The only difference was that while a blind man evokes sympathy and the immediate wish to help, my plight evoked ridicule. It requires enormous emotional and psychological determination for a deaf person to repeat the same word over and over again with little or no improvement, knowing that he or she is being laughed at.

I prayed that my mother would find an easier solution to my language problem. She did, by locating a neighbour whose brother was studying at the JJ School of Arts. This man was Pran Nath Mago, who was conversant with Urdu. He reassured my mother that he would take good care of me in Bombay.

Mago was only a few years older than me; his assurances were not enough for my mother to let me go to as distant a place as Bombay. In those days Bombay seemed as far away as London. It took two nights and two days to get there by train. No one in our family nor any of our acquaintances had ever ventured that far. Coupled with this was the fear of my leg ailment flaring up periodically. The possibility of my going to Bombay began to inexorably recede.

At around this time Chacha Trilok Chand told my father that he had accepted a job in Bombay. Though not a relation, Chacha Trilok Chand Kapur was closer to my father than any of his blood relatives. They had come to know each other soon after my father had settled in Jhelum to start his law practice. Unlike my father, who was new to the town, Chachaji's roots went back to 1870, when the British rulers built the first bridge to span the river. As the bridge took shape, the British established a large cantonment adjoining the town, and raised it to the status of a district headquarters.

Jhelum, a sleepy little settlement of boatmen who ferried people across the river, attracted quite a few business families from Lahore after the British took over. The 'Lahorias' as these families came to be called, formed a community of their own. The locality in which they lived came to be known as Lahorian di Gali (the street of people from Lahore).

Chacha Trilok Chand and my father had a lot in common. Both were lawyers; both were ardent admirers of Lala Lajpat Rai and had taken the Gandhian path. Furthermore, both had been to jail together, as had their wives. Though Chacha Tilok Chand later moved to Lahore, the bonds of affection that bound him to my father remained as strong as ever. His children and we brothers were roughly same age, and we usually holidayed together at Pahalgam.

Chacha Trilok Chand had moved to Lahore to work as the manager of the newly formed Lakshmi Insurance Company. After I had my accident in Pahalgam, my mother and I had to spend many months with him while I was undergoing an agonizing series of surgeries in a Lahore Hospital. My father had to stay in Jhelum to look after his work and rest of the family. Chacha Trilok Chand went with me and my father to see Sir Sikander Hayat Khan and Principal Suminder

Gupta to plead for my admission to Mayo. During my years in the school I spent a lot of time in his home. He was in fact my surrogate father in Lahore and did his best to help me emerge from the vault of silence that had engulfed me.

Being aware that children more than elders tend to be cruel towards the handicapped, Chacha Trilok Chand made sure that his children treated me as their equal. I was able to communicate with them and because of their support I managed to establish a link with my classmates and teachers. And of course, I could never forget that it was Chacha Trilok Chand's sons Harish, Romesh and Jagdish who had pulled me out of the foaming Ludder and rescued me from certain death. The news that Kapur Sahib, as others affectionately called Chacha Trilok Chand, was to move to Bombay where he had accepted a higher position in the corporate world, was enough to banish my mother's misgiving. With Chachaji there, Bombay was no longer a terrifying place in her mind.

Principal Charles Gerard of the JJ School was a kindly Englishman. He was not as worried about my inability to hear as he was of my lack of knowledge of English. He thought this would put a greater burden on the teachers especially since he was not allowed to recruit more staff to fill vacancies because of the war. But Chacha Trilok Chand, like my father, was not one to give up. He tapped his contacts in the higher echelons of the administration and the corporate world. He approached the senior executives of Burmah Shell and impressed on them that I had recently won a competition for designing a war poster, and won a scholarship sponsored by Burmah Shell. As such I was entitled to claim their support. Ultimately the principal not only admitted me but also gave me credits for the years I had studied at the Mayo School.

The Kapurs continue to be part of my life to this day. Harish distinguished himself as the only Indian to be elevated to the post of a professor at the School of International Studies in Geneva; he is also a commentator on international affairs for many leading Europeans journals. His elder brother Jagdish has established himself as a futurologist of distinction.

For different reasons, Prasher and Inder supported the idea of my going to Bombay. Inder thought that Bombay had the right climate for nurturing the seed of social commitment that he had planted in me. Bombay's film industry had attracted many of Punjab's leading poets and writers, including some of Inder's friends such as Krishan Chander, Rajinder Singh Bedi, Sahir Ludhianvi and Ali Sardar Jafri. He intended to put me under their guidance, particularly since I was beginning to show a flair for writing poetry. Prasher, on the other hand, saw things differently. For him the appeal of the JJ School of Arts lay in its association with John Lockwood Kipling. This despite the fact that the curriculum it followed had nothing to do with what Kipling had prescribed for Mayo in Lahore.

The thing I looked forward to most was learning the technique of painting murals. Inder also felt that murals could be utilized as a means of communication with the masses. Murals were one area where painting fused aesthetics with social commentary and political satire; in public spaces especially, murals could explosively depict historical events and function as visual inspiration for movements of social change.

On this point Prasher was in full agreement with Inder. He told me that Kipling, as head of the JJ School, had crusaded for Indian artists, most of whom he had trained to create sculpture-based murals for the buildings that were designed by English architects. The results confirmed Kipling's belief that although the synthesis between painting and architecture achieved by this method might only be skin-deep, it could become cohesive if the designing of buildings were also entrusted to traditional *mistris.*

When I joined the JJ School of Arts in 1944, the Second World War was at its peak. There was a large influx of American GIs into the city.

Many of these soldiers were painters. Because of this and the opening of the first-ever American Library in the metropolis, contemporary Western art began to make its appearance on Bombay's art scene.

At the same time the leading figures in Bombay's art world were K.K. Hebbar, Shiavax Chavda and N.S. Bendre, who formed the avant-garde. There were also academicians such as Gopal Deoskar and J. Lalkaka. A few of my fellow students were destined to become famous in later life. Pran Mago, Harkrishan Lal, Laxman Pai, S.H. Raza, Jehangir Sabavala and Francis Newton Souza, who were then in their final years of study. Among the newcomers were V.S. Gaitonde, and myself. Mago was recognized as the most original of this group of artists.

The atmosphere of the JJ School was quite different from the one prevailing at Mayo: it was more self-assured and aggressive. The chord that Lockwood Kipling had struck still resonated. At Mayo the walls of classrooms and hallways were lined with drawings of ancient buildings with their carved or painted details copied by students from the 'Jaipur Portfolio', modelled on miniatures. At the JJ School, the legacy of Kipling was not of his post-Bombay period which the Mayo School at Lahore exemplified, but of the academic European style which had prevailed at the JJ School before Kipling's arrival, and with which he was forced to compromise.

Pre-Raphaelite murals in Indian garb adorned its walls and plaster casts of Roman and Greek statues cluttered its corridors; they were evidence of Kipling's illusion that such hybridization would result in a harmonious synthesis at some late date.

I felt an alien in my new surroundings. And being unfamiliar with English, I was more isolated than ever before. I became very dependent on Pran Nath Mago.

In contrast to the indifference towards craftsmanship that had been the hallmark of the work created by those who had begun to imitate Western modernism, Mago's style of the paintings stood out as a testament to technical competence. It was a superb example of indigenous modernity. Mago's work validated the convictions of an Englishman who was as much against Macaulay's denigration of everything Indian as were the Indian nationalists.

Charles Gerard, the Principal of the JJ School, and Claude Batly, who headed the department of architecture were products of the art and crafts movement begun by William Morris, who had revived the traditional way of synthesizing diverse techniques of plastic expression and crafts.

But though both Batly and Gerard were opposed to Macaulay's anti Indian attitude, neither of them was bold enough to go as far as Kipling, who enthusiastically prescribed and supported the adaptation of traditional Indian approaches and methods. Both men believed in a compromise between traditional styles and Westernized modernity.

For Claude Batly, the problem was further compounded by the attitude of hundreds of Indian architects who looked down on the craftsmanship of the native *mistri*. In fact these Indians were Macaulay's bastard offspring, more loyal to British concepts than to their own roots.

Trends in art forms that gained popularity in England were faithfully copied in India. As the winds of modernism blew across the English Channel from Europe into England, and the stranglehold of the Pre-Raphaelite academic hierarchy loosened its grip, Indian artists, as was their wont, toed the line drawn by their English mentors.

In the beginning I stayed close to Mago because he knew how to communicate with me and also because he was a fellow Punjabi. In class, I required his help to follow the instructions of my teacher, who I simply could not understand. But as time passed, I grew more independent.

Mago left the JJ School in 1945 when I entered the third year. I found myself, among others, with F.N. Souza and V.S. Gaitonde. 'Gai' after having studied at some other school, was admitted into our class grade. Souza had been marooned in the same class for many years. I did not take much notice of him as he seldom attended classes. What made me remember him in later years was an incident that provoked him to slap our amicable teacher, a professor named Bhonsle. Souza was immediately expelled from the school. With Gaitonde my friendship was of longer duration. We had much in common; both of us were short-statured and very conscious of this. We heard of a doctor in Ahmedabad who had concocted a brew which, if taken orally, could apparently rectify this quirk of nature.

The cost of a rail or a bus ticket to Ahmedabad was beyond our means. Providence came to our rescue. We were selected to join a group to study art and architecture in Ahmedabad.

As soon as we got to the city we located the doctor's clinic at one end of a noisy bazaar. We made several rounds of the bazaar till the crowd lessened, and we had summoned up courage to face the Doctor Sahib. To our surprise he was no taller than us; he had evidently not tried out his invention on himself. This was very disconcerting, as in the preceding weeks we had mentally added many inches to our heights and worried over what it would cost us to have new garments made to fit our elevated statures. We left the doctor's clinic very crestfallen and disheartened. I tried to comfort Gaitonde by insisting our height were meant to indicate that we carried sparks of genius in our small bodies, and when they burst into flames the world would be dazzled by their brilliance. He was not very consoled by my citing the example of short men who had achieved great levels of achievement. His sardonic response was that going by my logic, Nepal should have a plethora of geniuses in the ranks of its Gurkhas. I do not know if Gai ever again consulted other specialists in the field of stature-building; I certainly did not, and made peace with my short self.

I did not see much of Gai after we left school. But I had the satisfaction of knowing that my theory of short men attaining eminence came true at least in Gai's case. He rose to be one of the greatest Indian artists of our times.

I don't remember how and when I first met Piloo Modi. He was planning to do a course in architecture and was orienting himself by circulating among artist and architects. But I recall that we were introduced to each other by a friend who was the son of senior bureaucrat. He also introduced me to Zulfiqar Ali Bhutto.

Piloo Modi attracted attention because of his enormous paunch; it seemed to me as if he had been born fat. Bhutto stood out as a dandy. He was always nattily dressed in well-cut suits and matching ties. He radiated self-confidence. At that time, Bombay was agog with the story of the sensational murder of a concubine by her nawab patron. The crime was committed in a house close to the residence of the Bhutto family. Naturally, what Zulfi had to say about it was regarded as authentic. He was a great raconteur with an eye for minute detail. What Zulfi said was translated by Piloo into the language I understood, a mixture of hand gestures, writing on the palm and making signs with the fingers. Since both Piloo and I were interested in politics, we were drawn towards Bhutto. I sensed that Piloo was more interested in politics than in architecture. I was not sure whether Bhutto really knew Mohammed Ali Jinnah, the founding father of Pakistan, or was only name-dropping. But since his house was close to Jinnah's and his pedigree gave whatever he said a tone of authenticity, we accepted his claims. He quoted Jinnah as if Jinnah had spoken to him personally. At that time a meeting between Jinnah and Bhulabhai Desai of the Congress Party was scheduled to take place as the prelude to a meeting between Jinnah and Gandhi after the latter was released from Poona Jail. We listened in awed silence to Zulfi Bhutto giving us an insight into Jinnah's mind.

As a supporter of the Communist Party of India. I fully supported the idea of a separate state for the Muslims if they wanted it. On that score I had no serious differences with Zulfi Bhutto. However, I did not fail to notice how self-righteous and irrational he became when talking about Hindus and Muslims being two different nationalities who could not live amicably in one country. Though it was common knowledge that his mother had been a Hindu dancing girl, no one dared to contradict him.

I met Zulfiqar Ali Bhutto once again in the mid-sixties when he visited New Delhi as the foreign minister of Pakistan. We met at Piloo's house. He did not seem to have any recollection of having met me in Bombay. However, he told me he had seen some of my paintings in the house of Faiz Ahmad Faiz in Lahore.

Piloo had a colourful career as a Politician. He was elected to the Lok Sabha on the ticket of the Swatantra Party. During the Emergency, he spent over a year in jail. He was then elected to the Rajya Sabha. He made a mark as an orator of great wit and humour. I met him on what happened to be his last night on this earth. He had been to a health farm in Bangalore and shed a lot of weight. His paunch had shrunk and he was proudly displaying the gap between his reduced belly and the waistband of his old trousers. The sudden loss of weight proved too much for his overworked heart. He died in his sleep. I recall that on the last day of his life he had read in the morning papers about the architectural controversy in which I was involved. He rang up my wife and exploded. 'Organic architecture! Synthetic architecture!' he bellowed into the phone. 'What nonsense! Kiran, tell him to grow up, tell him to shut up. Just draw a plan, get paid and fuck the rest.

My sessions with Ali Sardar Jafri were of a different kind. He was recognized as a poet of great promise when he was still in his early thirties. He cut a handsome figure—slender ad tall with dreamy eyes. He looked every inch a poet. He had made friends with Inder in 1941 when both were in prison. Inder introduced me to him as his younger brother who also composed poetry. He was generous enough to accept me as a *shagird*. The mentor-learner relationship did not last long as we both agreed that poetry was not my forte. But our friendship has lasted to this day.

Sardar had little appreciation of the plastic arts, but like other writers and poets, he was inclined to accept an artist's assessment of his own work. I liked him as a person and as a poet. Though strongly imbued with Marxism, his poems were lyrical, sensitive and imagistic. Despite my holding the same political views, I wished he would not include so much dogma in what he wrote. He was impervious towards criticism on political grounds, and gave the impression of having sealed himself in a hermetic ideological shell out of which he refused to emerge. I last met him in 1997. He seemed depressed and disillusioned. It was not due to age or poor health but the realization that the philosophy he worshipped and the political principles that so significantly shaped his aesthetics, had let him down.

Meeting American GIs who had enrolled as part-time students in the JJ School prompted me to practise my English as much as I could. My faulty grammar and stuttering did not evoke derisive laughter because their own attempts at speaking Hindi were no better. Having encountered and negotiated many cultures during their war assignments, they were impressed with Indians' command of English. However, they attributed it more to our colonized mentality rather than to any special gift for languages. That was also the opinion of Tony Rosenthal, the Jewish GI who sat next to me in class and to whom I got closest. He used my poor command over English to his advantage in his efforts to learn Hindustani; through me he was able to get the perspective of an Indian not as anglicized as the other students.

My knowledge of Jews was very limited, and based on the stereotypes created by anti-Semitic jokes and stories which depicted Jews as narrow minded, mean and obsessed with money. Till I met Rosenthal I had been unaware of the persecution of Jews by Christians throughout the Middle Ages. I had assumed that virulent anti-Semitism was limited to the Nazis. One outcome of Hitler's senseless genocide was that it brought about a radical change in the popular image of Jews. From being stereotypically regarded as tight-fisted and culturally insular parasites, they somehow assumed a position as the world's underdogs. I remember telling Rosenthal of the correspondence between Mahatma Gandhi and the German novelist and Nobel Prize winner Thomas Mann who had left Nazi Germany and settled in the United States. Though my grammar and pronunciation remained poor I became less self-conscious about my errors and more eager to communicate in English as much as I could, with whoever I could.

At about this time my legs started to bother me again. Ever since the surgeries on my femur, I had suffered periodic spells of acute pain which attacked the entire leg, from hip to toe. The spell usually lasted for the two to three months of autumn each year. If the attack was mild, I was able to combat it by taking painkillers. If the pain became too severe I went back home to Jhelum to be nursed by my mother. The malady was never professionally diagnosed.

In October 1946 I suffered a severe reoccurrence of this infection. Dr Rosenthal took me to the American naval hospital where he worked. His colleague in the orthopaedic ward took some X-rays and diagnosed my ailment as 'side effect of osteomyelitis'. The bone marrow of the femur had become frozen and was blocking adequate blood circulation in the leg. He advised immediate surgery to remove the affected bone marrow and pre-empt further complications. He cautioned me against being too optimistic as there was a possibility that the remaining marrow might again freeze within ten years.

I had no choice but to accept the surgeon's advice. My Bombay sojourn was terminated. In October 1946 Chacha Trilok Chand took me to Lahore to be operated on by Dr Ganesh Dass, who had operated on me earlier.

Dr Ganesh Dass was not as pessimistic as the American naval doctor. He cut through the entire femur and removed the frozen marrow. He assured my mother that there is no danger of it freezing again. The bone was lifeless as rock, it had no nerves that could nourish fresh marrow. He had drilled a hole in it to let blood pass down through the knee.

He warned me to be careful as a fracture of the femur would never heal. (I paid a heavy price for disregarding his words. Forty years later in 1980, I fractured my left femur and consequently had to spend four years in bed.)

5
PARTITION

By the time I recovered from the surgery, the country was in the throes of a violent internal crisis. The policy of direct action called by the Muslim League in Calcutta resulted in a chain reaction of Hindu-Muslim riots spreading from Calcutta to Bihar, from Bihar to Noakhali in East Bengal and then to the North-West Frontier Province and the Punjab. By the time the conflagration reached Jhelum district, it was totally out of control.

After his last imprisonment ending in 1944, my father did not resume his law practice: it was another example of his growing faith in Gandhi, who disapproved of the legal profession as a means of livelihood. Along with the loss of income from his legal practice, he lost income from his holdings of lands following the communal frenzy of 1946. Most of the tenants were Muslims unwilling to pay their dues to their Hindu landlords. He could no longer afford to keep me in Bombay.

Returning from Bombay in 1946, I set up a graphic art studio at Lahore. Instead of reducing my father's financial burden I squandered whatever remained of his savings. This was very foolish of me as life in northern India was fast deteriorating into chaos. No one could be certain of what might happen the following day.

I wondered why my father had not stopped me from this misadventure that wiped out all his savings. When I had suggested it to him, he had simply nodded and let me go ahead. Instead of receiving customers I would sit in my studio and watch never-ending lines of tongas loaded with Hindu and Sikh families going towards the railway station with their trunks and bedding rolls. They were in a hurry to transfer whatever they could of their possessions to the side of the border they felt would fall to India, and thus be safer for them.

At about this time my father was elected to the newly formed Constituent Assembly representing Rawalpindi division, of which Jhelum was a part. His membership was transferred to Karachi as soon as the country was divided into India and Pakistan. He was in Karachi awaiting his turn to take the oath of loyalty to Pakistan when both sides of the Punjab erupted in civil war on an unprecedented scale, leaving no doubt in anyone's mind that Hindus and Sikhs were not wanted in Pakistan.

I stayed on in Lahore watching different parts of the city go up in flames. The fires and rioting came nearer and nearer towards my home, which was close to the Nishat Cinema. I had just enough time to escape before hooligans came to loot whatever little I had. The only safe haven I could think of was Lajpat Rai Bhavan where my father's friend Lala Achint Ram and others associated with the Servants of the People Society were staying. I covered the distance of five kilometres at a run. There were many others also fleeing Muslims mobs who were venting their fury on Hindu and Sikh life and property.

After I was safely inside the Bhavan, I realized the magnitude of the calamity that had overtaken the city. The Bhavan and the adjoining DAV College hostel were overflowing with distraught families; more were pouring in every minute. The buildings were converted into the

Central Refugee Camp and a contingent of the Dogra regiment was provided to stand guard. We were still more than a fortnight away from the fateful day of 14 August when Pakistan was to become a sovereign independent Islamic state. But we still we did not know the fate of Lahore. Would it come to India or go to Pakistan? We tensely waited the Radcliffe Award which was to decide the issue. The air was thick with rumours. Most newspaper had ceased publication. This further added to the confusion. Those who stayed on in their homes came to the camp to get authentic news. But none was available.

Finally, on 13 August 1947, the Radcliffe Award was announced. It ceded Lahore to Pakistan. The next day the country of Pakistan officially came into being as an independent entity.

For my father, the culmination of what had been his life's mission was, to say the least, ironic. He had worked and suffered for the freedom of his country. Now freedom had come, but instead of one country there were two. Where did he belong? Like many others, he was confident that once the anarchic tide of violence subsided, the warring religious communities would return to living in peace on both sides of the newly drawn frontiers.

He had friends among the leaders of the new dominion, and was close to its founder, Mohammed Ali Jinnah. He had been given to understand that Jinnah intended to invite him to join his cabinet of ministers. He arrived in Karachi expecting to take the oath of allegiance to Pakistan and perhaps be the first and only non-Muslim to be included in the governing council. But by time he took oath as a member of the Pakistani parliament, the two nations were on the brink of war. Communal riots had spread all over the two Punjabs, Pakistani and Indian.

My father was flown to Lahore in a military plane in the hope of salvaging a murderous situation aggravated by the ruthless arson and plunder. In the evening when he met the Indian Prime Minister Pandit Nehru and Lady Mountbatten who had flown in from New

Delhi, he was a very shaken man. So was Nehru. Neither of them had any illusions about the two countries being able to live as friendly neighbours. Nevertheless, to my father's surprise, Nehru asked him if he thought there was any chance of stopping the communal carnage and preventing forced migration and exchange of populations. There were many at the table when Nehru put this question to my father. Why he singled him out remains a mystery. Or perhaps, as my father tried to explain to us later, Panditji only happened to turn towards him but was putting the question to himself. This was the state of bewilderment of all who sat round the table, including Raja Ghaznafer Ali, a newly appointed minister of Jinnah's cabinet. Ghaznafer Ali belonged to Jhelum. He had accompanied my father from Karachi to demonstrate his friendliness. The meeting ended on a note of frustration and despair.

The next day Raja Ghaznafer Ali drove with us to Jhelum, a hundred miles away from Lahore. Political differences had not affected the friendship between the two men. This was odd, as they were of completely different temperaments. My father was a recluse and somewhat puritanical; the raja was a jovial extrovert, and an unabashed womanizer. He had been a member of Sir Sikander Hayat's Unionist Party. When Sir Sikander died, Ghaznafer Ali joined Mohammed Ali Jinnah's Muslim League and became its only representative in the Punjab Assembly. After he had been inducted into the new cabinet, he suggested my father's name to Mr Jinnah for a ministerial post.

The drive to Jhelum was a nightmarish reminder of what had happened. At every milestone the faces of two men became even more grim and anguished. Before we came to the bridge on the Jhelum river, Ghaznafer Ali asked my father if he was still against non-Muslims leaving the district. Without waiting for my father's response, he leaned on his shoulder and said, 'Well, Lalaji, let us do our best to keep them here.' Though my father did not react, the raja concluded that this silence meant approval.

Both seemed to have overestimated their hold over their followers. The joint statement they issued on reaching Jhelum received wide publicity in the national media of both countries. Gandhiji and Jinnah approved of it. However, the actual situation made mockery of their efforts to restore normalcy. Everywhere they spoke they got a hostile reception. Hindus and Sikhs were incensed by my father's appeal to not leave their homes and accused him of making them *qurbani ke bakrey* (sacrificial goats). Although relations between local Hindus and Muslims had never been very close or relaxed, their differences rarely resulted in violent confrontation. Nevertheless, in small towns and villages, the divide was real and persistent. Hindu-Muslim estrangement was both cultural and social. Except for the Civil Lines which existed only in district headquarters, the two communities lived in clearly demarcated localities; their occupations were also different. Muslims lived off the land; Hindus and Sikhs in the towns of western Punjab were largely professionals, shopkeepers, moneylenders and traders. Even in the Mayo School hostel which never had more than a score of residents, the Hindu and Muslim sections were clearly demarcated. Though a façade of bonhomie was kept up, there was no conscious effort to bridge the ethnic and religious gulf that divided the students. Though we met on the playing fields, sat side by side in the classrooms and occasionally went to each other's rooms, we were housed in different wings of the hostel building and had separate kitchens and dining rooms.

Jhelum was no different from other towns in the region. Its population of about fifteen thousand was half Hindu and half Muslim. The Sikhs were considered a part of the Hindu community. Despite the segregation there was a lot of friendly give-and-take in everyday life, because the communities depended on each other for their survival. But this was rarely, if ever, extended to visiting each other's homes to share meals. Hindu taboos against eating with Muslims were the biggest stumbling block to social mixing. To the orthodox Hindu, some Muslim dietary habits rendered that community as unacceptable as Hindus of the lowest caste.

My father did his best to get the townspeople to overcome their prejudices, but he gathered very few followers. He established a branch of the Indian National Congress in Jhelum; it received no active support from the Muslims.

The fact that Hindus had responded with enthusiasm was all the more reason for Muslims to keep aloof. More galling to my father was the discovery that Hindus who had joined the Congress were very enthused by its call for national independence, but were unwilling to befriend Muslims or change their attitude towards untouchables.

My father accepted Raja Ghaznafer Ali's suggestion to appeal to the Hindus and Sikhs of Jhelum to stay on. But as the violence escalated, he came to the conclusion that there was no option for non-Muslims except to leave for India.

We were in Jhelum when suddenly hordes of *kabailis* (Afghan tribesmen) descended on the town. They were on their way to Kashmir to drive Dogras, Brahmans and Sikhs out of their state and annex it to Pakistan. Since Jhelum was the closest station from Mirpur, the border town of the state, it had been chosen by the Pakistani army commanders as one of the staging points for the invasion of Kashmir. The Pakistani leaders were wary of taking personal risks and hoped that the frontier tribesmen, ever eager to plunder and to abduct non-Muslim women, would do the job for them.

The tribes who lived in the no man's land between Afghanistan and Pakistan recognized neither law nor government. Their very presence struck terror into the hearts of the Hindus and Sikhs of north-western Punjab. For many centuries the main occupation of the tribal hordes was looting and kidnapping for ransom. Their chief targets were Hindus and Sikhs because in the tribal consciousness killing and robbing infidels elevated marauders to the status of *mujahideen,* warriors of Islam. Even the British with all their military resources had been unable to subdue these unruly tribesmen, and had left them to be controlled by their *jirgahs* (tribal councils).

The day the first band of tribals descended on Jhelum was unforgettable. They eyed our refugee camp as predators assess their quarry. They began with their traditional *khattak* dance, going round and round our terrified camp to the beat of the drums, firing rifles in the air while they danced to warn us of our impending fate. Had it not been for the pleading and cajoling by local officials led by Raja Ghaznafer Ali neither I nor anyone else would have lived to tell the tale. The experience finally convinced Ghaznafer Ali that it was time for non-Muslims to depart from the 'Land of the Pure'—Pakistan.

As the conflagration spread, Hindus and Sikhs in the thousands sought refuge in our *mohalla,* which soon became a refugee camp. Every newcomer had his tragic tale to tell—each bloodier and more spine-chilling than the last. I lost all sense of time. Death became a gruesome reality in our daily lives.

My introvert father rarely allowed anyone to witness his emotions, but there were moments when he seemed to sweat tension from each pore. At such moments he would sit huddled with his eyes shut. He was a God-fearing man, but seeing what God's creatures could do to one another shook his faith. Here were human beings behaving worse than wild animals. I wondered to whom my father now addressed his prayers.

With the ferocious *kabailis* having effectively increased the resolve of local Hindus and Sikhs to migrate to India, we began the evacuation, which turned out to be as bloody as the carnage that followed. Almost twice a week I would accompany a convoy consisting of dozens of trucks packed with several hundred people on the journey that for many would turn out to be their last. In spite of the armed Dogra contingent we were provided during each trip, the Muslim ambushes were difficult to withstand because the attackers outnumbered our guards.

The assaults varied in their character and intensity. If we were lucky, we were just ordered at gun point to surrender all our belongings. Those who resisted or showed any signs of reluctance, especially women who did not want to give up their jewellery, were seized and forcibly deprived of their valuables with horrifying brutality that left them badly injured and terrorized beyond belief.

Still, this was nothing compared to the escalating incidents of planned genocide. These not only resulted in the almost total annihilation of men, women and children, but were carried out in such a ruthless and bloody manner that they numbed the senses of those who were helpless witnesses and survivors.

Once at Lala Musa, a small town roughly fifteen miles from Jhelum on the way to Amritsar, the ambush ended in the general slaughter of all the men, the rape of women on the spot and abduction of the few before the rest were butchered. The murderers celebrated the carnages by impaling infants on spikes and going into frenzied bhangra dance, accompanied by wild drumming.

The fact that this gory event took place in a location that happened to be part of Pakistan did not mean that such atrocities were restricted to that part of the divide alone, or that Hindus and Sikhs were the only ones who were subjected to such demonic treatment. I witnessed no less inhuman scenarios enacted in areas that had become part of free India, the only difference being that the victims were those who happened to belong to the Islamic faith.

The trips I made with refugee convoys often did not terminate at Wagha, a hamlet that had become the border post between India and Pakistan, not at Amritsar which had become the terminal point for depositing refugees. I had to make sorties to Jalandhar, sometimes to drop off the stray girls and children we rescued from the kidnappers, and at other times to seek sorely needed assistance from the newly established East Punjab government which was camping at Jalandhar. Since my father was a government official, he gave me a letter of authority that enabled me to cross the border easily. We took an armed contingent with us to rescue women, but I escorted them directly from the recovery sites to camps on the Indian side on my own. This way my father ensured that in case there was any retaliation at least my life would be saved, if not his. This made me an unwilling witness to the slaughter on the Indian side. The worst among these was the attack on a Muslim girl's hostel in Amritsar. The inmates were stripped and forced to march in a procession through the Hall Bazaar, the town's main market. There these girls were gangraped and subjected to the most perverse treatment that any sadistic imagination could devise, before being murdered.

Our car was forced to a halt as the thoroughfare was parked with crowds who wished to watch this gruesome *tamasha.* Sitting in the car, I searched for signs of horror or compassion on the faces in the crowd. I could trace none.

The agonies of Partition left their impact on all those who were witnesses. Over time, the horrific scenes I saw no longer created in me the same intensity of revulsion I used to feel in the beginning. My senses succumbed to a gradual hardening. No calamity seemed to affect my numbed perceptions, which had frozen into a block.

One redeeming phenomenon of the sordid Partition epic was the way the unfortunates who formed refugee convoys would treat each other in an encounter. Though the instances of such encounters turning into massacres were not uncommon, these were outnumbered by instances when both sides sympathized with their common fate. They supplied each other with drinking water and other crucial necessities, but more significantly with profound emotional understanding.

One such encounter ended in a so-called 'Beas catastrophe'—a calamity enacted not by human but by nature, which that year seemed to be hellbent on destroying mankind as mankind seemed on destroying itself. There had been torrential rains and floods. An incessant spell of rain flooded all the fives rivers of Punjab in the month of September 1947, when the evacuation and migration of refugees was at its chaotic height.

Displaced and exiled people did not escape only in trucks or trains; a much greater number was struggling on foot and by bullock cart towards the borders that had just been carved into the subcontinent. These convoys were dozens of miles long, stretching so far that the vanguard would have crossed the border while the rear would still be several days from safety. More often than not the convoy disintegrated under ambush; rarely would an entire convoy successfully reach the other side intact.

The 'Beas catastrophe' affected not one but two convoys coming from opposite directions. They camped on the stretch of road that lay between the Beas river and one of its seasonal tributaries, about five miles away.

Pounded by torrential rain, and without any shelter, these afflicted souls were soon relieved of their suffering. Both Beas and its tributary rose in spate and sucked thousands of humans and animals into a foaming, thundering, watery grave.

Even weeks after the catastrophe one could not pass this stretch of road without burying one's nose in layers of towels, so overpowering was the stench of rotting corpses.

No burial or cremation was ever performed. And like most people, each time I passed the area I was more anxious about not catching some disease by inhaling the foul air than about the fact that so much life had been tragically destroyed here.

Fifty years after that fateful day, as I sit down to write these lines. I wonder which was the greater casualty: the loss of millions of lives and the uprooting of still many more from their homes, or the loss of compassion in myself and in other people. Compassion is a great trait that distinguishes humans from animals. How many survivors of Partition, from all faiths, could have retained this, after experiencing so much terror and anguish?

By March 1948, we had managed to send to India most of the families who had been brought into the camp from the area entrusted to my father. The task seemed endless, as there still remained young women who had been abducted, children who had gone missing and others mercifully given shelter by their Muslim friends. The exercise of rescuing Hindus and Sikhs was made perilous by the fact that our region had large numbers of retired soldiers who had been allowed to keep weapons and ammunition with them. The local administration was not equipped to deal with this kind of armed and dangerous populace. Despite the intense danger that the rescue missions involved, my father refused to abandon victims to their fate and escape to India. Most families of these missing people, who were in our care, also refused to leave till their relatives were found.

To add to our difficulties, the army personnel allotted to us for security were replaced by lightly armed Pakistani policemen. The war in Kashmir had hardened the attitude of the Pakistan government towards us. Because of Jhelum's strategic importance in the Kashmir operations, the government wanted us out of the way as soon as possible. We refused to budge and continued our efforts to rescue the lost and the abducted for another three months. We were able to save nearly three hundred people and dispatch them to India. How we did it is a long story. Each case was a tragic drama in itself.

I have never been able to erase the episode of Jaswant Kaur from my memory. She was recovered from Khewra, a place known for its salt mines. The village lay about fifty miles deep in the ravines. Jaswant Kaur, a Sikh girl of fifteen, was saved by her neighbour Ghulam Ishaq when her home was attacked one night by mobs from the neighbouring villages. In the melee her father and two brothers were killed. Her two sisters were abducted but her mother and a teenage brother managed to slip out to safety and joined a party of Hindus heading for the refugee camp, presuming that all her family massacred. Jaswant Kaur had hidden herself in a shed at the back of her house. Ghulam Ishaq found her two days later when he took the abandoned house for himself.

Ghulam Ishaq was a friend of the girl's father. He also presumed that Jaswant Kaur was the lone survivor of her family. Having daughters who were Jaswant's age, Ghulam Ishaq looked upon the young girl with paternal affection. This alone could not have saved Jaswant Kaur's life in the atmosphere of frenzy and phobia that prevailed in the region. So he announced his intention of marrying her. A *nikah* ceremony was performed but the marriage was not consummated. This was only known to his immediate family.

Kartari, Jaswant Kaur's mother, was brought to the camp in Jhelum with her son. Both were in a dazed state. Kartari was inconsolable and refused to leave the camp till her daughters were found. She had seen her husband and two sons murdered before eyes, but she was convinced that her daughters were still alive.

We had no soldiers or policemen to help us recover abducted women. My father tried persuasion. He had been legal adviser to the salt mines administration and had sorted out some family disputes in Khewra, so he decided to approach the villagers personally. One of his clients was Ghulam Ishaq. When my father called on him, he did not know that Jaswant Kaur was in Ishaq's custody. He asked Ishaq to help him in the recovery of three Hindu girls known to be missing from Khewra. Ghulam Ishaq pleaded ignorance of their whereabouts. To reassure my father of his sincerity, he came to Jhelum. Jaswant Kaur's mother fell at his feet and broke down. Ghulam Ishaq commiserated with her without divulging anything. Much as he was moved by Kartari's grief, he was not willing to part with her daughter because he had fallen in love with her. He returned to Khewra promising to do his best to find the missing girls.

It did not take long for my father to discover that Jaswant Kaur was in Ghulam Ishaq's house. His faith in Ishaq's sincerity was rudely shaken. He also came to know that Ishaq had married the girl and was powerful enough locally to resist any pressure from the administration. The only way out was to somehow inform Jaswant Kaur that her mother and brother were alive and staying in the Jhelum camp, and then plot her escape.

Anwar Khan, a police constable in the small contingent provided to us by local authorities, had been with us from the beginning and had become quite involved in our mission. He was the one who had told my father of Jaswant Kaur's whereabouts. He now managed to inform the girl that her mother and brother were alive and expected her to join them in the camp at Jhelum.

He told no one how he managed to reach her. By then Jaswant Kaur had gained Ghulam Ishaq's confidence and persuaded him to let her see her mother and brother, promising she would return to him. The night before they had left for Jhelum they consummated their marriage.

Once re-united with her mother, Jaswant Kaur went through another trauma. She found it hard to part from her. She confessed to feeling torn between her love for her widowed mother and her loyalty to Ishaq, who had been so protective and trusting. Ishaq had moved to Jhelum and visited her every day. The situation was fraught with danger. Ultimately Jaswant Kaur accepted my father's suggestion. One afternoon, she left with her mother and brother and a few others for Amritsar.

My father sent me with the group because he feared Ghulam Ishaq's wrath would fall on us. He then broke the news to the jilted husband. Much to my father's surprise, instead of exploding with rage, Ghulam Ishaq broke down and wept unrestrainedly. He was a giant with a glowing pink complexion which betrayed his Afghan ancestry. To see such a strong man so reduced by grief was a spectacle my father found hard to bear. It took a while for Ghulam Ishaq to compose himself. Then he told my father what he had gone through. He thanked my father for sparing him further embarrassment.

The story of Jaswant Kaur did not end there. Like several other women and children we 'rescued', she was left with my mother who had taken charge of a temporary refugee camp she had set up for rescued women awaiting others of their families to join them. As days went by their chances of leaving Pakistan become bleaker and bleaker. Many of them were pregnant and their families refused to take them back. The stigma of having unmarried girls bearing illegitimate children was not acceptable to their kith and kin.

This was what happened to Jaswant Kaur. The results of her cohabitation with Ghulam Ishaq began to show. At first her mother Kartari accepted the inevitable. But her teenaged brother Bhagwan Singh was adamant. The family *izzat* (honour) had been sullied. They would have to suffer the taunts of others for the rest of their lives. Kartari came around to her son's views and the two decided to abandon Jaswant Kaur to her fate. My mother's threats to expel them from camp had no effect. They slipped out of the camp, leaving Jaswant Kaur behind to survive as best as she could.

It was fate of women like Jaswant Kaur that determined the future course of my parents' life.

By this time my father's membership in Pakistan's parliament had been transferred to the Indian parliament. My mother was unwilling to abandon the women under her care and let them go to government-run refugee camps which had rapidly become like brothels. My father had very little choice in the matter. He could not think of being separated from his wife and spending part of his life away from her in Delhi. He decided to make his home in Jalandhar.

He resigned from the Indian parliament and started the Nari Niketan (women's home) at Jalandhar. It was gradually opened to women other than victims of the Partition. My parents jointly ran this institution for destitute women till my father's death in 1979. Then my mother took over and ran it single-handedly till she died in 1988.

The Niketan did not pull down its shutters. My father left his savings to the Niketan Trust. It carries on its good work under the supervision of my brother Inder. Apart from providing food and lodging, it also runs a high school for the children of its inmates, and for orphans.

The citizens of Jalandhar expressed their gratitude by naming the road that runs in front of Nari Niketan after my father. My mother, who survived my father by eight years, refused to accept any honours from the citizens or the government. She was happy that her husband had been honoured and was content to bask in his posthumous glory.

6

SHIMLA

Once the work of rehabilitating refugee women was over, I began to look around for a job. My father could no longer afford to support me. There was no question of my starting another graphic art studio of the kind I had earlier set up at Lahore. The best I could hope for was to get a job as a graphic artist. Fortunately, my father's friend Dr Gopi Chand Bhargava was elected the first Chief Minister of the Indian half of Punjab. The department of public relations which employed graphic artists was directly under him. In the summer of 1948, I joined this department at Shimla.

The job was a reasonably well-paid one. With it came a house that was too large for my needs. However, my joy at being able to earn my own money was short-lived. A government office is not the best place for an artist to give free rein to his creative faculties. My immediate boss, Lajpat Rai Nair, was an erudite man but not sophisticated enough to appreciate art. He also had his own problems. The director general of the department was Shri Virender, a scion of the family which had founded Urdu newspaper *Pratap*. He was the eldest son of Mahasha Krishan, its chief editor and member of the Congress Party in the Punjab Assembly. His status empowered him to boss over our department.

I had known of Virender since my childhood. *Pratap* and *Milap* were Urdu dailies which had much in common. Both were owned, edited and published by men who used 'Mahasha' as their title. Both papers were published from Lahore, catered to the same kind of clientele and propagated the ideals of the Arya Samaj. But they were implacably hostile towards each other. This went well beyond differences of opinion on provincial and national politics. They attacked each other with unfailing regularity.

Their readers enjoyed their slanging matches. Punjabis who could not read English read either *Pratap* or *Milap,* or both. My father preferred to read the *Tribune,* an old and established English-language paper with a liberal perspective on national and social affairs. For my mother, who could not read English, he procured one or other of these Urdu papers. He had hoped to get her interested in politics and social matters and in this he was successful. She quickly became an avid newspaper reader, and the habit became an addiction.

The Lahore papers reached Jhelum by the Frontier Mail at around noon. Father returned from the law courts a few hours later and looked forward to reading the *Tribune.* By then Mother had absorbed all the news she could from *Milap* and or *Pratap.* I shared her passion for newspapers, more so when my leg bothered me, and I was confined to my bed.

Newspapers played a very important role in our lives. As soon as we learnt to read Urdu, they became a part of our daily reading. I certainly derived more out of reading them than I did from school textbooks.

It did not take very long for my superiors to conclude I was a misfit and would not be able to draw pictures of the kind appreciated by

Urdu or other vernacular papers of the time. They began to look for excuses to get rid of me. I gave them a convenient one soon after I joined the department.

I was asked to design a poster against the hoarding of food grains and profiteering in general. The man I portrayed as the prototype of a black marketeer had an uncanny resemblance to the state food minister. Though I had designed the poster many weeks before the fellow was elevated to ministerial rank, he was incensed by the adverse publicity he received. Even before he took the oath of office, he had decided to teach me a lesson. He found my superior more than willing to oblige him. They were devious in the way they went about it. They knew that if I was sacked for drawing the minister's likeness, they could be in trouble themselves. So they dug into my past to see if they could discover some skeletons in my cupboard. They found what they were looking for in police files: my association with the Communist Party. I was proud of my leftist past and foolish enough to brag about it. Isher Singh Majhail, the minister in question, was an Akali and had many scores to settle with the Communists. He found me easy prey. I no longer had the protection of Dr Bhargava who had been replaced by Bhim Sen Sachar. I was ordered to either resign or be fired. I chose to resign.

During my years in Shimla, I had plenty of spare time to paint. I began with scenes of the Partition and its horrendous aftermath, which were still fresh in my mind. This theme was closest to my heart. It is possible that had there been no Partition I might have invented some traumatic and overwhelming scenario to express the anguish in my heart.

I was ploughing a lonely furrow. I knew no one who could assess the quality of my work.

Fortunately, one day in 1950 I ran into my old friend and mentor, Sardari Lall Prashar. Having lost the Mayo School of Arts to Pakistan, he had come to Shimla to try and set up something of the same kind in the half of the Punjab that came to India.

I had not met Prasher since I left Mayo five years earlier. Renewing my acquaintance with him proved very worthwhile. He was surprised to see my work. He was not a man of many words so the little he said in the way of encouragement bolstered my sagging spirits.

In 1949 there was a lot of talk about building a new capital for the Indian Punjab. Shimla was then the temporary seat of the Punjab government. It was swarming with the top brass of anglicized civil servants who feverishly imitated the lifestyle of their erstwhile rulers. They were pressurizing Nehru to invite a foreign architect to design the new city. Leading the group was P.N. Thapar, the seniormost ICS officer in the state, who held the post of financial commissioner (development). Thapar had recruited P.L. Verma, the chief engineer of Punjab, and Avatar Singh Malhotra, the finance secretary; both men shared Thapar's enthusiasm for everything Western.

Prasher, who remembered more details about the issue than I did, described the earlier controversial debate that had gone on over choosing architects to design India's capital when it was decided to shift the seat of government from Calcutta to Delhi.

The argument over the best architect to design the new capital for India had not been between the rulers and the ruled, but between imperialists on the one hand and liberals on the other. Among the latter were E.B. Havell who was principal of the School of Art in Calcutta, and John Lockwood Kipling, then settled in Lahore.

Havell and Kipling had regarded the decision to build a new capital on and around Raisina Hill as a wonderful opportunity to preserve the little that remained of the Indian tradition of architecture. They were outvoted by the imperialists who insisted on utilizing this opportunity to leave a legacy of their rule on Indian soil. They chose the British architect Sir Edwin Lutyens to design New Delhi. The Shimla conclave of brown sahibs had learnt nothing from this experience, and persisted with their demand to invite foreign architects to design a new capital for the Indian Punjab.

Pandit Nehru resisted the pressure put on him by Thapar. He had earlier criticized the grandiose designs of the Viceregal Lodge and the secretariats by Lutyens and Baker in New Delhi. If it had to be a foreign architect, Nehru's preference was for the American, Albert Mayer. Mayer was in India during World War II and had established a bond with leaders of the freedom movement, including Mahatma Gandhi and Pandit Nehru. He had impressed them with his ideas about building model villages and reviving cottage industries. Prior to Mayer's arrival in the Punjab, Thapar and his associates had tried to hire the American Frank Lloyd Wright as chief architect. Wright declined the offer on grounds of age and failing health. Mayer suggested the name of the Polish-American architect Javersky, a young man of surprising sensitivity towards Indian culture and architecture. Prasher and I, who had the privilege of meeting Javersky and seeing his early sketches, were impressed by how much he had imbibed of the atmosphere prevailing in India's bazaars and bylanes.

Young Javersky was not destined to have a hand in the designing of Punjab's new capital. On his return flight to India he died when his plane crashed at Cairo.

Thapar and his friends persuaded Nehru to accept three European architects to work with Mayer. They were Charles Edouard Corbusier, popularly known as Le Corbusier, who brought with him a team consisting of his cousin Pierre Jeanneret, Maxwell Fry and his wife Jane Drew, who was an architect in her own right. She was also the chief reason for Corbusier agreeing to accept an assignment to work in the remote land of heat and dust. Her liaisons with Corbusier and many others were as famous as Corbusier's buildings round the globe.

When Corbusier was appointed, Mayer left. Corbusier set up his office in Shimla. Young aspiring architects from all over India came in swarms to seek employment in the new venture.

At the time I was living in the YMCA where many of these hopefuls were staying. Among them was an American named Ted Bower. Bower had been a student and the alter ego of Frank Wright. He had come to Shimla to get acquainted with his mentor's *bête noire*, Corbusier, and study his plans to build a new city—or as he put it, 'to witness the seeding of a foreign culture, in an ancient land'.

How Ted Bower and I became friends is hard to explain. He knew no Hindustani. Whatever little English I had learnt in my interaction with Tony Rosenthal in Bombay had rusted for want of use. But to the surprise and envy of others in the YMCA we surmounted the linguistic hurdle easily, because we had a lot of other interests in common. For me, it was like a refresher course of my earlier days with Rosenthal. Bower was keen on learning what I understood of Lockwood Kipling's ideas, which he found to be conceptually close to those of his mentor and friend Frank Lloyd Wright. I was equally keen to discover what modern architecture was all about. Corbusier's arrival had triggered off a debate on the subject; its pros and cons were hotly argued across the country. Prasher told me that it reminded him of the controversy between the supporters and the critics of Edwin Lutyens' blueprints for New Delhi.

My friendship with Ted Bower brought about a positive turn in my fortunes. I valued this human connection much more than any exchange of information about precepts of architecture. Ted helped me to become more fluent in English. Though my enunciation remained somewhat unusual, I was less inhibited in my speech. I taxed Bower's patience and tolerance, but he bore it with grace and compassion. Bower gave me an insight into the fierce controversy raging between the upholders of regionalism and the champions of internationalism.

According to Bower, Corbusier disregarded indigenous styles and never made a secret of his contempt for anything which did not fit in with his preconceived notions.

Bower's analysis of trends in architecture proved to be prophetic. Corbusier based his plans for Chandigarh upon the time-worn cliche of 'form follows functions'. His admirers treated it as a sacred mantra. What they called functional architecture turned out to be more his own concepts rather than the users' or clients' notion of what they wanted. In common parlance, this phrase meant architecture for the sake of architecture. His buildings exhibit a marked indifference towards local cultures around which communities have traditionally created their habitats, in the ways birds construct their nests according to the shapes of their own bodies. Architecture that ignores this time-tested rule becomes artificial. Even decades after its construction, Chandigarh continues to manifest a duality of cultures: the culture of its inhabitants and the culture of its architecture. The two never seem to reconcile.

Corbusier's acolytes never cease to praise his pioneering work in India. They describe him as Pandit Nehru's own choice for the project. There is no truth in this assertion. Even if it had been so, it does not change my opinion that what Corbusier built has little relevance to the Punjabi ethos.

In a letter addressed to the then governor of the Punjab, Nehru wrote:

> Last night Mr Corbusier had dinner with me. In answer to my question as to what Indian style of architecture Chandigarh was going to have, he replied, 'You wear trousers, drive autos and have adopted the Westminster style of democracy and yet you ask for an Indian style'. This man worries me. Please keep an eye on him.

This letter still exists in the archives of the Prime Minister's secretariat.

Sometime late in 1951, before I lost my job with the Punjab government, I ran into Charles Fabri and his Indian wife Ratna who had been with me at Mayo.

I remembered Ratna because of her toothy smile. Though it occasionally admitted girls, the Mayo School was not co-educational because the social background of women wanting to study arts was very different from that of its male students. Finding little cultural and intellectual affinity with the crowd at the school, she had gone out of her way to cultivate me. Prasher encouraged her to do so.

Ratna Mathur, as she then was, came to know Fabri as her father's colleague in the Punjab government's archaeology department. When she met Fabri, she was in her teens and he was in his late forties, almost the same age as her father. I discovered what lay behind her attachment to Fabri. He was then curator of the Lahore Museum which was housed in an extension of our school.

The most widely discussed artist at the time was Amrita Sher-Gil, whose untimely death a little earlier had elevated her into a cult figure. There were scores of women artists who dreamt of filling Amrita's shoes. One of them was Ratna Mathur. She intended to join Bhubesh Sanyal's studio, but he had more students than he could accommodate. Charles Fabri persuaded her to abandon the idea. She was completely taken in by Fabri's claim that he had made Amrita Sher-Gil the greatest figure in art world. He convinced Ratna that he could do the same for her as she had the same potential as Amrita. He promised to raise her to great heights.

Ratna joined the Mayo school. Fabri took her under his wing. Ratna was convinced that Fabri had the magic formula by which he would open vistas of future greatness for her. Fabri came to see her in her classroom almost every hour and left her in high spirits. She applied herself to her work with demonic zeal and eagerly awaited his next visit.

Ratna was like one in a trance. Despite her father's strong opposition, she became Mrs Charles Fabri. Soon after came the Partition. Fabri opted to stay in Pakistan. This second blow broke her father's heart. He had a stroke and succumbed to it before the country was divided.

A year or so later Fabri changed his mind, migrated to India and settled in New Delhi. I resumed my acquaintance with him and we soon became close friends. His marriage was not harmonious. Bickering turned into stormy outbursts of temper; mutual allegations of infidelity were followed by dark hints of conspiracy and the overwhelming sense that each was trying to get rid of the other.

Fabri went to the extent of accusing Ratna of trying to murder him. Once Ratna invited my wife Kiran and me to dine with them in their makeshift flat on Ram Kishore Road in Old Delhi's Civil Lines. We were not able to make it, nor did we inform her in time that we would not be coming. Next morning when Kiran rang up to apologize, it was a very sick Ratna who answered the phone. She said she had been vomiting since midnight. It was food poisoning. She had eaten a slice of the cake she had baked herself. Fabri had fallen asleep waiting for us without touching the cake. When I tried to joke about what the cake could have done to old Fabri, Ratna became very serious and pleaded with me not to say anything about the episode in Fabri's presence. He had become highly suspicious of her. Fabri could not make an Amrita Sher-Gil out of Ratna Mathur. But she flourished as an interior decorator of remarkable originality. She won recognition as the pioneer of an ethnic style of interior designing.

Though the Fabris ultimately parted company with a lot of bitterness, it had to be conceded that when Charles fell ill, Ratna nursed him with much more devotion than a happily married wife would have done. Both of them died tragically. Charles' last days were full of financial difficulties; his age and failing health did not allow him to take on more work. He took his own life. The night before he committed suicide we met at an arts exhibition. Instead of going to the

Statesman office to write a review of the exhibition, as was customary with him, he handed an envelope, which I presumed contained his review, to the gateman. He came with me to my apartment. He was unusually calm and composed. I had absolutely no idea of what was going on in his mind. He was with me till midnight. He declined the lift home that he normally used to accept. A few hours later Ratna rang up to tell us that Charles was dead.

The envelope he had dropped at the *Statesman* office turned out to be the obituary he had written for himself. He was generous in the praise of his friends. Ratna died a few years later while still in her prime and busy as ever. The Fabris left behind their only child, a son who happened to be an albino.

My first meeting with the Fabris in Shimla was very significant. I invited both of them to see my work. Fabri's comments were most flattering; he was prone to exaggerate and write in superlative terms when he liked something. I was not aware of this at the time. He talked of great murals that were being painted in Mexico and compared my canvases to the best in that country. That was the first time I heard of Mexico as the home of mural art.

My earlier acquaintance with Mexico was through the myths of Mayan culture I had heard before I became deaf. According to *kathas* narrated by pundits in the Mohalla Chowk in Jhelum, Mexico was the *firangi* (foreign) name of *patal*, the underworld. I was fascinated by the idea of this mythological subterranean country. The significance of *patal desh,* according to these pundits, was that the Pandavas had migrated here after realizing the hollowness of their victory in the battle of Kurukshetra. The legend was given a 'scientific' gloss by a fraudulent anthropologist, Chiman Lal, who had been in jail with my father. In his book *Hindu America,* he propounded the thesis that the Inca and Aztec civilizations of Latin America had Hindu origins. According to him the Pandavas had named Argentina in honour of their warrior sibling Arjuna, and Yucatán, the coastal area of Mexico, was a distortion of the word 'Yogistan'.

After listening to Charles Fabri, I began to conjure up a new image of Mexico. More so as Fabri thought it was the place I should go to for inspiration. At about the same time I came across an advertisement issued by the ministry of education announcing a scholarship to study painting in Mexico. The year was 1952. At the time I was unemployed and living with my parents in Jalandhar. I spent hours trying to improve my English, and dreaming about Mexico.

I decided to apply for the scholarship. When it came to filling out the application form, I realized that I had nothing to support my claim except a diploma from the Mayo School of Arts. Fortunately, I remembered my connection with Charles Fabri, who had settled in New Delhi and was writing regularly on art for the *Statesman.* On a hot June afternoon my brother Inder and I knocked on the door of Fabri's apartment in the Shahjahan Road barracks.

As we pushed through the half-open door, we were astonished to see Fabri standing stark naked. Without being in the least discomfited he asked us to sit down and took his seat in front of his typewriter, which he had left to answer our knock.

I told him of the Mexican scholarship and asked for a recommendation. Without wasting time on formalities, he pushed a fresh sheet of paper into his typewriter and hammered out words which remain engraved in my memory. It was a glowing tribute to my talents as a painter. After handing me the testimonial he warned Inder not to build up too much hope about my chances.

Armed with Fabri's recommendation, we went to India Coffee House to show it to our friends. To my pleasant surprise they suddenly began to see in me talent they had never before suspected. Among these regulars at the Coffee House was an old classmate of Inder's—a stenographer on the board which interviewed applicants for scholarships. He did not pretend to have any influence but promised to keep us informed of what transpired at the interviews. Considering our limited contacts, we were delighted with his offer.

My main problem was with the enunciation of English, the language in which I expected to answer the board. Inder and my cousin Vijay Gujral coached me by making me answer a hypothetical set of likely questions.

One day our stenographer friend informed us that the Mexican cultural attaché had been invited to assist the board in the selection, and he had suggested that candidates be asked to bring at least two of their paintings with them. I was cheered by the news.

English not being my first language, the Mexican was not likely to be concerned with my enunciation or faulty grammar. I was advised to look straight at him when answering questions. But how was I to spot him among a dozen Indians who had similar complexions? Someone came up with the information that the Mexican's features were somewhat Mongol, with high cheekbones and slanting eyes.

The interview was set for 3 p.m. in the room of the joint secretary of the ministry of education. Holding one canvas each, Inder and I walked to the appointed room in the North Block of the secretariat. We were told to wait on the veranda where half a dozen other applicants were seated. The only one among them I was to meet in later years was Ram Kumar.

As I took my seat before the interview board, my eyes rested on a gentleman seated across from me, in the centre of the group; he had high cheekbones and slanting eyes. Throughout the question-and-answer session, I kept my gaze fixed on him. After the interview we met our stenographer friend near the grill that divides the secretariat blocks from the Rashtrapati Bhavan. He told us that my performance had not impressed the board. The diplomat had not attended the meeting. The man I took to be him was in fact the joint secretary, M.G. Siyadain.

I left for Jalandhar the same night.

A few days later our stenographer friend told Inder that the Mexican attaché who had the final say in the selection, had asked the board to recommend two artists, and wanted to see their work.

Humayun Kabir, who was then secretary for education, was keen that the board recommend Ram Kumar. In order to give their recommendations a semblance of fairness, the board members included my name because they were sure I would be turned down and Ram Kumar would get the scholarship. This was not good news except that it indicated that the door had not yet been slammed against me.

Then came another development. My architect friend Ted Bower had been in love with an Indian writer, Santha Rama Rau, who lived in New York. At her insistence, Bower had come to see her native land for himself. During the months Ted and I were together he often wrote to Santha about me. Suddenly she arrived in New Delhi.

She telephoned Inder and told him she wanted to meet me and see my work. I was in Jalandhar but many of my paintings were lying in my cousin Vijay's spacious bungalow on Barakhamba Road.

Santha had lunch with the Mexican cultural attaché. She had known him in Washington when her father was the Indian ambassador stationed there. When Santha told him of her appointment to see an artist's work, the attaché offered to accompany her. Having already seen the two paintings that the ministry had sent him, he had no difficulty in identifying them. All along Inder was unaware of the diplomat's identity.

It was only after Inder told Santha about my application for the scholarship that the attaché disclosed who he was and confirmed his decision to recommend my name. He was none other than the celebrated Mexican poet Octavio Paz, who later won the Nobel Prize for literature.

My selection had to be processed through the ministry of education. It had access to the record of my political background and the reasons for my dismissal by the Punjab government. It also hinted that I might face a problem when I applied a passport.

A few days later our stenographer friend told Inder that Octavio Paz had recommended my name to the ministry as his first choice.

To thwart me, the ministry tried another dirty trick. The letter informing me of my selection was destroyed. Another two were likewise typed out but not posted. The officials concerned could now presume that I was not interested in the scholarship.

I told Octavio Paz about this conspiracy. He advised me to write to the ministry telling them that I knew Octavio Paz had recommended my name and that I was accepting the scholarship. That did the trick. There was a bitter resentment in the ministry, but it had no option but to acknowledge my letter of acceptance.

The next hurdle was getting a passport. I knew that I would never get clearance from the Punjab Police. I had to think of other ways to obtain it. In June 1952 Nehru made a minor reshuffle in his cabinet and inducted Mr R.K. Sidhwa as head of the ministry of home affairs. Sidhwa had been in the same jail as my father. My father took me to see him and explained my predicament.

Sidhwa advised me to apply from Delhi. In the normal course of things the passport officer in Delhi would have referred the case to the Punjab Police, which would have taken a long time. Using this as a pretext, Sidhwa effectively sidelined reference to Punjab and had the Delhi Police give me a clearance. A passport was issued to me.

The news of my getting a scholarship to Mexico got around. I began to be taken seriously by the Coffee House crowd. One of the regulars was S.H. Vatsyayan. He was impressed by my work and suggested I hold a one-man exhibition in Delhi before leaving for Mexico. He and his wife-to-be, Kapila Malik, made arrangements to exhibit my paintings in the annexe of Freemasons Hall, located between Hotel Imperial and the main building of the Cottage Industries Emporium on Janpath. Vatsyayan wrote the introduction to the catalogue and persuaded Humayun Kabir to inaugurate the exhibition.

The morning after the inauguration remains ever fresh in my memory. It was well known that Charles Fabri went to the *Statesman* office after visiting an exhibition to write his review and ensure that it appeared in the paper the next morning. Neither Inder nor I got much sleep that night, waiting for the hawker to deliver the paper at dawn. When it came, the review thrilled us. It was on the top of the third page. The opening sentence set the tone for the rest. He declared me a genius.

By the time we had finished reading it a dozen times, the dak edition of the newspaper had reached Jalandhar and was seen by my father. When he spoke to Inder on the phone he broke down in a rare show of emotion. He felt that at long last I had managed to break through the walls of the dungeon I had been imprisoned in since I lost my hearing. Fabri's review was followed by a stream of other commentators vying with each other in the use of superlatives. Overnight I became a celebrity.

The Punjab government changed its attitude towards me and offered me a loan to meet the travel expenses not covered by my scholarship. I went to Shimla to collect the money and regain a little of the respect I had lost with my dismissal from my job. The visit did much to inflate my ego.

However there was one thing I did not accomplish on this visit. I was hoping to win the heart of a young lady I had seen soon after my arrival in Shimla in the summer of 1948. I had spotted her strolling on the Mall. She appeared to have a high-spirited nature and was conscious of her good looks and aware of men ogling her as she slid through the crowd. Basking in the attention showered on her, she would walk up and down the stretch between the Clark's Hotel at one end and Scandal Point at the other.

I was not the only one under her spell. She had a horde of admirers and was known among them as 'Miss .303' after the make of the rifle used during World War II. She was epitome of vivacious sensual charm and was said to be mature well beyond her eighteen years. As the summer wore on, my infatuation for her increased. It persisted through autumn and the snow and ice of winter. Instead of strolling on the Mall, most people went to the ice-skating rink. Miss .303 was a regular skater. I did not particularly enjoy skating as it was too rigorous a form of exercise for me and I liked to stay in my warm bed till mid-morning. But there I was—up at the crack of dawn, taking quick bath and arriving at the skating rink by 7:30 a.m. Once a day was not enough. I was there again in the evening, and did not leave till the girl departed at closing time.

All my efforts to attract her attention were in vain. Miss .303 scarcely noticed my existence. I fantasized about her, converted my fantasies into imaginary conquests and boasted about them to my friends. She remained beyond my reach. She was always surrounded by admirers who dwarfed me by their physical strength and social status.

On my last visit to Shimla I felt that since I had become a minor celebrity, I stood a better chance of making her acquaintance. I was out of luck. She had left for England. Shimla was thick with rumours that she was infatuated with a Pakistani and intended to marry him.

The change in the Punjab government's attitude towards me went beyond granting me a loan. M.L. Nanda, deputy inspector general of the Punjab Police, took me to his office and showed me the copy of a letter he had sent to the Delhi Police, with a copy to my father, ordering those remarks on my political activities be expunged from their records and my name be thus cleared. Nanda was distantly related to my mother and owed much to my father for the promotions he received after Independence. My father spoke on his behalf to his friend Dr Gopi Chand Bhargava, then Chief Minister of the state. The same Nanda had provided Shri Virender, Lajpat Rai Nair and the minister Isher Singh Majhail with information about my Communist past, that had ended my short and inglorious career as a government employee. At that time he had refused to see me.

Now that he had come to know of my father's closeness to Sidhwa, he suddenly remembered his being related to my mother and felt obliged to help me. The man changed colours like a chameleon. Two years later when Sidhwa was no longer a minister, he became inspector general of the Delhi Police. He went out of his way to prevent Inder's wife Shil from getting passport, on the same pretext that he used against me—my Communist connections. I was anxious to get out of India before government officials, particularly the police, changed their minds. I had to get the cheapest sea passage possible, which was hard to come by. Ultimately, I was able to get a berth on the *SS Multan* due to sail from Bombay in mid-August of 1952.

7

MEXICO

THE VOYAGE ON THE *SS SULTAN* IS STILL VIVID IN MY MEMORY—NOT surprisingly, since it was my first venture on the high seas in what then appeared to me to be a luxury liner. Thought the *Multan* was one of the largest in P &O's fleet of ships, it was on its last voyage before being consigned to the scrap heap. It was an entirely tourist-class ship with unrestricted access to all decks and restaurants. Since it had no class division it was exhilaratingly free of snobbery. Most of the passengers were students, the majority coming from Australia and New Zealand. It took us three weeks to cover the distance between Bombay and Southampton.

I was to take another boat from London to New York, and travel onwards to Mexico by train or bus.

Since this was the first time I was going to be absolutely on my own among total strangers, as soon as my train pulled out of Delhi railway station, I was filled with foreboding. I had brushed them aside when my parents and other members of the family expressed their apprehensions, but faced with the reality of my situation, all the bravado I had shown in the presence of my kin soon deserted me.

Though my English had improved since my friendship with Ted Bower in Shimla, and again in New Delhi where he had moved before returning to the US, it was not fluent or correct enough to be easily understood by strangers. Ted Bower did his best to reassure my parents, but noticing that I was still unsure of myself, he decided to accompany me to Bombay.

He spent much of the twenty-four hours we were together on the train teaching me the dos and don'ts of the society I was going to live in. On top of the list of 'don'ts' was holding hands or going about arm-in-arm with other males even a casual demonstration of physical affection between two males could be interpreted as homosexuality, which was stigmatized, attacked and ridiculed, often violently, in Western society. He had frequently noticed Indian men walking hand-in-hand, and found it very objectionable.

On top of his list of 'dos' was the advice that I should be less self-conscious about my handicap. He assured me that people in the West were more understanding and sympathetic towards the handicapped than people in my own country. He had other words of wisdom to impart. He assured me that in the world I was travelling to, merit counted more than in India. People sought the company of achievers. He told me about Francisco Goya, the Spanish painter of the Renaissance period who lost his hearing in his middle years. Even in that orthodox Catholic society, people went out of their way to communicate with him by whatever means were possible. Physical handicaps matter very little in the case of talented people. He mentioned the instance of Tony Rosenthal and his fellow GIs. They had desired my company because they found it worth their while. His parting words were, 'Your limitation will not be a handicap. Rather than causing you to be spurned, it may win you friends.'

Ted Bower's comments sustained my spirits through the long sea voyage. Once on board I became very gregarious and soon made friends with many fellow passengers. Among them was Bashka Nelkin, an Australian girl my age. She was travelling to Israel to involve herself in the task of nation-building. Through Bashka I made friends with Nairi Te Punga, a Maori girl from New Zealand who was five years younger than us. She was going to Oxford for further studies in anthropology. Bashka was not beautiful in the conventional sense, but full of zest and missionary fervour with regard to the project of working for the Jewish state. She found my family's involvement in the freedom struggle quite fascinating, but regretted India's anti-Israel and pro-Arab policy. Nairi Te Punga's chief assets were her brown complexion, a stunningly well-proportioned figure and full luscious lips. Like most Polynesians she had high cheekbones and dark sparkling eyes.

Though she had no intellectual pretentions, she was very curious about most subjects. I found her very desirable. Her eloquent body and seductive movements added emphasis to her poetic confessions. Bashka did not resent my preference for her friend. On the contrary, she began to encourage the closeness that was growing between us. By the time our ship entered the Suez Canal we had pledged undying love for each other. The only reason we were not able to take our love affair to its culmination was the lack of privacy on board. Men and women were not allowed berths in the same cabin. We looked forward to the end of the voyage so that we would have a chance to be alone.

The atmosphere that prevails in this floating world is almost an aphrodisiac. Love sprouts at the speed of wild grass. People are free to break the social taboos that exist on land. Bashka, in whom we both confided, took these happenings in her stride. She never said anything to discourage our growing intimacy.

On board I was always seen in the company of the two girls from New Zealand, one white and the other brown. Other passengers, particularly my fellow countrymen, were very intrigued. The only

Indian I was drawn to was a handsome South Indian youth going to Oxford. By sheer coincidence I ran into him again in London.

I was met at Southampton by my 'cousin' Harbans Kapur, son of Chacha Trilok Chand. He took me to London to stay with him. The next morning he took me to the Thomas Cook office to check about my onward journey to New York. My name was on the waiting list. To my dismay I learnt I could not get a confirmed booking for another month. The only alternative was to fly to New York. Besides it being beyond my means, no seats were available on flights for the next week.

We left the Thomas Cook office and took an underground train. When coming out of the tube station, I lost sight of Harbans. I waited outside the station for an hour. Then another hour passed. There was no sign of Harbans. Not knowing anything about London's tube stations, I did check other possible exits. As time went by, I began to panic. I had no money on me. All the traveller's cheques I had brought with me that morning had been cashed out to cover the difference between the sea fare I had paid for and the air passage I had asked for. Worse, I did not have Harbans' address. At that moment, the South Indian I had met on the ship materialized as if out of nowhere. He offered to help me find Harbans or his whereabouts. He took me to several places known to be the haunts of Indian students. He even lent me five pounds to buy lunch. I promised this South Indian whose name I did not know that I would return the loan the next day.

(That day came thirty-five years later. In the late eighties my son Mohit met the South Indian who had lent me money, in a friend's house. He told Mohit that I owed him five pounds he had lent me in London. Promptly I rang up my son's friend and learnt that the South Indian was none other than A.P. Venkateshwaran, then India's ambassador to China and later foreign secretary. He refused to accept the five pounds I owed him unless I added to it the accumulated interest at the rate of twenty percent, either in cash or in form of one of my paintings. I considered his demand usury of the grossest kind.)

Finally, we found someone who knew Harbans and took me to his lodgings. There I found a message from Thomas Cook. The only two seats available due to a cancellation were for the next day, one in the morning, the other on a flight at noon. I choose the second, hoping to get a final tryst with Nairi Te Punga.

I managed to get in touch with Nairi and Bashka and told them of my impending departure. Nairi came all the way from where she was staying to see me off at Heathrow airport. This was the last I saw of her.

The two weeks abroad the *Multan* had made me confident about my ability to get on with strangers. Besides the chance of spending a little with my Polynesian sweetheart, I had opted for the second flight because Ted's sister Mali Bower had promised to meet me at the airport. Before I crossed the immigration line at Heathrow, Nairi ran up to me and thrust a slip of paper in my pocket. I forgot about it as I had a lot to explain to British immigration officials about my transit visa for the US.

The overnight flight to New York was uneventful, but the minute plane landed at John F. Kennedy airport, my problems began. US immigration officials regarded all foreigners as prospective immigrants or Communist agents. What made my case suspect in the eyes of the authorities was the fact that while my visa was only for seven days, I had declared intention to spend as many days in New York alone. They informed me that it would take me an additional three days to cross the US by train—taking my total stay to ten days.

As if this was not bad enough, I had only five hundred dollars to meet my expenses for the duration, as well as pay for my fare from New York to Mexico. All this only added to the suspicions I had created in the minds of the immigration officials. My assurances that my stay in New York would be paid for by my sponsors cut no ice with them. Mali Bower, who I expected to be waiting for me at the immigration counter, was not there. On my pleading, the immigration officer agreed to ring her up. It was six in the morning. No one picked up the phone at the other end. I was told to sit in a corner and wait for the verdict.

Suddenly I remembered Nairi slipping a chit in the pocket of my overcoat. I opened it. It said that in case I found no place to go I should try the International Centre hostel for foreign students in New York. I gave the address to the immigration official and signed an undertaking that I would cross the US border within seven days. My impassioned appeal had an effect. After he had thoroughly scrutinized my scholarship papers he let me go. I took a cab to the International Centre on Riverside Drive.

I tried to get Mali Bower on the phone. There was no response. I decided to go to her apartment and took a bus to Greenwich Village. The kindly bus conductor took my map and marked the route to Christopher Street, circling the building where Mali Bower lived. When I got there, I found her apartment locked. In her letterbox I saw the telegram that I had sent her. Evidently, she had not collected her mail for quite a few days. My arriving earlier than expected had created confusion.

I started the return journey on foot so that I could see something of the city. By evening I found myself at Rockfeller Centre on 42nd Street. I took a lift up the tower and had a long look at the world's greatest metropolis. I bought a ticket to Radio City and watched a musical. I found it boring and walked out. In my confusion I dropped the city map. Once more I was gripped with panic. How would I get to the International Centre?

I did not have the nerve to stop anyone and ask for help; everyone seemed to be in a mad rush to get somewhere. Around midnight I got to 72nd Street where I managed to take a bus to the Centre. I had left it at 9 a.m. I got back around 1 a.m. the next morning. Except for the stop at the Rockefeller Centre and a bite at a hot dog stand, I had been walking nonstop for over ten hours.

The next day I stayed in the International Centre waiting for Mali to call me. I had left a message in her letterbox giving my address. She did not telephone. I had spent two nights New York and had only four more to go—of these four, two were for the onward journey. The immigration authorities that had checked me at International Centre had warned me in no uncertain terms that if I stayed in the country even a minute beyond the six nights and seven days granted by my visa, I would be arrested and deported back to India. I did not want to take any chances and decided to get out forty-eighty hours before the deadline.

Romesh Bhandari, the Indian Vice-Consul in New York, made arrangements for my onward journey. He sent one of his staff members to see me off at the railway station and sent a cable to the Mexican authorities informing them of my arrival.

I was told that in a non-smoking compartment I would find myself all alone. That was so till the train crossed the border into Mexico. Then the compartment filled up till there was no room to sit and passengers had to stand in the corridors. It was very much like a train journey in India. Though I was not able to converse with anyone, I noticed the informality and warmth amongst the passengers. They invited me to share their food; one woman put her baby in my lap to let me play with it. The countryside we passed was bleak and inhospitable. The land was flat, dusty and barren; the only vegetation was prickly cacti of different shapes and sizes. Occasionally I caught glimpses of nondescript villages, or peasants in large hats riding donkeys.

A few hours before we reached our destination the atmosphere in the train changed perceptibly. It was caused by the arrival of customs and immigration officials. They demanded the passports of all foreigners. While these were being inspected, customs officials got busy and began to manifest their tough, intimidating style. Like other passengers I was taken to the baggage van and ordered to open my cases. Around me was a litter of clothes, cosmetics and gadgets being checked for prices. The men in uniform reminded me of Punjab policemen—cocky, arrogant and rude.

Finally, it was my turn. To my utter surprise, the grim officials became all smiles. After a long scrutiny of my passport he sent for a woman seated at another table. They were intrigued by a piece of paper attached to my passport by the railroad authorities in New York. It stated that the bearer of the passport was deaf and should be communicated with in writing. The woman gave me a wry look and began scribbling questions dictated to her by the officer. I was cleared by customs. The immigration official then informed me through writing that the type of visa I had required reconfirmation by the immigration office in Mexico City. He warned me that I might be asked to show my documents over and over again, and advised me to get my sponsor's assistance.

It must have been nearly 10 p.m. when the train finally pulled up at the station in Mexico City. There was a lot of hugging and kissing all around me as passengers poured out of the train. I smiled at every face walking towards me, hoping it was that of the person who had come to receive me. Finally there was on one left to smile at. I dragged my heavy suitcase to one side and sat down upon it.

After an hour I concluded that no one had been sent to meet me. I felt very lonely and lost. For the first time since I had boarded the *Multan* I asked myself why on earth I had left home.

From a brochure in Spanish distributed in the train I scanned the list of recommended hotels. I could not pronounce their Spanish names, so I wrote the word 'hotel' on a piece of paper and walked to the nearest taxi stand. The cabbie I approached looked at me from head to foot and gave me a broad smile. Immediately I knew that he would try to cheat me.

In what seemed to be fit of patriotic fervour, he took me on a sightseeing tour of his city before he dropped me outside a hotel that I discovered the next morning was on a majestic *avenida* facing the rail station, and bore the grandiose name El Presidente. Though not a five-star or even a four-star hotel, I sensed it would be well beyond the meagre amount I had been left with. However, I decided to stay the night at El Presidente and then get my hosts to find me suitable lodgings.

None of the hotel staff spoke English. But they understood enough to instruct me how to get to the Palacio Nacional de Bellas Artes on Avenida Reforma, and marked the route on a city map. I was ready early the next morning. I decided to walk the distance to be well in time, before the opening of the offices. It took me a little more than an hour to walk to my destination. The front door was still closed.

I wandered around for another hour and at 10:30 a.m. I presented myself at the director's office. The secretary, a good-looking young woman, courteously ushered me into a waiting-room and asked me to wait till Señor Gamboa had finished with an interview he was conducting. After half an hour, I was told the director was still busy. Finally, the third time I asked, I was ushered into Señor Gamboa's august presence. He pleaded ignorance about my scholarship and asked his secretary to explain the situation to me. The lady took me to her cubicle and told me I could not have chosen a worse time to arrive in Mexico. The country was in the midst of re-electing its president and its administration, including the director of the Palacio Nacional de Belles Artes. Señor Gamboa had more important matters to deal with than my scholarship. Since there was no Indian diplomatic mission based in Mexico, there was no one he could approach on my behalf. The secretary was good enough to let me use the office telex to send a message to Romesh Bhandari in New York, and promised to let me know when she got a reply.

On the first day that I waited for the director to see me, I picked up the Spanish word *mañana,* meaning 'tomorrow'. After the aborted interview, I found a café which looked inexpensive. I had not eaten anything since I had entered Mexican territory. As I sat down and studied the menu, the only two items I could recognize were tea and coffee.

Fortunately a basket of bread and cakes was on the table. For the next few days, as I awaited the director's pleasure of granting me an interview, I dosed myself with *cafécon leche* (coffee with milk), bread and pastry. Later one of the hotel staff who spoke a few words of English gave me a menu which had items in both English and Spanish.

These small gestures of understanding kept me from leaving the hotel, which was otherwise well beyond my means. The manager agreed to give me time to settle my bill until my scholarship was activated. He ultimately charged me much less than their usual rates.

As there was no response from Romesh Bhandari I decided to look around for cheaper accommodation. Walking around the Avenida Insurgente I found a sign board reading 'Casa de Huéspedes', with its English equivalent 'Boarding House' marked alongside.

I entered the place and met the landlady who was German-Mexican. Many American students had been staying with her. She agreed to take me in. I was to stay with her till the end of my stay in Mexico.

Unknown to me at the time, the landlady, Julie Bastard, had a niece who was married to the renowned Mexican artist David Alfaro Siqueiros. It was through Julie that Siqueiros learnt of my presence in Mexico and the problems I was facing due to non-payment of my stipend. Soon after, a young Mexican woman artist came to see me and took me to meet Siqueiros. He was angry on hearing of the way I had been treated. He had spoken about it to the famous muralist Diego Rivera and a few other friends. A benefit fund was set up to help me. They also meant to take up the question of my scholarship with the ministry of external affairs.

Siqueiros sent me with the woman artist to make a courtesy call on Diego Rivera and see a few other well-known people. Their efforts managed to open the doors of the Mexican cultural establishment to me.

A few days later, in response to the telex I had sent to Bhandari, I was informed that the Indian Ambassador was to arrive in Mexico in a few weeks to present his credentials to the country's new President. Adolfo Cortinez, and would look into my problems during his visit.

The ambassador, Shri Gaganbhai Mehta, arrived in the city and took me to see the minister of external affairs. The best this official could do was to arrange a loan from his ministry pending the release of funds by the ministry of culture. By that time three months had already elapsed since my arrival in Mexico.

It was about then that I received a letter from Octavio Paz, who was posted in Tokyo. Inder had somehow got in touch with him and told him of my plight. Octavio advised me to go and see Emilio Portes Gil, who at the time was selected was the Mexican Ambassador in New Delhi. Gil had since returned home and was living in Mexico City.

As a former president of Mexico, Gil wielded considerable influence. Though I had never met him he was good enough to receive me. Gil was very upset on hearing of what I had gone through. He took me home to dinner. I received my stipend the next day.

In his telex informing me of Ambassador Mehta's visit, Romesh Bhandari had advised me to meet his colleague M.K. Rasgotra, then third secretary, who was accompanying the ambassador.

When I called on Rasgotra I ran into a comely Mexican journalist, Gossi Aguina Soto. The meeting proved to be most fruitful. It started as light-hearted banter. I discovered that she was not interested in me as a person but as an Indian, a rare species in Mexico in those days.

Indians were an uncommon sight in Mexico. Early this century four Indians had arrived by different routes: two had smuggled themselves into the country, the third was a Sikh member of the revolutionary Ghadar Party who had fled to Mexico from California. The fourth was Khankoje, who had been with Rash Bihari Bose, and was wanted for an attempt on the life of Viceroy Lord Harding. He had escaped to

California and then made his way to Mexico where he did a course in scientific agriculture and settled on a farm. It was through Khankoje that I met the other three resident Indians. I was disappointed. None of the four remembered much about India nor spoke any common Indian languages or English. Coming from different regions, they had evolved a vocabulary that only they could understand.

Gossi Soto was drawn to me out of curiosity. She had been attracted to Indians before she met me. She was no starry-eyed adolescent—she was twenty-four, well educated, well read and a woman of the world. She worked as a stringer for the *New York Times,* a position which gave her access to important people. Her love affair with India had started with a meeting with Aruna Asaf Ali who visited Mexico in 1947 with her husband Asaf Ali, India's first Ambassador to US. Aruna's escapades and underground activities in the 1942 Quit India movement had filled Gossi with an admiration for everything Indian.

Ambassador Asaf Ali's entourage had included two young officers. Ashfaque Hussain was married, but Prem Kirpal was a bachelor and as such ripe for plucking. I had no idea how far her attempts to seduce Kirpal succeeded: Gossi was prone to exaggerated descriptions of conquests. All I could be sure of was that the affair lasted as long as he was in Mexico, which was less than ten days. Later it was either on his advice or by her own choice that she began to explore the possibility of a permanent liaison with Ashafaque, who being Muslim, was not bound by laws of monogamy. He had visited Mexico a few times and she received a few letters from him while he was in Washington. By the time I arrived on the scene, he was back in India and too far way to keep the affair going.

Gossi then became involved with another Indian diplomat, who accompanied Ambassador Mehta to Mexico. This diplomat was an inhibited bachelor and enjoyed himself during his brief tenure at the Indian mission. After it became certain that he would not return to Mexico, Gossi decided to convert her friendship with me into a liaison. Both of us were fully aware that it would be temporary. We made the best of the limited time at our disposal. Gossi freed me of inhibitions I had about sex. Like most Indians of my age, I had been brought up with the traditional socio-cultural belief that sex was sinful and dirty. To start with I pretended that my interest in this good-looking Mexican was purely platonic. She was accustomed to Indian men approaching her with these false claims, and knew how to expose them thoroughly and ruthlessly. She did me a great favour. She severed the complicated knot of sexual inhibitions and ambiguities in which I had entangled myself. She made it easier for me to have physical relations with other women.

My contact with Gossi Soto did not terminate with the end of my stay in Mexico. Months before I left Mexico, her dream of going to India had come true, courtesy Ashfaque Hussain, who had taken over as secretary of culture in the ministry of education, a development I had duly reported to Gossi. She contacted him; he responded quickly and arranged a scholarship for her so she could visit India. It was a grant that had been long due in exchange for the one that the Mexican government had favoured me with.

But by the time I reached India one year or so after her arrival in New Delhi, the dice had been thrown. She had established herself in high social circles, which she efficiently charmed with her availability, good looks and intellectual calibre.

I tried to rekindle our old relations but without any success. Compared to those whom she had cultivated, I had neither resources nor stature. My delusion that she would reciprocate affectionately came to an abrupt end when, knowing that she loved being entertained, I made a plan to take her out to dinner. I mentioned this to Inder, with whom she had initially stayed and did even now, on and off. He thought this scheme foolish on my part, considering our financial resources, the high cost of food in good restaurants and her expensive habits. However, I was convinced that one evening with me would be enough to lure her away from the exclusive circles where such entertainment was routine.

Considering my serious commitment to the scheme, Inder had advised me to choose the Kwality restaurant next door which was perhaps within our resources. But being cautious by nature, he advised an advance visit to Kwality before taking Gossi there. This was to check the prices and choose a menu that would match my pocket.

The visit was not rewarding. The only item I found affordable consisted of *chhole-bhature*. When I mentioned it to Inder he laughed and advised me to save those ten rupees for some better purpose. I was bitterly disappointed, but bowed to his impeccable logic. Gossi soon married a Spanish diplomat and ceased to be part of my life.

Back in Mexico, I apprenticed myself to David Alfaro Siqueiros, who had interceded for me regarding my stipend. Along with Diego Rivera and José Clemente Orozco, Siqueiros formed the triumvirate that ruled the world of contemporary Mexican art.

Besides being an artist, Siqueiros was an active member of the Communist party. When Leon Trostsky fell out with Stalin and was being hounded by the Bolsheviks, Diego Rivera, who had by then become disillusioned with Stalinist Communism, offered Trotsky refuge in one of his own houses in Coyoacán a suburb of Mexico City. It was during Trotsky's stay in this house that the conspiracy to murder him was hatched, and Siqueiros took the responsibility of driving the executioner to Trotsky's place of refuge. He was supposed to wait in the getaway car but had to flee on hearing the commotion that ensued after the murder was committed.

Siqueiros escaped on a ship and forced to stay on it for the next one year as no country was willing to let him in. Finally, he was admitted to Ecuador and kept in detention in a house.

By the time this imprisonment ended, he had turned his entire house into an art gallery: floors, walls, ceilings and garden were all fused into a magnificent aesthetic composition, part painting, and part sculpture and part architecture.

It was not gimmickry, though many described it as such at that time. It has survived as one the best living examples of the synthesis of art and architecture. Even his critics conceded that it was his politics and not his art that they questioned.

Criticism of Siqueiros become very serious because of his involvement in Trotsky's assassination. At other times he was accused of petty violations, such as leaving his hotel in New York without settling his bill. He had defended himself by pleading that it was a minor revenge taken for the Yankee plundering of Mexico that had gone on for many decades. The case received much publicity and Siqueiros was declared persona non grata by the US for the rest of his life.

Siqueiros was indeed a man of many talents and one whose lust for experimenting knew no bounds. He pioneered many techniques which other artists used, and through which many achieved fame. Unfortunately, his obsession with Marxist dogma and his active involvement in radical politics robbed him of the credit that was his due.

Siqueiros invented the style of splashing automobile paint on canvas which later brought renown to the American artist Jackson Pollock who had served his apprenticeship under Siqueiros a few years before me. The same is true of the gestural brush strokes which earned Willem de Kooning a place in the world of art and become the bedrock of action painting.

Siqueiros had only himself to blame for not letting his unquestioned gift as an artist come to full bloom. The ideologue in him overwhelmed his powerful creative faculties. If I had the courage I would have quoted Oscar Wilde to him: 'Beauty ends where intellectual expression begins.'

Siqueiros' home was a beehive of leftist activity. He kept an open house for Communists from all over the world. On Sundays everyone was made welcome. In his house I made friends with many Latin Americans, some already at the peak of their careers. Among them were the Chilean poet Pablo Neruda and Fidel Castro who had fled Cuba after a failed coup in 1953. Nobody called him Castro: Fidel was the name he preferred to be known by. Along with the Canadian expatriate painter Arnold Belkin, who was also to make a name for himself in the years to come, I often ran into Fidel. We had little in common with him. Fidel was totally preoccupied with politics. He sought my company because he was curious about India and its political institutions and systems. Arnold had told him of my family background and our involvement in India's freedom struggle. Since neither Fidel's English nor my Spanish were adequate for communication Arnold acted as our interpreter.

Like so much else, Fidel too would have faded from my memory had it not been that on my second visit to Mexico in 1961, I called on Siqueiros. He had just returned from Cuba where he had been invited as a state guest by Fidel Castro, who was in power. It was only then that I discovered Fidel's last name.

Pandit Nehru, with whom I had discussed my interaction with Fidel, reminded Castro of it when they met during the UN Conference in New York. At first Fidel could not recall having known me till Nehru told him about my deafness. That jolted his memory. We were to meet once again when Castro came to New Delhi to attend the NAM conference in 1980. But by then Mrs Gandhi had distanced herself from me because of my criticism of the Emergency. She ensured that I was not invited to any function in the visitor's honour. She went even further and forced engagements upon Castro in the time he had put aside to meet me. He thought it prudent to let her have her way.

Arnold Belkin who become one of the greatest figures in Mexican art, remained a friend and functioned as the bridge between Fidel

Castro and the rest of us. He had preceded me as apprentice to Siqueiros. He had also preceded me as the lover of Rocio Saigon, queen of the Mexican Ballet, who became my passion once my longing for Gossi Soto began to abate.

Arnold introduced me to Rocio and did all he could to get me a ringside seat in her court. This was presided over by Miguel Covarrubias, a famed illustrator and chronicler who was then at the peak of his career. Though Covarrubias was forty years older than Rocio he had ousted Arnold from her favours. Arnold never forgave the other man for robbing him of his inamorata, and hoped I would avenge the insult by stealing Rocio from him.

I did not completely fulfil Arnold's expectations. But I did succeed in diverting some of Rocio's interest from Covarrubias towards me. She was very generous in granting favours to her admirers. At the time I was so besotted by her that I forgot my limitations and my humble status compared to Covarrubias. Finally Arnold realized I had failed, and developed a sense of guilt for having tried to exploit me and severely disrupting my emotional equilibrium. He tried to discourage my pursuing Rocio any further.

I met Rocio once again in the mid-eighties a full thirty years after I had first met her. This was in my home in New Delhi. Time had not been kind to her. Covarrubias had died soon after I left Mexico in 1954. Heartbroken, she had retired from the stage in despair and moved out of Mexico City to live in the countryside near Veracruz. She married an amateur architect and had children by him. It was hard to believe that this once bewitching beauty with whom I had been so obsessed was the same middle-aged matron sitting in my house.

I was constantly reminded of Mexico's ambivalent and paradoxical attitude to sexuality whenever I meditated on my own affairs or witnessed the turbulent romantic liaisons of my friends. Early one morning while returning from the airport after seeing someone off, I passed through a locality where Arnold was living. I decided to call on him. It looked like another Casa de Huéspedes. I knocked on his door. Instead of letting me in he popped his head out of the door and signalled to me to wait in the sitting room. When he came down, he was full of apologies for not having invited me upstairs. He explained that it being early morning, he had his girlfriend in bed with him.

I accepted the apology but could not repress my curiosity about his current bedmate. He had said nothing about his new girlfriend in our frequent meeting. She turned out to be half-German and Half-Mexican, like my landlady Julie Bastard. I asked him how old she was. Arnold pretended he had not heard me. I repeated my question. This time he replied that all he knew about her was that she had been in school with my landlady. That would make his new bedmate an old woman of sixty-five. When I told him, he simply shrugged his shoulders: her age was of no consequence to him. As long as she provided him free boarding and lodging, he was happy to pay her by providing sexual services. He suggested I should come to a similar arrangement with my landlady. I modified his suggestion by saying that I could settle for a landlady of forty-five or so but no older. He promised to look out for one. He found a few ladies willing to accommodate me—they were ready to provide either food or lodging but not both, on the terms offered. They lived at some distance from the city centre; what I would save by my sexual effort would be spent on bus fares. So I politely turned down Arnold's kindly proposals.

I cannot give a better example of the Mexicans' quirky attitude towards sexuality than of a bill introduced in the Senate a little before my arrival. It sought to grant pensions to retiring prostitutes. The senator who introduced the bill argued that services provided by certain lady up to the ripe old age of seventy-five without ever infecting a single one of her clients should be rewarded with a pension. The bill was supported by all members of the Senate. It would have become an act of Parliament but for the last-minute intervention by the President. However, while vetoing the bill the President graciously conceded that the lady in question deserved this consideration, but he felt that it would set a precedent for other retiring prostitutes to make similar claims. A solution was found by establishing a private fund, heavily subsidized by the state treasury, to ensure that these ladies lived in reasonable comfort till they died.

I first saw Frida Kahlo painting in 1953, in her first-ever solo exhibition. She came to the inauguration against her doctor's advice. She arrived in an ambulance and was seated on a throne-like bed decorated with posters of her paintings. The gallery Arte Contemporaneo was crowded with celebrities of the Mexican art world and leftist politicians.

Her paintings were autobiographical, bewitching and stunningly powerful. They heralded what come to be known as narrative art. The exhibition was to elevate Kahlo to cult status almost immediately.

I was told that her work graphically depicted the physical and emotional suffering she had undergone.

Frida Kahlo had been stricken by polio at the age of seven. She had been in and out of hospitals all her life, suffering from multiple ailments. She had been written about in medical journals round the world. She was of Jewish descent, the daughter of a Hungarian photographer and painter. From her student days, her life had revolved around the famous artist Diego Rivera. She was said to have announced her intention of having a child by Rivera, who was twice her age. She managed against all odds to marry Diego, then divorced him only to remarry him after a few years of separation.

Despite her obsession with Rivera it was surprising that her work did not bear the remotest influence of his style. A chance encounter with a young Argentine writer named Raquel Tibol, who came to stay in the Casa de Huéspedes, made it possible for me to meet Frida Kahlo many times. Raquel was working on a series of articles on Mexican artists.

As her interview with Frida progressed, Raquel kept other guests in the Casa fully supplied with details about the artist's life and work. Most of the information was about Frida illness. Recently she had been compelled to have her right leg amputated. It was a case of 'osteomyelitis'. The mention of this word brought back stark memories of my childhood agonies. I began to take greater interest in the Argentine lady's stories. She sensed the depth of my curiosity and began to visit me in my room. She also told Frida Kahlo about me.

Early in 1954 Frida asked the Argentinian to introduce me to her. I was very excited. I read her medical history, which she described vividly to people who came to interview her, and later become valuable source material for her biographers. Her paintings expressed her physical and emotional pain. Having been through the same ordeal I developed an affinity for her.

Before taking me to see her Raquel gave me another insight into Frida's life, something she had not mentioned in her detailed descriptions at the dinner table. Though a full-blooded Communist, long year of intense suffering had made Frida turn towards spiritualism.

She had recently read a volume of Jiddu Krishnamurti's lectures delivered during one of his visits to Mexico. Raquel thought one of the reasons Frida had shown an interest in meeting me was perhaps that since I was also a Hindu I must be familiar with the sacred texts which discussed the path to *nirvana*. This made me very anxious, as my knowledge of the Upanishads and the Gita was less than minimal. My commitment to Marxism had made me indifferent to scripture.

However, I looked forward to seeing Frida. Being received by her was regarded as a rare privilege. Raquel took me to Frida's residence in Coyoacán. Diego had gifted it to her after Trotsky's assassination in the same house.

Frida was lying in bed on her stomach. She had recently undergone spinal surgery. She continued with her painting as she had throughout

My parents, Avtar Narain
and Pushpa Gujral

At the Mayo School,
Lahore, 1940

Gujral House at Pari Darwaza, Jhelum

My family in Jhelum, 1935. Standing: my father and Inder; seated: my mother and me

Portrait of My Father, 1957,
oil on canvas

With my sisters, Niti (l) and Uma (r), and Inder

Glory, 1954, acrylic on board

Self-Portrait, 1956, oil on board

Pilgrim, 1953, acrylic on canvas

Mourning En Masse, 1952, casein on cardboard

Untitled, 1952, oil on masonite board

Self-Portrait, 1954, oil on hardboard

In Mexico at an exhibition, 1954

In Mexico, 1953

Kiran at my show in New York, 1961

Untitled, 1960, mixed media on canvas

Adam and Eve, 1960, mixed media on canvas

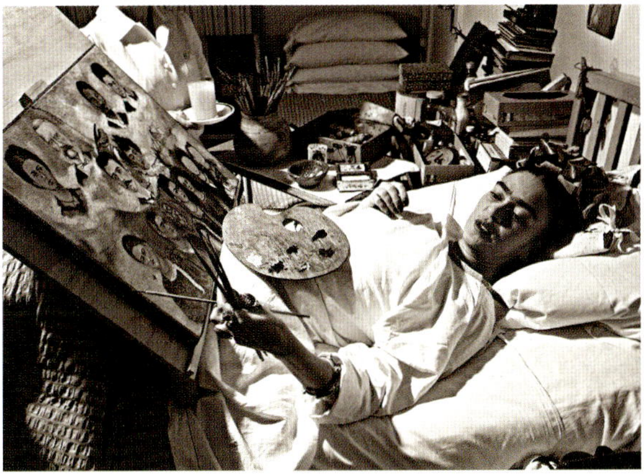

Frida Kahlo painting

With Diego Rivera,
Mexico City, 1954

At Frida Kahlo's funeral—Diego Rivera (right) carrying the coffin, 1954

With Frida Kahlo,
Mexico City, 1954

In Mexico, in front of my artwork

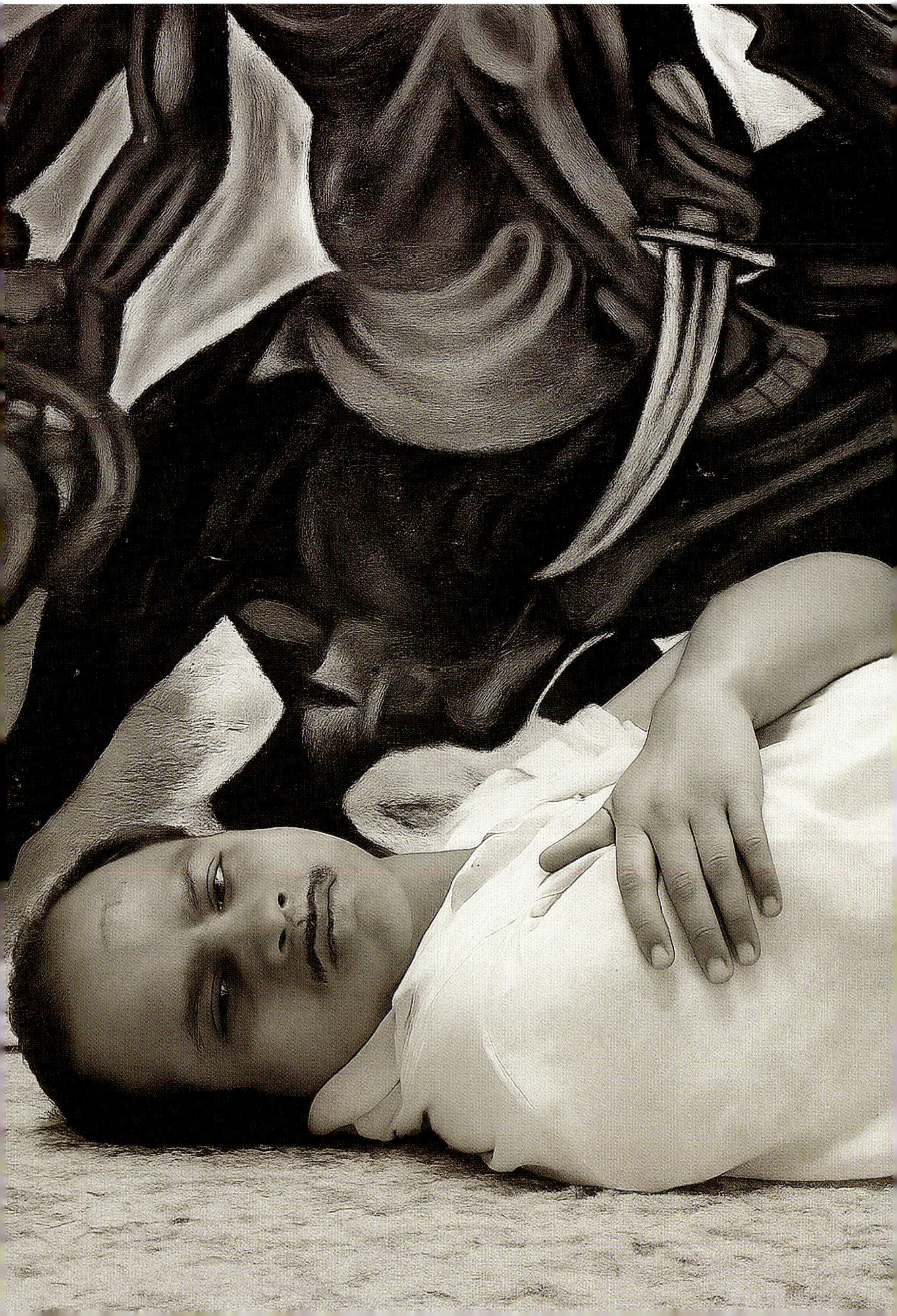

With Kiran at a show in Paris

Kiran with Shrimati Indira Gandhi at our wedding reception, 1957

Kiran with Pandit Nehru and me at our wedding reception

With my extended family and friends, 1958

With Kiran and her ceramics at Tilak Marg

With Pandit Nehru at the inspection of the portrait of Sardar Patelji

Portrait of Nehru, 1957

With Shrimati Indira Gandhi, in front of her portrait

Portrait of Indira Gandhi, 1957

Kiran at Tilak Marg with her ceramics

Kiran's ceramic installation at our home in New Delhi

LALIT KALA AKADAMI

NATIONAL EXHIBITION OF ART

CERTIFICATE OF AWARD

GIVEN THIS AWARD (OF Rs. 1000/-)
FOR OUTSTANDING MERIT
TO Satish Gujral
FOR EXHIBIT No. 120 ENTITLED
"DESPAIR" ENTERED INTO THE
NATIONAL EXHIBITION OF ART
ORGANISED BY THE
LALIT KALA AKADAMI IN 1956

Secretary Vice-chairman Chairman

Dated, the January 15, 1957

Received the Lalit Kala Akademi award in 1956

Mural at the Punjab Agricultural University campus in Ludhiana, Punjab

Untitled, 1971, oil on canvas

Untitled, 1971, paper collage

With Kiran

With Inder in front of our father's portrait

Receiving the Padma Vibhushan from honourable
President K.R. Narayanan in 1999

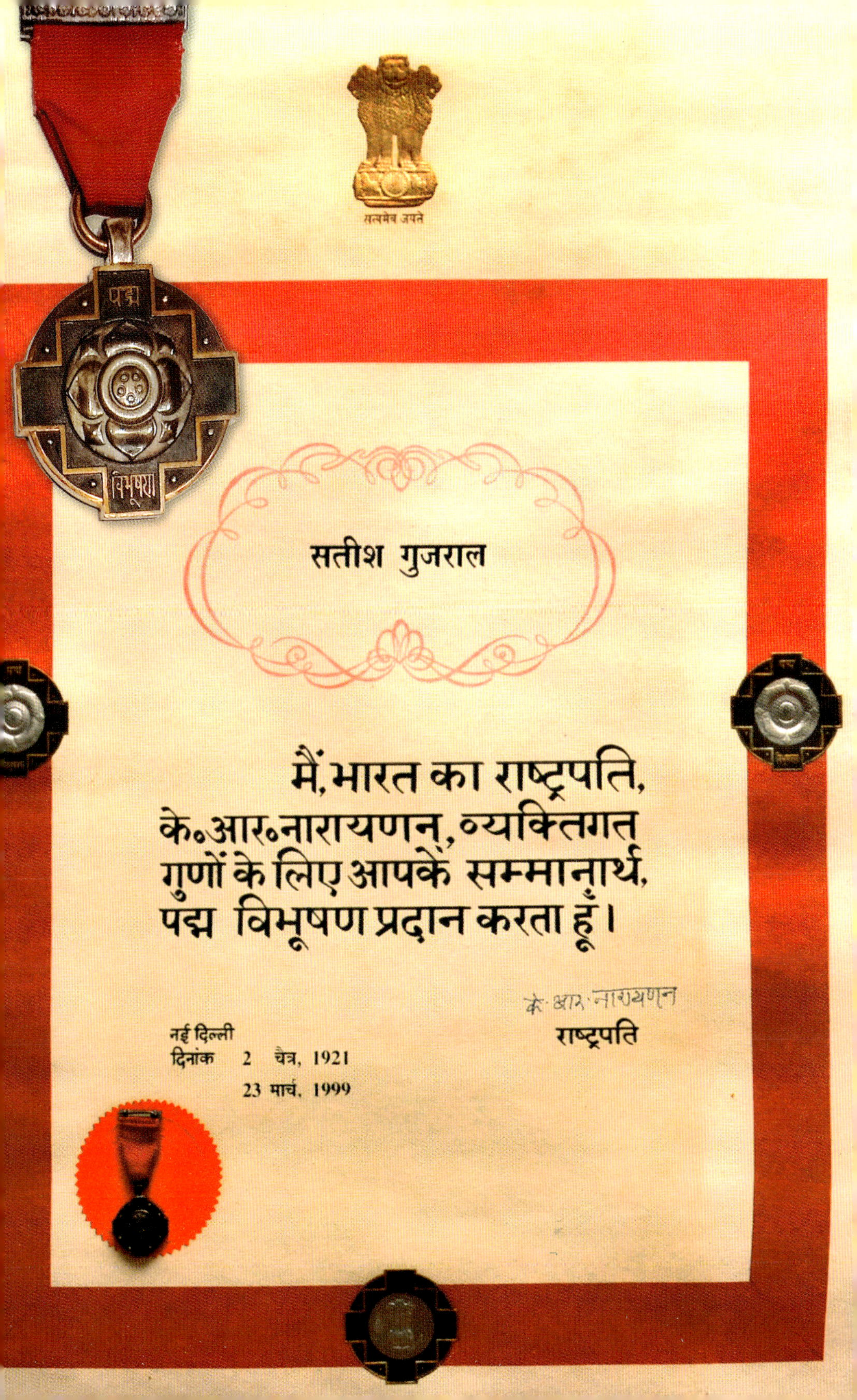

सत्यमेव जयते

सतीश गुजराल

मैं, भारत का राष्ट्रपति,
के॰ आर॰ नारायणन, व्यक्तिगत
गुणों के लिए आपके सम्मानार्थ,
पद्म विभूषण प्रदान करता हूँ।

के॰ आर॰ नारायणन
राष्ट्रपति

नई दिल्ली
दिनांक 2 चैत्र, 1921
23 मार्च, 1999

With Shri Krishan Kant,
former Vice-President of India

With Dr Karan Singh

With Maharani Gayatri Devi

With the honourable President
Shri K.R. Narayanan, 1997

With Her Excellency Queen Elizabeth II on her visit to Delhi, 1997

With Shrimati Sheila Dikshit, former chief minister of Delhi

Receiving the Lalit Kala Ratna Puraskar from the honourable President Dr A.P.J. Abdul Kalam in 2004

The Belgian Ambassador's residence, New Delhi

ROYAUME DE BELGIQUE

ORDRE DE LA COURONNE

Sur la proposition du Ministre des Relations extérieures,

il a plu à SA MAJESTE LE ROI

de conférer, par arrêté royal du 27 octobre 1983,

la décoration d'OFFICIER DE L'ORDRE DE LA COURONNE

à Monsieur Satish GUJRAL, de nationalité indienne, architecte et artiste (peintre, sculpteur et céramiste),

en reconnaissance des services rendus.

Pour le Ministre des Relations extérieures,

Le Fonctionnaire Délégué,

With Kiran, receiving the Order of the Crown from Prince Albert of Belgium, 1983

Central Stupa of the Ambedkar Sthal at Lucknow,
Uttar Pradesh

Chancery at the Belgian Embassy, New Delhi, 1980–84

The Al-Moughtara Farm in Riyadh, 2001

L–R: Pravina Mehta, Aditya Prakash, me, B.V. Doshi, Raj Rewal and Achyut Kanvinde. Vistara: *The Architecture of India*, 1986

L–R: Inder Gujral, Indrani with Ram, me, M.F. Husain and Charles Fabri

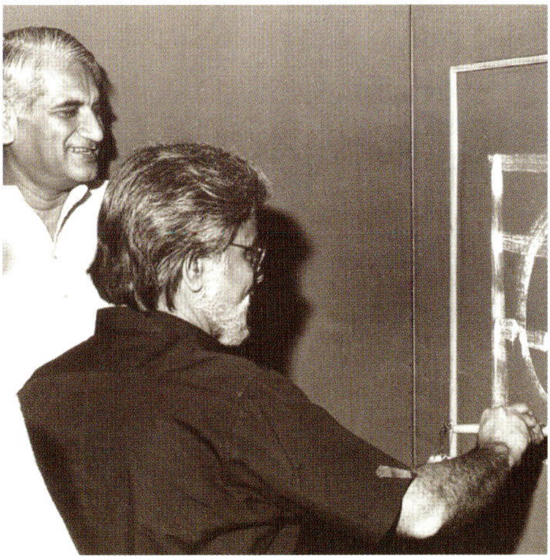

With Charles Correa. Vistara: *The Architecture of India*, 1986

With Mohit

her illness. She rested her chin on a pillow and had a specially designed easel placed before her. She asked me to sit beside her pillow. In her illness she was a pathetic sight, yet her face had a strange radiance. Like most Mexicans I met, she began by expressing profound admiration for India, its culture and spiritual traditions. She went on to discuss the Upanishads. Raquel come to my rescue by changing the topic of conversation to the illness which had afflicted both of us. Frida asked me to tell her how it had begun and what kinds of medical treatment I had received. We developed an immediate rapport that lasted till her death, which occurred six months later.

Frida was a very generous woman. She showered me with gifts each time I called on her: it was a basket of art material one day, a package of books on another. She also sent me fruits and other delicacies every other day. During these months I seldom saw Diego Rivera, who lived separately. He moved in with her when it became obvious that her end was near. He noticed Frida's affection for me. When she died, he included me among the few given the honour of keeping vigil by her coffin as she lay in state at the Palace of Fine Arts. I was also privileged to be one of the pallbearers on the journey to the crematorium. Others included the former President, Lazaro Cárdenas.

I have strong memories of Frida for yet another reason. Her bent towards Hinduism induced her to make a final request that her body should be cremated rather than buried. At the crematorium of the Panteón Civil de Dolores, Diego and some family members laid Frida body onto a chute. As the chute slid into the oven, the intense heat forced the corpse into a sitting position; her hair rose to form an aureole around her head. The macabre scene haunted me for many years. Far from being a nightmarish reminder of a tragic death, it has become one of my most precious memories.

We had to wait four hours to collect her ashes. Diego gathered them with his own hands. Before he put them in a red cloth he had brought with him, he took a fistful and put it in his mouth. This was to mingle Frida's being with his, he said.

On our way back from the crematorium, Diego asked me to come with him to the Teatro de los Insurgentes and see the mural he was painting. It was clearly an invitation to assist him in finishing it I accepted with alacrity.

This assignment roused my interest in mosaic and the use of different materials for making murals. Diego had chosen to paint it in acrylic, a method recently developed by a Mexican chemist José Gutiérrez, who had also been helping other muralists to experiment with mediums based on silicon and automobile paint.

Midway through the mural, he decided to cloak it with glass mosaic, a traditional medium, which the artist-architect Juan O'Gorman had used in his mural for the library building at the new Universidad President Aléman, in Mexico City.

While Diego went on to finish the mural in acrylic with his band of assistants, in which I was included, mosaic craftsmen started the process of cladding the painted parts with glass tiles. It was fascinating to watch them. One could compare the painted and the glass-covered portions side by side. It was easy to perceive which part of it was organic and architectural. This experience influenced my later searches for materials other than paint. Diego was happy with the way the mural's covered section was progressing. Contrary to his usual habit, he invited a few friends to see the results when the work was still incomplete.

Among those who came to see the mural was the American architect Frank Lloyd Wright, an old friend of Diego's. Wright's approving nod heartened Diego the most. Ted Bower had often spoken to me about Wright, but seeing him in flesh and blood was something different. Though he was almost as short as me, he gave the impression of being much taller. He held himself erect with his chin slightly raised and nose in the air. He always wore a felt hat. Even when he stood beside

Diego who was much teller and fatter, Wright managed to hold his own. When everybody was seated, Diego asked us if anyone wished to put questions to Wright. Since I had boasted of my acquaintance with Wright through Ted Bower, and was the only one who could speak English, the honour to question him was bestowed on me.

I first referred to Ted Bower's correspondence with him on the town planning and architecture of Chandigarh. Wright acknowledged my introductory remarks with some surprise. Then I put my question. 'How come, Mr Wright, you who are one of the greatest architects of our time and a close friend of Diego Rivera, have never thought of having murals on any of your buildings?

With a faint smile, Wright looked directly at me and replied, 'Well, an architect needs an artist to resurrect a dead wall, but I never design dead walls.' It took me a little while to understand what he meant, as my colleague was slow in writing it down for me. But his words took root in my mind. They became more relevant when I later took to designing buildings myself. Any medium that depends on another to enhance its validity only admits its inherent weakness. Murals and sculpture can be used in architecture as ornamental additions, but they cannot help in strengthening a building's spatial or utilitarian aspect. After this realization, I began to look at Mexican murals from another perspective. Whatever their plastic or aesthetic merit, in most cases they made no contribution to the buildings that they adorned. The disillusionment was shattering, but it helped me in making a more objective assessment of Mexican art and the true value and function of murals.

In 1953, when I had been in Mexico for less than a year, Siqueiros organized my first exhibition in a leading gallery of Mexico City. The reception by the media and the cognoscenti was most heartwarming. For a while I toyed with the idea of settling down in Mexico. I was encouraged to pursue this idea when Portes Gil informed me that my scholarship had been extended for another year. That evening at his house, Gil assured me that I would get a resident visa if I wished to extend my stay beyond the second year.

I began to weigh the pros and cons of settling in Mexico or returning home. There was not much for me to look forward to in India. The exhibition of my work before I left Delhi had earned me some renown but very little money. Nor had I been showered with feminine affection in the twenty-seven years I had spent in my motherland. I wrote home and told my family what I was thinking. My parents and brother Inder were very alarmed. As a compromise, Inder suggested that after my scholarship expired, I should spend some time in New York before making a final decision.

To people back home, New York seemed much closer than any other part of the American continent, principally because there was a lot of coming and going of Indians through that city. Also, we had a diplomatic base there, so it was possible to monitor Indians. For my family, Mexico barely existed on the globe. In the absence of any other Indian source of information from there, my letters to them were the only evidence of my being alive. If I failed to write my weekly letters, they became apprehensive. In those days letters between Indian and Mexico took fifteen days to reach their destination. Also, an American visa was something granted only to the very privileged. Inder wrote to say that my chances of getting one from the American embassy in New Delhi were less than zero.

Fortunately, my exhibition in Mexico City had won me new admirers. Among those who bought my paintings was Nick Webster, a scion of the dictionary publisher who had made his home in Mexico. He assured me that he could get me an American visa if I chose to live in the States. But he could not understand why anyone with any sense would want to live in New York instead of in Mexico City.

Casa de Huespedés, where I lived, housed a lot of American students, most of whom were studying in Mexico City College, an American institute located at the end of the street. Few had any affection for their homeland, especially as it was in the midst of senator Eugene McCarthy's witchhunt for people suspected of leftist leanings. None of these students encouraged me to visit America.

Then an American girl named Ruth Reves came to stay in the Casa de Huéspedes. Being a theatre student, she made a dramatic entrance into the dining room at lunchtime on the first day of her arrival. When she was introduced to me, she described having played bit roles in Ram Gopal's troupe in her previous incarnation as a ballet dancer. We were immediately drawn towards each other. We made love on the very first night of our meeting.

And we continued sharing the same bed thereafter. This was to be my last and also my longest love affair in Mexico, and for the duration of my stay in New York. It was uppermost in my mind when I thought of making my home in New York. Ruth was enthusiastic about everything in the Big Apple, where she had her home.

Having seen my work, she felt a move to New York would open up new vistas for me and stop me absorbing more Mexican influence, especially that of Orozco, who she thought was dominating my work. Her criticism was well founded, as I too had begun to feel I was becoming too influenced by him. As a final temptation she offered to accompany me to New York.

José Clemente Orozco was part of Mexico's artistic triumvirate, along with Rivera and Siqueiros. But he did not share their political views. Though he had died a few months before I came to Mexico, his ghost haunted the nation's artistic milieu. I felt his presence everywhere I went. Neither in his life nor in his work did Orozco betray much concern with the political or social dogmas that coloured Siqueiros' approach to art. Despite being a hermit he was able to suffuse his work with human emotions. He had nothing but contempt for those who professed altruistic ideologies. Orozco seemed to subscribe to the aesthetic postulate of Oscar Wilde that I had wanted to quote to Siqueiros: 'Beauty ends where intellectual expression begins.'

There was much else that made Orozco a lone wolf in the world of Mexican art. He shunned the limelight. Though like Diego Rivera he also received commissions to do murals in the United State, Rivera received much more publicity in the American media. This despite the phobic and hysterical American attitude towards anything even remotely leftist. Rivera's image was blatantly ideological and revolutionary; Orozco's were the opposite. Diego's deliberate idolizing of Marxism in his murals at the Rockefeller Centre was bound to create controversy. And he knew it. Orozco had chosen Gandhi as an alternative to Marx for his murals for New York's School of Social Research.

The furore created by Diego's mural at the Rockefeller Centre ended in its being erased, with much publicity for the artist. Nothing more than a ripple was caused by Orozco's murals. They remained little noticed, despite their undeniable aesthetic merit.

I was amazed that despite having only one arm, Orozco was able to produce great works of art. At Guadalajara, the former capital of Mexico, he had painted the inside of a dome of a church. Finding it difficult to climb up and down to examine the progress of his work, he tied his brushes to bamboo poles ten feet long and painted with them while lying on the floor. It is astonishing how, despite this severe physical handicap, he was able to produce art of quality that will live forever. The lyricism and raw power that he infused into his figures surpasses the giant bodies painted by Michelangelo in the Sistine Chapel.

Prior to murals, Orozco had systematically painted themes from the wretched lives of Mexican prostitutes in brothels. These images were created during the years of the Mexican Revolution—the succession of violent political coups and military dictatorship that dominated the country from 1911 to 1920. After the Revolution was over, he turned to making cartoons, which also won him wide acclaim. Legend had it that he had lost his arm fighting for the Revolution, and was very moved by the plight of poor prostitutes who had to serve scores of men for a pittance. His cartoons were testimonials to his revolutionary zeal.

Rather than cashing in the publicity he received, he expressed strong disapproval of it in his autobiography, published a little before his death. He exploded all the myths about himself. His arm, he wrote, was blown off in his infancy when he accidentally exploded a stick of dynamite his father was planning to use to destroy the house of a woman who had spurned his advances. He confessed that, far from fighting for the Revolution, he was mortally scared of violence and had found sanctuary in a brothel. The stay inspired him to depict the lives of the victims of men's lust. What else could he paint while living in a bordello?

As for the 'revolutionary spirit' of his cartoons, he cartoons, he had been prompted to draw them because after the Revolution the only job he could find was with a newspaper sympathetic to this cause. He would have had no qualms about drawing anti-revolutionary cartoons had the paper asked him to do so.

There were good reasons for my fascination with Orozco and his art. Though he was no ideologue, his work was infused with profound compassion and a humanistic spirit. Had it been otherwise, I would have found Rufino Tamayo more attractive than Orozco.

There is a stage beyond which influence turns into imitation. An artist must rigorously guard himself against it. Ruth believed I had reached that stage and should look to expand my horizons. I agreed. She asked Nick Webster to get me a visa for United States, as my scholarship was coming to an end. It took him little time getting it; it took me much longer to arrange my exit from Mexico.

To begin with I was required to submit photographs of my paintings and have them stamped by no less than three agencies: the department of archaeology, the Academy of Fine Arts and customs. This ensured that indigenous works of art were not smuggled out of the country.

I had saved up a little money from the sales of my canvases. I thought I had enough to meet my expenses for the first few days in the United States. I had not reckoned with the Mexican bureaucracy. Government servants in Mexico are not meant to live on their salaries but on what they can extract from the public.

Finally, one morning in October 1954, I boarded the train from the same station I had arrived at two years earlier. I had crates of my paintings safely tucked away in the luggage van. I was to travel to Laredo on the Texas border by train, and once on US territory, proceed by bus to New York. That was the cheapest way to travel.

Ruth Reves saw me off. I had wanted her to accompany me but She had a return air ticket she had got at a bargain price while coming to Mexico. It could not be refunded. She agreed to meet me in New York.

The train to the American border took twenty-four hours to traverse Mexico. It halted on the Mexican side that allow US officials to check visas before it crossed the bridge into the United States.

After my passport had been examined and stamped, I relaxed and gazed out of the window. To my shock and dismay, I saw the crates of my paintings lying on the platform. I jumped out of the train with the customs clearance papers I had obtained before leaving. Though I had a copy in my possession, the originals had not been forwarded to the border customs. Before I could get the officials to do something, the train started to move with my personal luggage in it. I was advised to jump on it and return later to retrieve the crates.

Next morning, I was back at the border bridge to return to the Mexican side. To my horror, U S. officials informed me that I had only a single-entry visa and if I crossed over I could not return without a fresh visa, which was only obtainable in Mexico City. I pleaded with the US immigration officials, to no avail. Finally, after some days of utter frustration, I managed to get Ruth on the phone in Casa de Huéspedes. She flew in the next day, crossed the border, charmed the

Mexican authorities and returned with the crates of my paintings. She went back to Mexico City to finish her course at City College. I proceeded to New York by bus. Crossing the huge continent took more than two days and nights.

Before leaving Mexico I had sent photographs of my work to Romesh Bhandari with the request that he explore the possibility of my exhibiting it in that city. I knew I would not have more than a few dollars left when I reached New York. The cost of packing my paintings, their freight, my bus fare, and above all, humouring officials to get necessary clearances, would not leave very much in my wallet.

While sponsoring my visa Nick Webster had assured me that he would be responsible for all my living expenses in the United States. This was only meant for official records. I was expected to fend for myself. Fortunately, Romesh Bhandari responded to my letter. He requested Harold Leventhal to organize an exhibition for me. Leventhal had been instrumental in arranging an exhibition of Jamini Roy's paintings in New York. I had read a review of it in *Time* magazine.

As a GI during World War II, Harold had been posted in India, where he had developed a lifelong interest in Indians and Indian culture. He had met Nehru and Gandhi as well as several artists, including Jamini Roy. Back in the US he had become a sort of unofficial cultural adviser to the Indian mission. In later years many creative artists such as M.F. Husain, Satyajit Ray and others were to benefit from Harold's generosity and resourcefulness. I got in touch with him soon after reaching New York. Harold was not in the art business, nor in entertainment. Films and music were his main interests.

Harold was able to arrange Jamini Roy's show at the ACA Gallery largely because of his leftist leanings, which he shared with people in control of that prestigious space. Though the cultural air was fouled by Senator Eugene McCarthy's constant diatribes against 'socialists', the gallery ignored such vituperative bullying. Harold's optimism about my work was based on his view that the ACA Gallery liked to exhibit just the kind of work I did. He had not reckoned with the fact that all galleries were booked for months in advance. Bella Fishko, then curator of the ACA, told Harold there was no way she could accommodate me that year. But after seeing my canvases she promised to help me sell a few of them. Encouraged by this response, Harold suggested the exhibition be held at India House, when the season opened a month or two later. I took a room in an American-style Casa de Huéspedes on West 82 Street of Riverside Drive and awaited Ruth's arrival. She was due within a month.

During this interim period I met Sid Hammer, an American painter of my own age who was introduced to me by Bella Fishko at the ACA Gallery. Sid Hammer represented a group of young, talented and industrious American artists who for one reason or other had not been successful, or had been unlucky. Modern painting had been permeated by non-figurative and abstract trends, exemplified by the work of artists like Mark Rothko and Robert Motherwell.

Sid was an extremely generous and sensitive man. He was portly, and this made me look even smaller than I was whenever I stood next to him. He lived in a basement flat two streets across from my lodgings. He managed to live partly on his wife's earnings and partly by doing windows displays. He had strong leftist leanings. From Sid I learnt much about the art business in New York. Though a bitter man, it was to Sid's credit that he never used strong language or indulged in exaggeration.

The stories he told were funny and full of sardonic wit. One was about a gallery owner who was convicted on a charge of swindling. He had devised a novel way to promote sales. He scanned obituary notices in newspapers and then approached relations of the deceased, saying that the deceased had reserved a painting in his gallery. Grieving widows were his prime targets. They were taken in by his eloquence.

He took good care to price the paintings according to the means of the deceased person's family. He was caught when he made a blunder regarding the date on which he said one of his dead 'customers' had visited his gallery and made the reservation. He had calculated the date in accordance with the news report which said that death occurred after a 'short' illness. The 'short' period happened to be several weeks, making it virtually impossible for the deceased to have left his bed. Massive commotion ensued on his arrest. There were dozens of others who had been similarly duped.

Yet, compared to what went on in art galleries in Paris, the art business in New York was less murky. American corporate culture had penetrated the elite business of private and individual patronage, and made it undistinguishable from other, savagely competitive, commercial investments.

Nothing exemplified this better than the emergence of Pop Art and the crowning of Andy Warhol, who unabashedly declared that the most important thing in life was money. He had made his debut by painting dollar bills, and followed this by painting cans of Campbell Soup because, as he claimed: 'I used to drink it.' His subsequent evolution as a creative artist could not possibly have been any different from the way it turned out. An art critic of the *New York Times* described how when he requested Warhol's secretary for an interview, he was told by the ever-helpful minion that if it concerned painting he had better contact Mr X in Warhol studios since this man did all the painting, and if it was for a movie, he should contact Mr Y because it was Y who produced Warhol's films.

Andy Warhol, it was alleged, went to the extent of appointing a look-alike for attending social functions because he wanted to be seen in more places than one at the same time. The most infamous example of such impersonations took place during his grand one-man show in Stockholm, to which his only contribution was his signature on his 'paintings'. It was no surprise that most Pop artist were born in the advertising business.

Warhol was hailed as the true representative of American culture. Whether this was meant to be a compliment or a scathing satirical judgment remain to be proved. I never encountered Warhol except for a fleeting glimpse of him at Sid Hammer's house where he was a frequent visitor in the early fifties. He used to create blown-up comic strips and window displays assisted by Sid. Though Sid Hammer was initially critical of Warhol's emergence as a cult figure of Pop art as of Pop art itself, he eventually became a part of Warhol's underground movie ventures. Although he did not get any credit for it, it solved his financial problems. He spent his last year in an upmarket apartment in Greenwich Village.

If this was the image of artists and art dealers in New York, those who fancied themselves as collectors were in a class by themselves. Doing the rounds was the story of a leading executive of Wall Street who was somehow convinced by an enterprising Italian dealer that he could enrich his collection with the original of the *Mona Lisa* by Leonardo da Vinci. This international masterpiece would need clearance by Italian customs. He suggested that the original be painted over with a landscape which could be easily erased when the canvas reached its destination. The plan worked perfectly except for one hitch. After removing the landscape, the New York restorer asked the collector if he also wanted him to remove the portrait of Marilyn Monroe which he had detected beneath the figure of Mona Lisa!

More serious was the case of the chairman of the Chrysler Corporation. He had spent hundreds of millions of dollars acquiring European Renaissance paintings. He had to suffer the mortification of these being certified as fakes. The revelation exploded in his face when he presented them for purpose of tax deduction.

As an artist, poor Sid was not destined to go far in what was a gruelling, unforgiving and competitive business. Though he had three exhibitions courtesy Warhol, whom he had known since they were together at the Carnegie Institute of Technology in New York, they received scant notice. He died unhonoured and unsung but not as poor as he had been. Sid did not consider himself a failure, as he had his fair share of exposure and publicity. He proudly showed me folders with clippings from newspapers. They were invariably advertisements announcing his shows. When I asked him about reviews, he pointed to a prominently displayed clipping, which for the most part carried city news and had on its masthead the name and the date of the New York Times. The write-up on Sid was short and oddly titled 'The Ppower of endurance'. Below it were a few lines justifying the headline. It went as follows: 'There are artists about whom whatever reservation you may have, you have to admit their power of endurance. Such is this artist Sid Hammer. For a decade now he has been coming up with ever larger bodies of work but has never succeeded in drawing notice. He has endured this indifference on part of the critics and the collectors. He is back again. There is no reason to believe he will not continue to persist. We wish him good luck, next time.' When I told Sid that I felt the review was negative, he brushed me aside. 'It is the *New York Times*. How many artists can get a mention in this paper? What it says is not important. It is the appearing in it that matters.' In a way he was right. There were hundreds of art galleries in New York, and dozens of museums. With so much on view week after week only the *New York Times*, to cover them, and that too only once or twice a week few artists could hope to get a mention in the columns of the prestigious paper.

Ruth had given up her flat in New York before she left for Mexico, where she had planned to live for the rest of her life. She received a monthly alimony from her divorced husband. It was not enough to meet the cost of living in New York, so when she returned she stayed with her parents in a distant suburb. She found a shabby room for me on Riverside Drive, on 82nd street. However decrepit, it was more than I could afford with my meagre savings. Fortunately, Romesh Bhandari allowed me to store the creates of my painting on the premises of the Indian consulate.

It took Ruth one and a half hours to get to my place. Immediately she would cook whatever she had picked up on the way for my breakfast. Then we would go around visiting friends in Greenwich Village. They included artists, actresses, dancers and writers struggling to make their living. Ultimately Ruth realized that I needed to continue painting and selling what I produced in order to be able to survive instead of wasting my time in socializing.

We started by doing the rounds of art galleries. We did not have any success. The winds in the city's art world blew in favour of abstract expressionism, with Jackson Pollock and Willem de Kooning reigning supreme. Figurative work had no takers, whatever its merit on the commercial circuit. Even those who appreciated my work were unable to accommodate me because their galleries were booked for the entire season.

Just as I was about to give up, one of Ruth's actor friends asked me if knew anything about yoga. He was acquainted with a rich woman who was obsessed with this discipline. If I could impress her with my knowledge of yoga, she would introduce me to affluent people who collected works of art.

Ruth also happened to know this lady. She assured me that my ignorance should not dishearten me, as the woman in question was not so much interested in the physical aspect of yoga as in the tantric mumbo-jumbo that went with it. She had heard the dancer Ram Gopal expound tantrism, which no one in his audience understood. If I picked up a smattering of Sanskrit words, I could pass off for a learned pandit.

I was reluctant to indulge in such chicanery. But Ruth had her own ideas on the subject. She took me to the New York Public Library and dug out a few books on yoga and tantrism. She read them first and marked passages and words to help me pass my test. I was persuaded to go along with the plan.

The lady in Greenwich Village was told about me and was excited at the prospect of meeting me. I was presented as a young sage with yogic credentials, and well known as a painter. She invited me and Ruth to dinner the same night.

As we boarded the train for Greenwich Village from Grand Central Station, Ruth shored up my flagging morale by reassuring me that our hostess knew no more about yoga than I did. In the hour that it took us to reach our destination, I kept repeating the words and key sentences I had memorized sitting on the steps of New York Public Library. By the time we were shown into the lady's house. I had quite a repertoire of incomprehensible Sanskrit phrases mixed with some rustic Punjabi ones.

That evening was a grand success. According to Ruth I performed well; my commentary was full of sagacious advice, and most convincing. Ruth did not let any of the other guests present break the spell I cast on everyone with my torrent of words in a languages which no one could understand. Not even I.

During the buffet dinner following my 'discourse' Ruth revealed to the old lady my other talent: painting. She announced to the esteemed hostess and her guests that these paintings were graphic depictions of deep yogic and tantric states, visualization in a transcendental mode. Thanks to Ruth's ingenuity and her rich lady friend's generosity I was able to stay on in New York for some months.

One 'success' was followed by another. Harold Leventhal's exhibition of my painting at Indian House received a good review in the *New York Times*, and I was able to sell some canvases to ensure a comfortable sojourn in New York. I fared better in New York than I had in Mexico.

A few weeks after the show at India House a young man came to see me. Even before we could shake hands he gestured and spoke through sign language; 'You are deaf? So am I.' This was the prelude to a friendship that was to last for many years and give me an insight into the world of the deaf and the dumb in the golden land of opportunity.

Seymour Gross was born deaf and dumb in an affluent American Jewish Family. His wealth was partly inherited; he had added to it by his own efforts. He ran an insurance agency in partnership with a similarly handicapped friend, Martin Kaplan, who also taught at the University College for the deaf and dumb in New York.

Meeting Martin and Seymour gave me entry to what seemed to be another world within our world. It was a club to which membership was exclusive. Only those could join whose hearing and speech was impaired, forcing them to communicate through an unspoken language familiar to me. It reminded me of my days in the school for the deaf and the dumb in New Delhi. This society was surprisingly widespread, interlinked and active across the length and breadth of the United States. In New York alone it had over a dozen centers with facilities for social interaction. These provided crucial psychological assurance to the members that they were not missing out on anything. They had created islands of their own within the ocean of the 'hearing world'. As I learnt more about them, I discovered how completely they had equipped themselves to overcome the handicap that nature had inflicted on them. They provided themselves with plugs attached to their beds to help them respond to the doorbell or teleprinter. These plugs not only illuminated bulbs when the bell rang, they also caused a kind of vibration under the beds to wake deaf sleepers in the event of some mishap. All kinds of equipment were subsidized by the state and made affordable. There was even a country-wide directory listing teleprinters and phone numbers of people similarly disadvantaged. These included names of shops and hospitals fitted with necessary equipment to assist these people when in need.

Seymour Gross was among the wealthiest and Martin among the best educated of this tribe. About the time I met Gross he had been trying to break out of the shell of the community of the deaf and the dumb. He was dating a strikingly beautiful girl whose hearing and speech were intact. She was well educated and worked as an agent for a car manufacturing unit based in England. She had managed to pull her lover out of his self-imposed exile. She had read a review of my exhibition which mentioned my being deaf, and thought that by getting to know me Seymour might to able to get the better of his handicap. She persuaded him to call on me.

Though Seymour's girlfriend Gloria accompanied him to the clubs he frequented, and was well-versed in sign language she never seemed to be at ease in the crowed, nor was the crowed comfortable in her presence.

I could not help asking Gloria why she bothered to come to the club. She was candid in her reply. She loved Seymour without being obsessed with or ashamed of his handicap. She said she never felt superior because she could hear and he could not. On the contrary, she suspected rather justifiably that Seymour thought her adoration for him was tinged with sympathy or pity. She strove to rid him of his complexes, which she thought were the result of the isolation he had created for himself by restricting his social activities to the community of the handicapped.

I mentioned this to Seymour. He agreed that he was aware of her efforts to extricate him from this community. She had once succeeded in doing so and he had kept away from that circle for almost six month. In the end he could not bear the strain of adjusting himself to the hearing world; and returned to the company where he felt more comfortable.

Six years later when I visited New York again, I learned that Seymour had left Gloria, or perhaps she had left him. He was living with Susan, a girl similarly impaired, and seemed quite happy being with her and the community.

After a year in New York, I felt I had shed the spell Orozco had cast on me. His place was taken by Rufino Tamayo. I began to see Tamayo's work as if with a new pair of glasses. I had not met him during my stay in Mexico as he was cut off from the mainstream and I could not afford associating with him and risk being ostracized by artists who worshipped Siqueiros and Rivera. Tamayo believed in the Biblical adage: Who is with my enemy is my enemy'. Considering my style, he was certain to regard me as part of the enemy's camp. Ruth welcomed my transfer of loyalties. Though there was not much I had painted that indicated Tamayo's influence the seed had been sown and sprouted in paintings I later did in Europe and India.

About this time I also met Tambimuttoo, a Sri Lankan poet and literary critic who had spent his youth in London in close proximity to Krishna Menon. He had now moved to New York with his Indian wife. Krishna Menon introduced me to Tambimuttoo during my show at India House. I soon become closer to Tambimuttoo than I had been to his mentor who was then vociferously promoting India's causes at the UN.

Tambimuttoo was a very erudite scholar and had a discerning eye for painting and sculpture. In England, he had become friends with Herbert Reed and John Berger, both critics of renown, as well as John Irwin, the curator of the Indian section of the Victoria and Albert Museum. He wrote to his friends telling them about me. The crowning achievement of Tambimuttoo's days in London had been his launching of the Penguin series on modern English poetry.

Tambi was a lanky man who looked like a brown-skinned version of the Hollywood star Gregory Peck. He cut an odd figure in his *sherwani* and *chooridars*. His apartment was close to mine on Riverside Drive. This gave us many opportunities to be together. He was often alone as his wife worked at the consulate from dawn to dusk.

In communicating with me, Tambimuttoo preferred to write. He wrote reams in response to any simple question I asked. I found this very intriguing. His calligraphy was as beautiful as his choice of words. I looked forward to our meetings and missed him on the weekends when his wife was at home.

Tambi told me that he had written to his friends in England who were looking forward to meeting me and seeing my work. I thought it was time I saw something of Europe. Early in 1955 I left the shores of the United States.

Ruth spent my last night in New York with me. We talked and made love till the early hours. Both of us realized that we meant more to each other than we had admitted to ourselves. In those last hours together, for the first time we talked of the possibility of our staying together for the rest of our lives. It was odd that we made this pledge when there were just a few hours before the liner I was booked on, the *Queen Mary*, set sail for Paris. And only the day before, Ruth had signed a contract to act in the much-talked-of play, *'Tis Pity She's a Whore.* She had been very keen to get this role, which later catapulted her to fame.

We were not destined to meet again. Six years later in 1961, when I visited New York, The first thing I did was to ask my wife Kiran to telephone Ruth at her father's house. The man who took the call was her father. He told Kiran that Ruth had died the previous night, and he was keeping vigil over her body. She had been thrown off her horse while out riding. The fall had fractured her skull.

Before the *Queen Mary* slipped out of New York harbour, I ran into Electra Arenales, the niece of Siqueiros' wife Angélica. She was a ballet dancer. I had known her rather casually during her frequent visits to Mexico city where she stayed at Casa de Huéspedes with her mother's aunt, our landlady Julie Bastard.

Electra's father was the go-between in New York where the conspiracy to murder Trostsky was hatched. He was in Mexico City when the murder took place. As Siqueiros fled, so too did he. He sought sanctuary in New York for reasons of security.

Electra had given me her address in New York. Ruth advised me not to contact her as her father was a marked man on the FBI list. This was the time when Senator McCarthy's witch-hunt for suspected Communists was at its height. However, I did meet Electra off and on, but not as often as I would have liked.

Electra was a stunning beauty in her early twenties. Married to a nondescript painter, she was a promiscuous bohemian and made no secret of it. Though the wedding had taken place barely six months earlier, she was on her way to Paris without her husband to 'refresh' herself, as she put it and meet celebrities whose names she could drop when she returned to New York. Although I had yet to make the celebrity list, she did not repel my advances. It was a short four-day crossing over the Atlantic. There was not much time to be discriminating, and she wished to keep me in good humour. She enjoyed hearing of my escapades in Mexico which were partly true and partly consisted of gossip I had picked up about people we both knew.

Electra was armed with introductions to quite a few well-known people. The first on her list was Louis Aragón the French leftist-intellectual and poet, a friend of Siqueiros. The minute we reached our hotel in the Latin Quarter near the metro station Saint Germain, Electra started to make appointments.

I did not expect her to take me along. But the next afternoon, after we had done some sightseeing, she told me that I was to accompany her to Louis Aragón's as he kept an 'open house' every Saturday. When we arrived at Aragón's residence, we found it was packed with bohemians of different nationalities. Electra disappeared into the noisy throng. I wandered around like a lost soul. Till the end of the evening, I did not meet my host.

I ran into Motiwala, a Parsi who had been my classmate at the JJ School of Arts in Bombay. He had left India at the time of independence to settle in Paris. Though jovial, Moti was a snob. Had he seen me coming along a street in Paris he would have looked the other way, or looked through me as if I did not exist. But here it was the house of Louis Aragón, which meant that was no longer a nobody. When we were at the JJ he had never deigned to speak to me. Since at the time I was not able to speak English, he had treated me like an untouchable. I was not anxious to renew his acquaintance. Motiwala did not give me a chance. Without as much as a by-your-leave, he took me in his embrace as if I was his long-lost brother.

Motiwala's affection for me grew as he saw Electra emerge from the crowd, leading a hefty old man towards me. With great enthusiasm she introduced me to her new companion: he was no other than Fernand Léger, the celebrated artist of Picasso's generation. Though both Electra and Léger disappeared as fast as they had appeared, Motiwala was most impressed with my new credentials. He summoned his French wife from almost nowhere and described how long we had been close Friends.

The next day Electra left hotel without so much as saying goodbye to me. But she had done me a great favour by impressing Motiwala with my importance. It proved invaluable during my stay in Paris.

Contrary to the image he projected, Moti had a heart of gold. Though I told him the truth about how I had gained entry to Aragon's house he continued to demonstrate great affection for me and had me over for dinner at his home almost every other evening.

Motiwala had joined the master etcher, Hyter, at his atelier in Paris as a student. He had graduated to become an apprentice and then Hyter's associate professor. He did not have much creative talent but had acquired mastery over Hyter's technique of engraving directly on copper plates and filling the recesses with printing inks. This had to be repeated with each individual print.

I wanted to join the atelier and learn the technique but Moti had just about then left Hyter and set up his own studio. There was some delay in the installation of printing units at his new studio, and I was unable to learn from him.

As none of Moti's successors spoke English and Hyter was at the time in New York, I was up against the problem of communication. Fortunately, one evening another Indian artist joined us for dinner at Moti's place. He was Krishna Reddy, a sculptor who had moved from Shantiniketan to Paris.

Till then Krishna's only concrete achievement was having gone through two marriages. He was now contemplating a third. That night he suddenly showed an interest in graphics and offered to accompany me to Hyter's atelier. I spent just one day there as I found Hyter's technique did not suit my style of painting. But it made all the difference to Krishna Reddy's Fortunes. Using Hyter's technique, he went on to win laurels while poor Motiwala died in obscurity.

After a few months Tambimuttoo advised me though his letters to shift London. I did so in the spring of 1955. The contacts I made through him proved to be as good as claimed they would be.

Of Tambimuttoo's friends, the first I called on was John Irwin. He was most cooperative. He told me he had arranged an exhibition of my paintings at the Victoria and Albert Museum. The show was to open in June 1955. He had got the Asia Society to bear the expenses of printing the catalogue and other sundry expenses. I could not have hoped for better. Our high commissioner in London at the time was Mrs Vijayalakshmi Pandit. The president of the Asia Society had requested her to inaugurate the exhibition. She had agreed to do so. This was one thing that John Irwin did not approve of. During a dinner in his house, his wife told me they had suffered an unhappy demonstration of Mrs Pandit's manners.

She was known to accept invitations and not show up at the last minute if she felt she would get nothing out of it. This is exactly what she did with me. Hours before the opening Mrs Pandit disappeared and sent a minor functionary of the high commission to represent her. There and then I swore never to ask anyone to inaugurate my exhibitions, VIPs or non-VIPs. No one has yet given me credit for setting an example that artists should not kowtow to people who know nothing about art. I find this sort of sycophancy very nauseating. I received good notices in the British press. John Berger covered the exhibition for the *New Statesman*, Herbert Reed for the *Spectator*, and the president of the British Art Critics Association (whose name I cannot recall) reviewed it for the *Guardian*. The only art journal of those times in England which had worldwide circulation, *Studio*, had a lengthy spread in its issue the following month.

More than the media coverage, what cheered me most was the presence of Roop Krishna and Mary on the opening day. I had discovered Roop's whereabouts by writing to Prasher in India, as no one in Indian community or the High Commission was aware of his existence. His approval meant a great deal to me. From that day on I dropped in at Roop's basement flat facing the South Kensington tube station almost every other evening.

Roop and Mary that had cut themselves off from all Indian contacts after they migrated to England in 1946. For all those years they kept their distance from their countrymen living in London and refused to read Indian newspapers. Knowing Roop as I did, I was not surprised. He was man of strong likes and dislike—mainly dislikes. Words such as compromise, accommodate and tolerate did not exist in his lexicon.

Roop also had the remarkable capacity of erasing people he did not like from his memory. Once in the course of small talk I asked him what he thought of Amrita Sher-Gil. For a moment he could not even recollect the name; then he drew a long breath and asked me, 'You mean that stupid Hungarian girl? Ah, only that old Hungarian hack Charles Fabri thought she was a genius.' I protested and told him that everyone in India agreed with Fabri's assessment of her worth. He slapped his Forehead and replied, 'Well, you get what you deserve.' It was then that he told me he had thrown Amrita's paintings from the balcony of his flat above the Rama Krishna bookstore in Lahore.

'Amrita,' Roop continued, 'had returned to India painting in the manner thousands of students had been doing in the dormitories of the École des Beaux Arts in Paris. There was not much to her talent except a good hand at drawing bold lines.' He had told her that to her face. But she had a big ego and a high opinion of herself. The only way to cut her down to size, according to him, was to toss her canvases out into the street. Roop was convinced that Amrita's arrogance was based on a feeling of racial superiority. She had later accepted the same advice from the expatriate English artist J.B. Pittman, who had initially suggested that she seek Roop's opinion. Though Amrita's work improved vastly in the years between her visit to Roop Krishna and her death in 1942, Roop continued to rate her poorly. Much as I tried to influence him in Amrita's favour, he refused to budge from his position. He gave no one any grace marks. To him an artist had to be judged by the rules of grammar of his chosen language. This in Amrita's case was Western, and she did not measure up to Western standards. According to Roop her vocabulary was *passé*, outdated by fifty years. Western art had radically changed from the conceptual experiments of early Impressionists like Paul Gauguin whom Amrita had adopted as her role model. Roop could not accept Amrita as a modern by comparing her with her Indian contemporaries. The argument was to resurface in India in later years, but no one gave credit to Roop Krishna for having refused to worship at the altar of the goddess that Amrita had become.

Roop and Mary died in oblivion soon after I left England in 1955. In her last letter to me Mary quoted one of her own lines, written many years earlier when she lived in Lahore:

Seek O seek not for light,
For with light goeth again sight;
Cometh inertia of sense and mind,
That makes the beholder blind.

Roop Krishna tried to persuade me not to return to India, especially after he learnt that I had sold quite a few of my canvases in Mexico and New York. Ruth had been writing to me in the same vein from New York. Her success on the stage had won her an offer to act in Tennessee Williams' *A Streetcar Named Desire*. But however tempting the prospects of living in Mexico or New York, there were compelling reasons for me to return home to India. My father and brother bombarded me with letters telling me of the publicity I was getting in the Indian press. They boosted my ego. I felt I could now get even with the people who had humiliated and belittled me.

I was still making up my mind I ran into Balwant Gargi at the Piccadilly Circus underground station. I knew Balwant was a successful playwright; his Punjabi plays had been frequently translated and staged in Urdu. I had no personal acquaintance with him, though we had seen each other on innumerable occasions in coffee houses at Lahore, Shimla and New Delhi. He never showed the slightest interest in me and gave me the impression of being an intellectual snob. However, that day as we passed each other he suddenly turned round and before exchanging greetings embraced me in a bear-hug.

I can gauge the extent of the interest a person has in me by the effort he or she makes to communicate with me. Of those eager to cultivate me, first come those who put all their energy in reaching me though a mixture of words, gestures and invisible writing with their index finger, using the air or their palms as slates. Then come those who take a shorter cut by always writing, either on their palms or on paper. Those who can't be bothered to make the effort, I treat with equal disdain; give as good as I am made to take. I was surprised when Balwant, after hugging me, used gestures and writing on his palm to talk to me. Only after we sat down for tea at the then fashionable Lyons Corner House on Regent Street did I understand what lay behind this switch from calculated indifference to spontaneous warmth.

Apparently, report of my modest achievements in the West had made me acceptable to India's literary and artistic elite. That evening and those that followed with Balwant did more to persuade me to return home than any number of beseeching letters from my family.

8

NEW DELHI

A FORTNIGHT LATER I CALLED THE INDIAN HIGH COMMISSION FOR assistance in getting a berth on a boat bound for Bombay. Ships were heavily overbooked, and I needed a permit to import my own paintings. The process was as complicated as getting a visa to the United States. I was advised to see P.N. Haksar, the senior functionary at the High Commission. He was kind and helpful. (We became friends for life. Haksar later became Mrs Gandhi's right-hand man). He told me that the paintings I had done abroad and those I had brought from India without proper registration would be subject to customs duty. How were they to be priced? How was the duty on them to be assessed? Haksar advised me not to fix my date of departure before the matter could be sorted out with the government at home. This might take many months, if not years. Haksar thought the easiest way out would be to declare the paintings as 'used articles'. He advised Indian customs to be accommodating.

Balwant Gargi and I were on the same boat to Bombay. Gargi, with whom my friendship had grown stronger with time, remains to this day somewhat beyond my comprehension. Though seemingly guileless and transparent, he conceals his real self behind a torrent of words. He is a short, stocky, pudgy man, as far from being a lady's man as anyone I know. And through the years I have known him, he has lived a hand-to-mouth existence, never knowing where his next meal will come from. Nevertheless, women are infatuated by him. He is always seen in the company of pretty girls. Once during his stay in the United States he married a stunningly attractive American called Jeanine, a few inches taller than him. The couple bought a lot of American gadgets, including a big convertible. When he drove from Bombay to New Delhi, he broke journey at Agra to show her the Taj Mahal. He was mistaken for a taxi driver and interrogated by the police for not possessing a cab-driver's licence!

Gargi's marriage did not work out. It was not the beautiful Jeannie who was unfaithful but her hefty husband who could not resist the temptation of tasting forbidden fruit—a Sikh divorcée. While Jeannie had given Gargi a son and a daughter of his own, he was cavorting with this Sikh lady, mother of two daughters. Jeannie returned to her home in Seattle with her daughter, leaving her son with her ex-husband. She refused to see them ever again.

On landing in Bombay, Balwant rang up Mulk Raj Anand who had a small flat on Cuffe Parade. He invited us to visit the same evening. He had a few admirers over and pressed us to stay for dinner.

Mulk had a purpose in extending hospitality to me. I was aware of his interest in promoting me. In an issue of *Marg,* the magazine he edited, he had published an article about me, in which I was described as a 'meteor'. Mulk was a Communist, as were most of the guests. The dinner durbar was delighted to make me a member of the charmed circle. I soon discovered the reason for this. During the dinner Ali Safdar Jafri and Mohit Sen told me that they had seen an article on me written by Rajani Palme Dutt, secretary general of the British Communist Party. Indian Communists were impressed. I had met Rajani with John Berger in London and he had written a very appreciative article on my exhibition in the British Communists Journal, the *Daily Worker.* I was not aware that the same article had been reproduced in India. I was elated. Despite my disillusionment with propagandist art and the Soviet Union, I still had warm feelings towards leftists.

Mulk advised me not to settle in New Delhi but in some remote place, like Shimla. This would distance me from the scheming and opportunistic atmosphere of Delhi's art circles. I was not inclined to accept his advice as I did not intend to cut myself off from the centre of India's artistic activity. He also advised me to have nothing to do with the newly formed Lalit Kala Akademi under Barada Ukil.

Mulk was good enough to arrange a one-evening exhibition of my work in his flat. The week I spent in Bombay gave me a foretaste of the gang wars between rival groups of artists that I was to face in New Delhi.

Bombay's artist community had a caste system of its own. On top were the 'Brahmins' who had gained recognition and were reluctant to admit upstart newcomers in their midst. They included men like K.K. Hebbar, Shiavax Chavda, N.S. Bendre, Jehangir Sabavala and Rasik Raval. In the second grade but soon to make the top were M.F. Hussain, H.A Gade, V.S Gaitonde and Mohan Samant. This second group was gaining prominence because they were 'progressive' and enjoyed the patronage of European art critics who had stayed on in India after the British had gone. The most important of these critics was Rudi von Leyden, a Dutchman who headed one of the Tata corporations. S.H. Raza, F.N. Souza and Akbar Padamsee, who also belonged to the second rung, had migrated to Europe. Though no longer physically in Bombay, they made their presence felt from a distance. Through Bombay's art critics they waged unending wars against enemies at home and against each other.

At the time I arrived, this emerging group had fortified itself in a piece of property belonging to the Bhulabhai Desai Trust on Nepean Sea Road.

There were good reasons for Bombay becoming the Mecca for Indian artists. All the large corporations of thc country had their head offices in the city. Some enterprises like the Tatas and Air India bought paintings to adorn their offices. Bombay also had magazines like *Marg*, financed by the house of Tatas, entirely devoted to art; and the *Illustrated Weekly of India* belonging to the *Times of India* group of publications, which devoted a lot of space to artists and sculptors. The *Weekly* and its Hindi counterpart *Dharmyug* had all-India readership. These journals gave Bombay artists greater importance than they deserved. They supported the Bombay Progressives, who claimed to have introduced modern Western trends in Indian art; a similar claim was being made by Pradosh Dass Gupta and his colleagues who assumed the title of 'Progressives' in Calcutta in the early forties. Art critics resented my forthright opinion that Roop Krishna was the true pioneer in this regard, as far back as the late twenties. Karl Khandalawala, who had known Roop Krishna, was the only one who agreed with me, but even he did nothing to project Roop Krishna because of his personal dislike of the man. They did not see eye to eye in judging Amrita Sher-Gil's work. Roop gave her a poor rating while Karl thought she was the only genius the country had produced and paid her fulsome tributes in his coffee-table book on her published after her death.

I brought up the subject with von Leyden who was the self-anointed apostle of the Bombay Progressives. He was not as negative in his reaction and conceded that Bombay was not representative of the whole country. In 1946 he had organized an exhibition of the works of the Calcutta Progressives in Bombay. He tried to get artists of the two metropolises together. But von Leyden evaded committing himself to my point of view. Twenty years later I ran into him in Vienna, where he had settled after retirement. I bought up the subject a second time. By then von Leyden was a disillusioned man and had lost interest in the politics of Indian art. But he admitted that it would be difficult for him now to repudiate all that he had stood for. He had fathered the myths that the Bombay Progressives were the actual leaders of the movement to energize Indian art with modern European concepts.

It was the same with Karl Khandalawala, whom I met many times in Bombay and Delhi. Shortly before he died in 1991 I had a long session with him in Calcutta. Like von Leyden, Karl had mellowed with age and was overcome with a confessional urge. He told me of his encounter with Roop Krishna in Lahore. He had gone to see him while doing research on Amrita Sher-Gil. Roop found the very idea that anyone should write a book on Amrita quite revolting, and asked Karl if he had been Amrita's lover. When Karl denied the allegation, Roop asked him why he was going to all this trouble over a girl who was just starting to learn how to paint. Karl, who was a young man at the time, was very upset by the insinuation and swore never to have anything to do with Roop Krishna. It had taken him many years to get over his aversion to Roop and admit that Roop had some justification for his judgement of Amrita's work. I was sorely tempted to ask Karl if there was any truth in the rumour of his having been one of Amrita's many lovers, but I lost my nerve at the last moment.

In the autumn of 1955 I was back in Delhi. As the train pulled up at the New Delhi railway station, I realized I had barely enough money in my pocket to pay the coolies their fee. I was not unduly worried. I was back home among my own people.

The family had become poorer during the years I was away. My father had resigned his parliamentary seat and was helping my mother in the management of Nari Niketan in Jalandhar. They survived on the small sums of money Inder sent them. Inder's situation was not very good either, as he had neither the heart nor the head for business; his real interest was politics. He had ceased being a Communist and had joined the Indian National Congress. He was working with Sucheta Kriplani, the firebrand wife of Acharya Kriplani, then president of the party.

He had a small two-bedroom house on Hanuman Road, behind the present-day Park Hotel. It had a narrow veranda in front. We portioned the veranda and made a cubicle which became my bedroom and studio.

During the years I was away, the art scene in Delhi had changed beyond recognition. In the early thirties, the Ukil brothers, Sarada and Barada, dominated the capital's art circles. The elder brother, after retiring as an art teacher in Modern School, had founded the Sarada Ukil School of Arts on Janpath, close to the outer ring of Connaught Circus. After Sarada's death, his younger brother Barada took over the school. He was more a manager and a go-getter than an artist. He founded the All India Fine Arts and Crafts Society, which had a makeshift exhibition hall on prime land close to Parliament House. At about the time I returned, he had commissioned New Delhi's leading builder, Sir Sobha Singh, to put up a three-storeyed stone and marble building with an auditorium, art galleries and office rooms on another piece of prime land, where it is today. Upto the time of independence in 1947, it was the AIFACS under Barada Ukil that mattered in art circles.

Independence brought Hindu and Sikh artists from Lahore to Delhi. They were followed by artists from East Bengal and other parts of India who felt they had better prospects in the fast-growing city. Barada Ukil's position as the commissar of culture was challenged by Bhubesh Sanyal, who was supported by artists such as Pran Mago, Sailoz Mukherjee, Harkrishan Lal, Kanwal Krishna, K.S. Kulkarni,

Ram Kumar, Dhan Raj Bhagat and Biren De. The dissenters grouped under the name Shilpi Chakra. By the time I reappeared on the scene, Barada had consolidated his hold. He had manoeuvered to have himself appointed secretary general of the newly formed Lalit Kala Akademi, financed by the government but meant to function as an autonomous body.

I heard many stories of artists who fell by the wayside for having dared to question Barada's dictates. I did not want to earn his displeasure, but destiny determined otherwise.

Soon after my arrival, some members of the Servants of the People Society, in which my father had been active, commissioned me to do a portrait of Lala Lajpat Rai to be put in the Central Hall of Parliament.

Barada Ukil was a member of the parliamentary art committee, as he was of almost every other committee which had anything to do with the arts. He sent for me to brief me on the way the committee, which meant himself, would like me to paint the portrait.

I should have consulted an astrologer to advise me on the auspicious date and hour to call on the almighty Barada. I had to pay dearly for this oversight.

Barada Ukil cut a Romanesque figure. He was more than six feet and two inches tall, with a muscular frame. He exuded an air of self-esteem. He was always chewing something or the other; this probably gave him an appetite for people as well. He did both with equal gusto. Nobody was sure of how successful he was with women except that he made himself out to be irresistible to the opposite sex. Amongst the many conquests he claimed was Amrita Sher-Gil. Though a married man with children, he had spread the story that Amrita Sher-Gil had agreed to become his second wife. Amrita was no longer there to contradict him.

Though most of Delhi's artists bowed to Barada Ukil's hectoring, there were a few who either ignored him or stood up to him. They had a powerful supporter in Charles Fabri, who never missed an opportunity to needle Barada. He mocked Barada's boast of having enjoyed Amrita's favours as he, Charles, claimed to be the only one she had deemed worthy of receiving them.

The fact that I was a favourite of Charles Fabri was good enough for Barada to scorn me. He went by one simple rule: 'an enemy's friend is my enemy'.

I was not fully aware of the hostilities between Barada and Charles Fabri when, accompanied by Inder, I went to call on Barada. He held court in the circular annexe of Jaipur House which later became a part of the National Gallery of Modern Art.

To add to my misfortune, when we were shown in we found Fabri sitting with Barada. Instead of waiting till Fabri left, I asked Barada for instructions he wanted to give me regarding the portrait of Lajpat Rai. Barada raised his hand like Ceaser giving a command and said, 'Paint it in Amrita Sher-Gil style.'

I was bewildered and looked towards Charles Fabri. He did not wait for my response. With a spiteful look on his face he spat out at Barada: 'Why tell him to paint in the Amrita Sher-Gil style? You thought nothing of her when she was alive.' This was more than Barada could take. He yelled back in rage. 'You *firangi*! How dare you say I hated her. The whole world knows we loved each other!'

Barada turned to Inder with an expression of injured innocence. 'Amrita in love with you?' Fabri retorted sardonically. 'She hardly ever acknowledge your existence.'

Fabri got up to leave. But Barada had not finished with him. He came round the table and held Fabri by his shoulders and shouted, 'You say I did not know her? I say you did not know her. Remember she and I had come to Lahore together! We stayed in Faletti's Hotel. We registered ourselves as Mr and Mrs Ukil. You came to see me and I introduced you to her. I also remember you borrowed two cigarettes from me while leaving. You came back the next day to return them. You are an ungrateful beggar!'

Barada was foaming at the mouth. Although I could not hear the angry words they hurled at one another. I could see their faces distorted in anger. Inder filled in the gaps by rapidly transcribing the abusive exchange on the palm of his hand.

The visit was fiasco. I was forced to choose between Barada and Fabri. I left little doubt that in Barada's mind about whose side we were on. I allowed Fabri to escort us two brothers out of Barada's august presence.

A month later I submitted my portrait of Lala Lajpat Rai to the parliamentary committee for approval. Barada had no difficulty in having it rejected. We decided to fight back. Fabri and Inder agreed that the portrait should be put up for public viewing.

But we ran into opposition. The members of the Servants of the People Society headed by Diwan Chaman Lal, MP and Lal Bahadur Shashtri, who had recently become a cabinet minister, were opposed to a confrontation with the art committee. They felt it might jeopardize the chances of the portrait ever hanging in the parliament. They knew that Prime Minister Nehru was not very keen on having Lala Lajpat Rai's portrait in the house. What was I to do?

Lala Feroz Chand, a former editor of the *Times of India,* advised me not to succumb to pressure. Feroz Chand, a former editor of the *People,* a daily of the Congress party published from Lahore during the days of Gandhiji's call for non-cooperation in 1930. He was more an intellectual than a politician. As a member of the Servants of the People Society, he had done his best to have the portrait accepted. He was now entrusted with the task of trying to persuade me not to take a confrontational stand with Barada.

AIFACS was the only art gallery in Delhi that displayed canvases. This was under Barada Ukil. Someone suggested we try Modern School at Barakhamba Road. It had a hall where art classes were held and would be suitable for exhibiting a large portrait. The art section at the school was headed by Kanwal Krishna, whom I had recently met.

Kanwal was sympathetic but did not think it would work. Krishna Kulkarni and Dhan Raj Bhagat were of the same opinion. All three had suffered Barada Ukil's autocratic ways and their protests had only worsened their positions. However, Kanwal took me to see the principal, M.N. Kapur.

Kapur, though amused at the reason for my wanting to exhibit the portrait, readily agreed to let me to do so. Fabri was naturally delighted. The exhibition was fixed for an evening early in 1956.

I cannot forget the prelude to the opening. Early in the morning Diwan Chaman Lal came to see us at Inder's house. He had been close to my father for many years. Both had been in the same jails and later had been together as members of the Constituent Assembly. He tried to exploit his relationship with our father to browbeat us into dropping the idea. He admonished Inder for playing politics which could jeopardize my future.

Sensing that we were not impressed, he tried another approach. He told us how very difficult it had been to get Lajpat Rai's name included in the list of those whose portraits were to hang in Parliament House. He revealed Nehru's hostility towards Lajpat Rai that went back to the days of Nehru's father Motilal and Swaraj Party. Nehru, according to Chaman Lal, considered Lajpat Rai a Hindu communalist not fit to be portrayed in the parliament of secular democracy. Chaman Lal had spoken to Barada before coming to see us and assured us that Barada was willing to compromise if I agreed to some minor changes in the portrait.

By sheer coincidence Fabri dropped in. Chaman Lal and Fabri were old friends. Chaman Lal tried to solicit Fabri's support for his compromise proposal. Fabri dismissed the idea and admonished Chaman Lal for even suggesting it to me. Chaman Lal immediately reversed his position and told me to go ahead with my exhibition with his blessings.

After Chaman Lal left, Fabri who knew what my artist friends had advised, said, 'Well, you may lose this battle but you will win the war.'

The days that followed proved his prophecy right.

The one-portrait exhibition did not set the Jamuna on fire. But its impact was beyond my wildest expectations. Fabri had his opinion of the portrait published on the front page of the *Statesman*. This had never happened before. He poured ridicule on the committee which had rejected the portrait, and accused them of being philistines who knew nothing about art and unfit to be entrusted with the responsibility of pronouncing judgment on the merits of a painting.

Fabri's words were compensation enough for the rejection. But there was still more to come. A few hours later there was a call from the Prime Minister's house asking me to bring the portrait to Teen Murti House as Panditji, who read the review, wished to see it.

Panditji grazed at the portrait for a while before he said with a smile, 'I like it. But let me tell you, Lajpat Rai was not the lion you have made him out to be.' He ordered coffee for us and narrated an episode from Lalaji's life. Nahas Pasha, an Egyptian nationalist leader on a visit to Lahore, met Lajpat Rai and asked him if his party had any influence in the army. Lajpat Rai who was so frightened by the thought of the possible repercussions of any answers he gave, that he spent all the time he had with Nahas Pasha trying to convince him that the Congress was merely the 'King's loyal opposition'. What had vexed Nehru was not what Lajpat Rai had said but the manner in which he had spoken: it was cringing and cowardly.

The same evening Prime Minister Nehru overruled the committee's decision and ordered the portrait to be hung in Parliament House. He went further. On my request he also agreed to unveil it.

After the ceremony, Panditji made a short speech. He called me to the stage, put an arm around my shoulder and continued speaking. He told everyone present how the portrait had been turned down and why he had intervened and overruled the committee's decision.

Inder and I returned home so full of emotion that we could not speak to each other. We sat on our little lawn in absolute silence for many hours. To speak would have been sacrilegious. We were drifting in a dream world of suppressed elation and euphoria. What did the future have in store?

I had come to Nehru's notice. During my first exhibition after returning to India, Indira Gandhi had come to see it on the closing day. She wished her father to see it. Since he was not in town, she suggested we have a private showing at Teen Murti House, the Prime Minister's official residence. So I had a one-evening, one-man exhibition for one man, the Prime Minister of India. What was more, Indira conveyed to us her father's wish that I paint his portrait. I was extremely flattered. I had been told by many artists that Nehru had turned down every request to sit for a portrait. He knew it was another form of sycophancy. The only exception he had made was in the case of the famous British sculptor, Jacob Epstein.

The invitation gained us brothers entry into the house of the first family of India. We became closer to Indira Gandhi and then her father Jawaharlal. Indira began to invite us to the house regularly. She wanted me to get to know what her father was really like as a human being before I started to put his likeness on canvas. She had done the same when Epstein wanted to sculpt him. In the course of trying to get to know Nehru, we got to know Indira Gandhi better than we got to know her father. The two had very little in common. He was an extrovert, full of zest and spirit. She had inherited more of her mother's traits and was withdrawn and melancholic. This sadness could be discerned in her face as well as in the photographs of her mother.

An oppressive sadness dominated most of the paintings I was creating those days. Naturally I was strongly drawn towards Indira and more keen to paint her than I was to do her father's portrait. I confessed this to her. She was flattered and agreed to sit for me. So I painted Indira Gandhi's portrait before Jawaharlal Nehru's.

Since Inder always accompanied me to these sessions he got to know Indira quite well. They were about the same age and shared the same interest in India's political history.

It is ironic that the very portrait that brought us three together was to be the reason for her cutting me out of her life in later years.

A few days after I finished Indira's portrait, Fabri who knew her well, suggested we arrange an evening at our house and invite a select group of artists, art-lovers and critics to see the portrait. The evening was a great success. Indira graced our little home and amused everyone by telling them of people's reactions to the painting while I was still at work on it. The one person she avoided mentioning was her husband Feroz Gandhi. He had interrupted one of the sittings and given me a withering look that clearly indicated his contempt for my efforts. I was not wrong in my surmise. Inder Malhotra, the journalist who was a close friend of Feroze, later told me that Feroze was surprised to find me wasting my time and talent painting a woman who had nothing to distinguish except the fact of her being the daughter of the Prime Minister. He had quoted Professor Harold Laski, whose classes both Feroz and Indira attended in England, as saying 'She is a stupid girl with not a single idea in her head.'

I have vivid recollections of sudden changes of expression on Indira's face during very sitting. I had to track and capture her moods each day she sat for me. In the process her dominant and characteristic look eluded me. Nor did I try to fix it in the final version. This is because I lose interest in my own painting as soon as I have put the final stroke on the canvas.

Let me try to explain this better. The closest analogy that comes to my mind is having sex with someone. As long as the act lasts, one is totally absorbed in the partner; as soon as it is over, one feels detached and distant from the very person on whom a minute ago one had expended so much passion. That being so, Fabri's review in the *Statesman* the next morning came as a bit of a shock. While he applauded my craftsmanship, he felt I had failed to portray the essence of Indira Gandhi. According to Fabri, I had depicted her as someone cold-blooded and ruthless, which Fabri was sure she was not. My portrayal of the future Prime Minister of India played an important role in determining the relationship between the Gujral brothers and Nehru-Gandhi family.

I put the portrait away instead of delivering it to the Prime Minister's house. I kept wondering why I had given Indira Gandhi that particularly compelling and disturbing expression. Had I unconsciously depicted the moment her husband Feroze had violently entered the room? We came to the conclusion that perhaps behind the facade of smiling gentility was an embittered woman concealing vengeful and arrogant traits.

Inder recalled that while Indira Gandhi was sitting for her portrait, Nikita Khrushchev and Nikolai Bulganin had visited India. It was known that the entourage of the Soviet leaders included a Russian general who had ordered progroms of ethnic minorities inhabiting areas in the path of the Nazis' advance towards Moscow. He suspected they would collaborate with the Nazis if given a chance, and had ordered their forcible deportation to the hostile interior territories of Russia. Hundreds of thousands had perished in this state-supervised version of ethnic cleansing. Inder had mentioned this to Indira Gandhi. Her reaction shook him. She said she did not think it was such an outrage, and faced with similar kind of disloyalty, she would have done the same thing. Nehru, whose portrait I started a few days later confirmed that his daughter was unforgiving towards those she suspected of harbouring designs against her, of being a threat in any way. He asked Inder to let him see Indira's portrait. Inder did his best to prevent Panditji seeing it. He told him that some people thought it showed Indira as a very determined woman with a sadistic streak.

Nehru clamly replied, 'That is what she is.'

He liked the portrait and ordered it to be hung in his reception room. We were relieved that the matter had ended amicably. Indira's reaction to Fabri's review was by no means adverse. She never said anything about my having made her look stern and unforgiving, and cordially accepted the painting.

However, the story of Indira Gandhi's portrait did not end with its adorning the Prime Minister's wall. Two decades later the controversy resurfaced. Indira Gandhi as Prime Minister had imposed the Emergency, which deprived people of their democratic rights and arbitrarily jailed thousands of citizens. When she ended the Emergency and called for elections, she was thrown out of power. There was a spate of books, each vying with the other, to find skeletons in Mrs. Gandhi's cupboard. Among the most hard-hitting were Uma Vasudev's *Two Faces of Indira Gandhi* and Janardhan Thakur's *All the Prime Minister's Men*. Both referred to the portrait episode and Fabri's critique. The primary source of material these writers had were old copies of the *Statesmen* and gossip picked up in the India Coffee House. But Indira was somehow given to understand that I was the man behind it. Since I had expressed harsh disapproval of the imposition of the Emergency, she willingly believed the allegations against me and refused to have anything to do with me for the rest of her life.

As I look back and assess the impact of my portrait of Lala Lajpat Rai on my career, I realize that it was indeed the most important watershed in my life. I succeeded in breaking the stranglehold of Barada Ukil on the Delhi art scene and carved a niche for myself as a painter who had muscled his way into the art would and the Prime Minister's house.

There was more to this painting than the nod of approval given by Nehru and the fact of my work finding a place in the pantheon of heroes of the Indian freedom movement. It was at the inauguration of this portrait at Modern School that I first set eyes on Kiran Ram Nath.

Kiran was in the final year of the local arts college which was then located at Kashmere Gate in Old Delhi. She came to the exhibition with Inder's friend Bhupinder Hooja and his sculptor wife Usha Rani. Later, the Hoojas came over to our home and brought Kiran with them. She wanted to see other paintings I had done. As the evening progressed, so did my fascination for the girl. She was lovely to look at, cultured in speech and asked intelligent questions about art. And I enjoyed her praise of my work.

I had been back in New Delhi for three months when I met Kiran. All this while I remained a focus of controversy and very much the most talked about artist in the capital. Like Inder, I had become a regular patron of the India Coffee House. I was there every morning to pick up gossip, munch cashew nuts, sip cups of coffee and ogle the girls. For me the special attraction was my old Shimla flame Uma Vasudev, alias Miss .303. She had returned from England still unmarried and had established her court in the Coffee House.

In her new incarnation, Uma had become a journalist. She published and edited a journal of her own. The attention she showered on me was in stark contrast to the indifference she had shown towards me in Shimla. My desire to seek her company was rekindled; the more I saw of her, the more I wanted to see her. What deterred me from getting closer to her was the battery of admirers who surrounded her. They were a mixed assortment of minor celebrities; there was the journalist Inder Malhotra, the playwright Balwant Gargi, the socialist Ram Manohar Lohia and the bureaucrat (later politician) Natwar Singh. The list was endless.

Inder was alarmed at my growing obsessiveness. He had a clear vision of the kind of woman who would make a suitable wife for me;

'Miss .303' did not conform to this image. He tried to impress this on me as he noticed my increasing emotional involvement with her.

Uma Vasudev, who was to remain my friend for life, was a complex character. She was not cut out to be a one-man woman. Unfortunately she discovered this after her short-lived and unhappy marriage, which left her with two daughters and not enough money to live independently. She was lucky to have parents who had no son. They provided shelter when she had nowhere else to go.

Uma Vasudev's looks proved to be both an asset as well as a handicap. Few men could resist her charm, and she received all the attention any woman could ask for. At the same time it deprived her of the will to strive and exploit the enormous talent she undoubtedly had. She liked to be the centre of attention wherever she was. That was never a problem. But her creative talents remained dormant. As the years took their toll, she became a graveyard of unfulfilled potential. She tried frantically to make up for lost time. She had started feeling it was too late.

The application of single-minded devotion to one's talent is not something you are born with or inherit; you have to work relentlessly till it becomes a part of your life. Like teeth that replace those lost only up to a certain age, habits such as sustained effort and rigorous concentration cease or fail to take root after a certain point of time if they are not constantly nurtured and reinforced.

Kiran arrived on the scene just in time to prevent my rekindled infatuation for Uma Vasudev from getting out of control. Inder was relieved that my attention had been diverted from the flamboyant 'Miss .303' to a staid but an equally attractive girl.

Kiran was the daughter of a leading dentist of Delhi Dr Ram Nath, who like hundreds of thousands of us had migrated from Lahore after the Partition. He had a cousin, also a dentist, who had a French wife. Inder, who had had a fleeting acquaintance with both dentists, mistook Dr Ram Nath for the husband of the French woman.

Inder and I thought that my chance of winning Kiran were brighter if her mother was foreign. She would not be as prejudiced against a deaf man as the common run of Indian women and the fact of my being a painter would mean more to her than to a traditional Hindu *shrimatiji*. Kiran was not aware of our confused perception of her parentage, nor did the subject come up till I proposed to her. It was only then that the reality surfaced, and surfaced with a vengeance. We discovered that her mother was not French; her mother was dead and had been replaced by a stepmother, her mother's young sister, her *masi*. She was adamantly against the marriage. So was Kiran's father. He was appalled to learn that his pretty daughter was contemplating marrying a deaf painter. Bhupinder Hooja tried his best to convince Dr Ram Nath, but failed in his mission. We sought the intercession of Prime Minister Nehru and his daughter Indira Gandhi.

Marie Seton, the English film historian and a close friend of the Nehrus, who was also known to me, narrates in her biography of Nehru that one day Nehru asked her how the Satish Gujral-Kiran Ram Nath affair was progressing. At the Prime Minister's suggestion Marie Seton called on Dr Ram Nath to plead my case. The doctor refused to yield. We were left with no choice but to defy him and decide our future ourselves.

We fixed 28 June 1957 as the date for our wedding. We did not consult any astrologer or brother to match our horoscopes. The date was chosen because it happened to be the first Monday after the expiry of the four-week compulsory waiting after we had issued the notice of our intention to marry under the Civil Marriage Act.

The only obstacle that we faced was the lack of Kiran's birth certificate, a compulsory document to be attached to the application for the permit to marry. We thought that her graduation certificate, to which she had become entitled a few months earlier, would suffice. Even this was not available for a long time. I asked my friend Bishamber Khanna, who was a teacher at the art college, to ask

Bhubesh Sanyal, then the college principal, to expedite the process. To Bishamber's surprise, Sanyal disclosed that he had been holding back the certificate because of a request from Kiran's father who had known Sanyal since the Lahore days. Bishamber confronted Sanyal and asked him point-blank if he was under the illusion that just by withholding the certificate he could prevent the impending marriage. This worked. Sanyal thought it prudent not to create bad blood between himself and Inder, who he knew would soon be confronting him with the same request. He issued the certificate but made Bishamber pledge that he would not tell anyone of his initial reluctance to comply with our requests. Bishamber Khanna's determined intervention at this crucial time created a bond of friendship that grew stronger in passing years.

The night before 28 June, when I was dropping Kiran home, I kept reassuring her that all would go smoothly. But I needed more reassurance than she did. I felt a strange anxiety whenever I thought of what lay ahead. It was a hot summer night. The entire family, my parents, two sisters, Uma and Niti, Inder and his wife Shil were in a celebratory mood. We had our dinner on the lawn. While the others were in high spirits I was overwhelmed by a mixture of fear and uncertainty. What was I pulling Kiran into? It seemed as if Kiran's father had insinuated his forebodings into my mind and was intensifying them by remote control. I began to see his point of view. What if Kiran had been *my* daughter instead? Would there have been any reason to celebrate her marriage to someone like me?

Inder intuitively knew what I was thinking. After everyone else had gone he stayed on to talk to me. He had never seen me so crestfallen and unsure of myself. Was I suffering from fears of sexual inadequacy? I assured him I had nothing to fear on that score. He took my hand in his. In our years of closeness we had developed a language that was not dependent on words. We sat in silence for quite some time. I felt his self-confidence flow into me. I was reassured and decided to go ahead with my plan to sign the marriage register the following day.

Early the next morning I met Kiran on Parliament Street across from the lane that led to her father's house. It was near the police station and the magistrate court. She did not seem to be assailed by any doubts. We entered the courtroom together, signed the register and came out into a new world as man and wife.

The signing ceremony at the court was a drab affair. Only members of my immediate family were present in the room. The reception that followed was quite another matter. The reception that followed was quite another matter. The artists community in the capital turned up in full force. Among those who graced the occasion were Nehru and Indira Gandhi.

My father was moved by the gesture. He pressed Nehru's hand in gratitude and reminded him of the day in 1930 when he had visited our home in Jhelum. I was a toddler then. Holding me, he had climbed the stairs to the roof, from where he delivered his speech. This was soon after Nehru was elected president of the Indian National Congress session at Lahore. At this session he had proposed and carried the momentous resolution declaring complete independence from Britain as the party's goal.

We spent our two-week honeymoon in Nainital. When we returned to Delhi, Inder informed me that the Prime Minister had issued an order allotting me a two-room apartment in the barracks, then called Constitution House adjoining Hyderabad House on Curzon Road. The rent was to be Rs 350 a month. Though nominal it was beyond my means. Fortunately I mentioned this to Tom Keehn, head of the Rockefeller Foundation in India. Tom had become quite friendly with me. He had his office in the premises of the Cottage Industries Emporium, from where he doled out patronage to people or institution connected with the arts. He came to our rescue. He recommended Kiran name for a job in the design section of the handicraft board; the salary would enable us to pay the rent for the premises allotted to us.

As soon as Kiran working in the emporium, she sensed how people perceived our relationship. Since she had taken a low-paying job and was the wife of a handicapped person, they thought she would be easy game. Not a day passed without someone or the other making a pass at her under the guise of sympathy. After two months, she had had her fill of lecherous office Romeos and decided to quit. This kind of unwelcome male attention has followed her persistently through her married life. This despite the fact that since she quit her job, we have hardly ever been separated for more than an hour or two.

In the two months at the emporium Kiran quickly learnt about the commercial potential of Indian handicrafts. With my help she set up a small workshop in the courtyard of our house to design and fabricate wood jewellery, small wooden objects and batik prints. Though these did not earn us much money, their sale helped us to live in some comfort.

9

VOYAGES

About this time I started feeling that I had come to a dead end with the style of painting I had been doing since Partition. In one sense it had been invaluable, since it had brought me recognition and some money. It had given me an identity. Giving it up would have been like stripping myself and standing naked in the marketplace of art. I spent sleepless nights pondering over my dilemma I became irritable and short-tempered. Kiran sensed the turmoil within me and implored me to confide in her. I told her what was tormenting me. She understood the nature of the crisis and encouraged me take the plunge.

I took the leap into the unknown. The catalyst that pointed me in a new direction came about in an unexpected way. During my days in Shimla with Ted Bower, I had come to know Pierre Jeanneret, a cousin of Le Corbusier. After designing the layout of the new city and some of its main buildings, Corbusier had entrusted their implementation to Jeanneret, who stayed on in India while Corbusier came twice a year to check how the work was progressing. Jeanneret and Ted Bower had become close, as Bower was the only man on the project who could speak French. At the time Jeanneret had great difficulty in speaking English.

Although I could not communicate directly with Jeanneret, Ted kept me briefed about what passed between them. They talked incessantly as we three strolled round Jakhoo Hill every evening.

Jeanneret's appreciation of Corbusier's work was somewhat grudging. They were cousins and at one time been in love with the same girl. The affair had long been over and the wounds inflicted on Jeanneret had healed. He stoutly defended Corbusier against Bower's criticism but without offending him. He had shown interest in my impending visit to Mexico. After hearing Fabri's favourable comments on my work, he had recommended that I go to Mexico.

According to Jeanneret, mural painting required a technique and discipline of its own. Along with some knowledge of painting and sculpture, it required a knowledge of architecture. A muralist had to operate within the parameters set by the architect. If the muralist chose to ignore architectural compulsions, his work did not enhance the beauty or strength of the building. Jeanneret believed the Mexican muralists had to some extent exemplified aesthetic and conceptual brilliance.

Jeanneret had many friends in Mexico. They included the artist-architect Juan O'Gorman, who had built the library of the New City University, and Mario Paani who designed Hotel del Prado in Mexico City, which was later destroyed by an earthquake. He had given me introductions to his friends when I left for Mexico. I got to know both O'Gorman and Paani during my stay in the country. By the time I returned home, Jeanneret had moved from Shimla to Chandigarh, which had by then begun to look like a city, I called on him when I visited the new city for the first time. It was early in 1961.

The city had developed exactly the way Bower had predicted. Even at that early stage its synthetic character had become apparent. It was difficult to pronounce it either a success or a failure. There was an utilitarian anonymity and neutrality about its construction.

Jeanneret offered me a wall in the newly-built Gandhi Bhavan at the University, which he had designed. He hoped that I would demonstrate on it what I had learnt in Mexico.

To what extent the mural succeeded is besides the point. The commission freed me form earlier concepts of painting to which I had shackled myself. It was the beginning of my preoccupation with space. In that early mural with a rough wall as my canvas, I attempted to treat space not as something separate from humans but as an integral part of our being, with no visible line to divide the two. It was a concept I was later to extend to designing buildings as an architect. I had found the freedom that allowed me to negotiate and organize external space in a manner that would harmonize with my inner being and allow it to expand and flourish.

The transformation in my style set the turmoil within me at rest, but at a great price. Overnight I was left with no admirers. The older set thought that marriage had made me complacent and comfortable, and deprived me of the angst which had earlier fuelled my creative powers and driven me to express myself in radical and original images.

This new-found concept was put into practice after I had finished the portraits of Nehru and Indira Gandhi, and had followed them up with those of Mirza Ghalib and Krishna Menon. My acquaintance with Menon might well have ended after I left New York, but for the evening when Indira Gandhi arranged a private viewing of my paintings at the Prime Minister's residence. Menon was there. He took it upon himself to conduct a guided tour of my work for Nehru and others whom Indira had invited for that evening. I was fascinated by Menon's sharp features which seemed to be ever-mobile, ever-changing. I offered to paint his portrait. He was flattered and agreed to sit for me.

It was during these sittings that Krishna Menon talked to me about Marie Seton, the film historian. Though she had earned a place for herself in that world, she was somewhat domineering and given to name-dropping. Two of the celebrities whose names she mentioned constantly were the famous director Sergei Eisenstein and, later, Krishna Menon. She and I shared many common friends. Some were Mexicans: Marie had spent a few years in Mexico doing research on Eisenstein who had worked in that country. When I first met her in London, she had a grant to write on Indian cinema and Satyajit Ray. She arrived in India at about the same time as I returned home. Independently of each other, we met in the Prime Minister's residence. It did not take Marie Seton much time to win Indira's confidence and affection.

Marie Seton was also given to boasting about her sexual conquests. She claimed to have had an intimate relationship with Krishna Menon. She 'confided' to me that Krishna had fallen for her long before he became India's first High Commissioner in London. He was then only a left-wing agitator running the India League. I have little doubt that she must later have claimed that she got me the assignment to paint Menon's portrait. I was not far wrong in my estimation of the woman. As for her claim to have been close to Menon, I vividly recall one of his portrait sittings when she kept hovering around us. When she went out of the room, Krishna burst out, 'Get this woman off my back!'

Such outbursts were typical of Krishna's reactions towards people who pestered him. 'This woman,' he told Inder and me later, was in the habit of 'fantasizing' about him. He assured us that he had only a nodding acquaintance with her during his tenure as India's High Commissioner. He had been instrumental in getting her the grant, as he had done for dozens of others. It was only after Marie had forged links with Indira and moved into Teen Murti House that Krishna thought it prudent to keep her in good humour.

That same evening Marie Seton burst into our quarters at Constitution House. She was in tears. She poured out her story to Kiran. She accused Krishna of treating her with shameful cruelty. He had been so tender and considerate when they had first fallen in love with each other, but now he brushed her off like a piece of dirt, she sobbed.

At the best of times, it was not easy to fathom what went on in Krishna's mind, but I was more inclined to accept his version rather than Marie Seton's hysterical description of the alleged relationship.

Ghalib, whose portrait I painted next, was not among the poets whose works my father had given me to read when I was bedridden as a youth. As I said earlier, it was not an oversight on my father's part. He did not want to expose me to poets who wrote so explicitly about love and physical desire.

I had to wait till I joined the Mayo School at thirteen to read Ghalib and other Urdu romantic poets. My father was fond of Hali, whose *Musaddas* he loved to recite both in the original Urdu as well as its Punjabi translation. His choice of poetry for me was ideological, revolutionary and patriotic. He was more liberal and sophisticated in his choice of prose for me: I could read anything I liked, provided it did not include love and sex.

If in Ghalib I found sophisticated turns of phrase and seductive images rich in colour and form, through Muhammad Iqbal I discovered the fountain of youth which lay dormant within me. It was not so much the content of what Iqbal had to say but the way he said it. There was music and power in his choice of words, which calmed and excited the reader simultaneously. My admiration for Iqbal did not decrease inspite of my father's strong disapproval of his politics, which my father considered downright communal. His convictions were reinforced when Iqbal openly advocated for a separate Muslim homeland, an idea that later was realized in the violent birth of Pakistan.

A person whom I came to know personally, and admired as a writer, was Dr Zakir Husain, later to be elected the first Muslim President of India. He had commissioned me to illustrate his charming collection of stories for children, *Abu Khan ki Bakri.* During this assignment I met Zakir Sahib several times. He was touched by my passion for Ghalib's poetry and in 1956 commissioned me to do a portrait of the poet for Aligarh Muslim University.

At about this time Faiz Ahmad Faiz went back to New Delhi after being released from a Pakistani jail. He brought the manuscript of poems he had composed during his years of imprisonment. He had appropriately entitled the collection *Zindan Nama* (The Prison Journal). He asked me to design its cover.

My acquaintance with Faiz went back to the time when he joined the Hailey College of Commerce in Lahore as a junior professor. He had befriended Inder who was studying in the same college. His first book, *Naqsh-e-Faryadi*, had just been published. It was an instant success, especially with young Urdu-speaking Punjabis. Faiz lived in an annexe in the college grounds, which included the students' hostel. Every other evening student admirers would gather in his home to listen to him reciting his poems. He did not have a very good voice nor did he seem very comfortable reading his work, but the spell he cast would linger on after every session.

Faiz was a slightly built man who was handsome in his own way. His wry smile conveyed aloofness, yet bewitched people. He went out of his way to befriend me. I found his poetry refreshingly different from anything I had read. Reading Faiz, my inner self unfolded.

I had not seen as much of Faiz as I would have liked. I saw something of him when he shifted from New Delhi to Lahore, to take up the editorship of the *Pakistan Times.* I lost contact with him after

Partition, till we met again when he visited Delhi in an attempt to have his poems published.

Time had not only aged us but changed our attitudes and perspectives. The years of imprisonment and the subsequent political evolution of Pakistan had hardened Faiz's belief in Marxism. He expressed it through his poetry. It was intoxicating and powerful. Though it bristled with ideology, it somehow remained as lyrical as the best Urdu romantic poetry. He never sacrificed his exquisite exploration of the symbolic mode to intellectual analysis or propagandist rhetoric.

When I told him what I thought of his poetry, he felt a little uneasy at first but was by no means offended. He admired my style of painting (I was still engrossed in depicting the trauma of Partition) and was impressed that the change in my aesthetic perceptions and political commitments had not affected my art. He told me that if he had been a painter and not a poet, he would have painted the way I did. When he saw the cover I designed for his *Zindan Nama*, he affirmed his statement. Our friendship lasted till the end of his life.

My obsession with space and rough surfaces lasted for about five years. Another commission for a mural for the Oberoi Hotel in New Delhi set me on a new course. And again architectural considerations induced me to look for a different medium. This was in 1963. Ever since my collaboration with Diego Rivera on his mural for the Teatro de los Insurgentes, which he later cladded with pieces of glass mosaic, I had been thinking that there were more effective ways of making murals than by simply using oil paint. I had toyed with the idea of using unconventional materials while working on a mural for Chandigarh University but did not have enough time to experiment with them. Besides, the building I was to work on was the Gandhi Bhavan, scheduled to be inaugurated on Gandhi Jayanti, only a short time away. So there were political considerations I had to bear in mind. Also, I spent more time than I had envisaged in conceiving the mural in its totality and breaking away from the style I had followed in my Partition paintings. However, when it came to the Oberoi Hotel, I was determined to find a new medium as well as a new style suited to that medium.

Rivera's use of tiles did not seem to me to be appropriate. The fact that the paint was clothed in glass was by itself a negation of the logic which demands a symbiosis of medium and content. Any kind of covering is at best an ornamental addition, without the material's organic character.

I called on Sardar Gurcharan Singh, one of India's leading potters and ceramicists, who had his workshop near Safdarjung Hospital. I had occasionally worked with him to make my own decorative pieces.

Gurcharan Singh was a kindly old Sikh as generous with his advice as he was with the use of his premises. But he was unwilling to let me use his place for experimentation because his own work would come to a standstill. I was still deciding what to so when I received a commission to do a mural for the Indian pavilion at the World Trade Fair in New York. As the mural was to be made in New York, I had to look for a ceramic workshop in that area. I soon found one with the help of the American Crafts Council. It was in Portchester, an hour-long train ride from Grand Central Station.

In the preceding months, I had been trying to develop a style of ceramic sculpture. The workshop in Portchester became a launching pad in this quest. In the two months that I worked there, I came to grasp the basics of this exciting technique that was to be my fundamental medium for the next decade.

The basic requirement was a kiln that could be fired by electricity or gas. Neither was available in India. India was also very short of foreign exchange. There was little possibility of my getting a permit to import it.

Fortunately for me, Indira Gandhi, who was a member of the committee organizing the Indian pavilion, happened to be in New

York. I approached her for help to get an import licence for a kiln. When I told her I had the necessary dollars from selling the paintings I had brought with me, she agreed to help me. I bought the kiln in New York and shipped it to India. I planned to install it in my garage on Tilak Marg.

The kiln arrived within a few weeks. Now I was up against the municipal authorities. They refused to give me another electric connection because of the high voltage necessary to operate the kiln in a residential area. It seemed as if I would never be able to do my Oberoi mural in ceramics. By coincidence, at the same time war broke out with China and the Oberois had to postpone inaugurating their new hotel. Meanwhile Dr Zakir Husain had become Vice-President of India. He used his influence to get me a shed in the newly built industrial complex in Okhla, close to Friends Colony.

I installed my kiln in this shed in 1963 and began my ceramic experiments. Kiran also used it to make pots. But it was not in constant use, as murals did not come my way too frequently. In the twenty years we had this kiln, I made only five murals with materials produced from it. These included the Oberoi hotels in Delhi and Bombay, Shastri Bhavan in New Delhi, the Delhi High Court, a small mural for the Chandigarh Museum, and one each for the Northern Railway headquarters and the IBM office on Bahadur Shah Zafar Marg in New Delhi. The mural at the Oberoi hotel in New Delhi and the one in the IBM office no longer exist. They were dismantled in the course of the two buildings being renovated.

During this time, I found I had developed specific and unique images. From early stylistic experiments, I was able to evolve a technique for making paper collages. I continued doing so for the next ten years.

While I was in New York making my ceramic mural for the Indian pavilion, I also had an exhibition of my paintings. It was visited by the author Ved Mehta, who was blind.

I had met him briefly earlier but could hardly claim to have known him. However, I had read almost everything he had written and had become a devoted admirer. He had recently published *Fly in the Fly Bottle,* a collection of interviews with philosophers and thinkers. Like his earlier publications, this book was also acclaimed by the critics. I had good reason to be drawn towards Ved Mehta. We came from similar social backgrounds and our families had known each other. Above all, like me he was handicapped—he without sight, I without hearing—and that brought us close to each other.

Ved was among the very few who had converted a defect into an advantage—even made it a source of strength. He had been able to substitute sight with vision, the perceptual and cognitive gift that enables one to see the invisible. There was an elusive touch of genius in him. However, I found it rather baffling that he went out of his way to describe scenes and people not as seen by his inner eye, but portrayed them as people with normal vision would do.

I wanted to tell Ved about a prison in ancient Spain which was dug into the earth in the shape of a well. It was so deep that neither sunlight nor sound could penetrate to the bottom. Thus, it eliminated all sense of time and space in the minds of those condemned to live in it. Only one of the hundreds lowered into it had escaped and lived to tell his tale. Ved and I were two men who had emerged from a similar, completely dark, soundless vault. Each of us had gift, and along with this came the responsibility of describing our experiences to the world, and narrating how our aesthetic consciousness had been shaped by our handicaps, instead of moping about our afflictions or wasting time talking about the life already familiar to millions of 'normal' people.

Which is worse, to be blind or to be deaf? Ved thought the inability to hear was a worse fate than the inability to see. I thought it was the other way round. Perhaps our perceptions were based on our personal experiences: he had overcome blindness, I had prevailed over deafness.

I asked Kiran what she thought. By then we had lived together for nearly a decade and were fully acquainted with the phenomenon of mutually adjusting to my demands and limitations. She looked at the mural I had just finished, put her hand over my eyes and said, 'Could you have seen my face the way it is if you had no vision?' People tell me Kiran has a lovely voice and can sing very well. She missed my not being able to hear her singing, but consoled herself by saying it would have been much worse if I had not been able to see her face.

As I mulled over the question of whether it was better to be able to see than hear, I recalled memories of songs of K.L. Sehgal and K.G. Dey, of the full—throated rendering of *Heer* by local bards in the late evenings when people of our mohalla gathered in the chowk under streetlights. And of the roar of the stream at Pahalgam that initially disturbed our sleep but soon became a lullaby. A visible object can provoke the memory of real sound or the fantasy of imagined sound, but can sound alone evoke or duplicate the sense of a solid, existent, natural, visible world? The more I thought about it, the more I was convinced that I would not exchange the faculty of sight for hearing.

To me, the absence of sound is not as frightening as the idea of blindness. I continue to experience darkness without knowing what it means to be blind and whether it is as deeply wounding as being deaf. What I do know is that it is easier to slight one with impaired hearing than one with impaired vision. People tend to mock the deaf with an assumption that what is not heard cannot hurt; this is a grievous error. A deaf person can immediately sense an insult though a highly developed empathy, which in many cases can prove to be a curse. Any kind of sensitivity be it aesthetic, emotional, physical or psychological, often leaves a person vulnerable to deliberate as well as casual abuse.

By the time I took to ceramics our first two children, Mohit and Alpana, had been born and the third, Raseel, was on her way. Indira

Gandhi had taken over as Prime Minister and had included Inder in her cabinet as a minister of state.

Octavio Paz had once again returned to India—this time as the ambassador of Mexico. The fact I most remember about Octavio's second term was his marriage to the wife of a senior French diplomat. I contributed rather unwittingly to this event. It was in my house on Tilak Marg that Octavio first met this lady. They continued to meet in my house without inviting suspicion. The courtship was brief and ended in the poor Frenchman having to leave India minus his wife. Octavio wasted no time in marrying her. Years later I ran into the French diplomat somewhere in Scandinavia. He had not forgiven me for allowing my house to be used for an adulterous liaison that had affected him so profoundly. However he expressed his disapproval of my behaviour in admirably restrained, oblique language.

Octavio's contribution to Indian art during his second tenure was his promoting the stray group of painters who gathered round Jagdish Swaminathan. The group swore to make mincemeat of all established artists. My name headed the list of those chosen to be put through the grinder. My friendship with Octavio suffered a setback but soon returned to normal after his marriage.

Kiran and I were finding it difficult to make ends meet. The ceramics workshop was proving to be somewhat of a white elephant, devouring money that we could not afford to part with. Ironically, most people thought it was a money-minting machine; it was in fact a money-gobbler.

We had started our married lives in a two-room apartment with a front veranda at the Constitution House. It has originally been built as an army mess for American soldiers posted in Delhi during the Second World War. It had long outlived its prime and had decayed into a shabby barrack with peeling walls and leaking roofs.

The only point in its favour was its central location. It was, as I have said, situated on Curzon Road next to Hyderabad House and within walking distance of Connaught Circus, the heart of New Delhi. When we returned from our honeymoon and took possession of it, we found that the sparse furniture in the flat was antiquated and chipped. It had suffered from misuse by a succession of occupants. With a few alterations that we could make ourselves, we made the place habitable. Our masterstroke was to pull out two small durries my mother had given us to use as underlay. We put them on the floor of our sitting space as carpets. They added a comforting touch of colour to our drab surroundings. They caught the eye of John Bissel. He was then working as a consultant with the handicrafts board, as was Shyam Ahuja. Bissel spread the word to interior decorators in the United States. Shyam cashed in by mass-producing these colourful durries and became India's 'Durrie King'.

The simple innovations that we made while decorating our flat created the impression that I had lots of money to throw around and was one of the richest artists in India. The truth was that for years in Constitution House we lived a hand-to-mouth existence, with Inder occasionally putting some money in our depleted bank account. Although myths were circulated about my seeming prosperity, similar things were not said about an artist like M.F. Husain who was getting paid a lot more for his work than any of his contemporaries. Perhaps the simple reason for this was that Husain roamed about barefoot and lived in a miserable *barsati* which contained nothing remarkable except his paintings.

The first time Husain dropped in to see how I was doing and how we lived, his attention was attracted by the small desert cooler I had installed. I had got this in a barter deal with its manufacturer, Jeewan Lal Gauba. I had to give him one of my paintings in return.

Husain was interested in buying the cooler because he was contemplating marrying a Czech woman he had met on a visit to Europe. Uncertain about how she would endure Delhi's infernal summers, he thought he would try and make the environment for her as pleasant as he could.

The idea of taking another wife was born during his tour of Czechoslovakia. Being a guest artist, he was provided an escort to show him around and act as his interpreter. The young girl assigned to him matured from girlhood to womanhood during Husain's short stay in her country. Though a married man with a brood of children, Husain proposed marriage to her. His proposal was immediately accepted. Being a Muslim, he was entitled to take up to four wives at a time. The girl was a Christian and Christianity frowned upon bigamous marriages. So the marriage ceremony could not be held either in church or in a civil court. Husain worked out a plan to overcome the hurdle. He would return to India, divorce his Muslim wife, return to Prague armed with a *talaqnama*, and would solemnize his union with the Czech woman in a court.

Unfortunately for Husain, things did not turn out the way he had planned. Having completed the divorce formalities in India, he returned to Prague. His lady-love refused to respond to his telephone calls. She had applied for a passport, but the Czech police suspected her motives for wanting to go abroad and refused to give her clearance. She thought it safer to keep her distance from Husain while she was trying to get around the police. Husain was disgusted. He tore up the *talaqnama* and returned to his wife, swearing that the affair had been a *tamasha*, a charade. Meanwhile I was left with the air-cooler I had bought for him.

The description of his Czech misadventure narrated by Husain to his biographer (a lady admirer) is somewhat different. According to this version, it was only the Czech girl's interest in the *Upanishads* and his thirst for exploring the Western mind that made them seek out each other's company. Alas, neither the Czechs nor the Indians understood that it was motives as lofty as these that lay behind their relationship.

Husain was not the only artist to be misunderstood in his own country. The case of Francis Newton Souza was even more bizarre. He was my classmate at the JJ school of Arts, Bombay. He had joined the school two years before me, but his examiners grossly underrated its talents and failed him two years running. So he found himself in the same class in 1944 when I joined as a freshman. While I was promoted to thc sccond and thc third year, Souza stayed on where he had started. He could well have been there today but for an unfortunately incident that cut short his student days. As I've said earlier, he slapped a professor named Bhonsle and was expelled. Souza's version of the episode does not tally with the facts known to me. According to him, slapping professor Bhonsle was an act of rebellion against colonial rule, like the 1946 naval mutiny. He construed his expulsion from the school as the death rattle of the remaining citadel of the British empire: the JJ school of Arts, founded by a dealer in opium. I was impressed by Souza's fervid imagination. He claimed that he was a fully mature artist while he was still inside his mother, and that he had painted his earliest murals on the insides of his mother's womb. I had to concede seniority to him. While I was picking up techniques in Mexico, Souza had already created murals thirty years earlier while still waiting to be born!

Long before Salvador Dali had established the effectiveness of gimmickry in the making of an artist, Shantiniketan's habitués had discovered that physical appearance went a long way in making an artist acceptable to the public. The expatriate writer Nirad Chaudhuri described the exercise as a 'carnival of fancy dresses and equally fancy ceremonials'. But the heights to which Husain took these theatricals made his predecessors in the craft appear childish. With Husain, gimmickry became an art form by itself—people found his antics much more entertaining than his actual work.

Souza outdid Husain in outrageous comments but he could not create an image to match that of the bearded, barefoot imitation *darvesh*. For several years it was debated whether Husain's stunts were self-generated or whether he had somebody to advise him. At first most people thought that Rudi von Leyden had meticulously planned them. He had organized a show in the late fifties in Bombay during which Bhimsen Joshi sang and Husain appeared on the stage to draw response that complemented Joshi's classical melodies. Those who knew Husain from his earlier days discounted this theory. They maintained that he had always demonstrated an instinctive flair for such narcissism.

He was noted for outlandish combinations of upper and lower garments; his choice of footwear ranged from military-style boots and leather skins to finally wearing no shoes at all.

I had not heard of Husain when I left for Mexico in the early fifties. It was during my stopover in Bombay on my return home that Mulk Raj Anand spoke of him as an artist who had achieved prominence during my absence. Since he was not in Bombay at the time, I was not able to meet him or see his work.

When I reached New Delhi, I went to the newly opened National Gallery of Modern Art to see Husain's *Zameen*, which had won the first prize the previous year. Then one day Husain walked into my studio-cum-bedroom in Inder's house on Hanuman Road.

Few people were able to communicate with me with as much ease as Husain. He had the advantage of being able to write Urdu on the palm of his hand with his index finger. Urdu lends to a kind of shorthand much better than English. We became friends.

We decided to organize a 'Six Artists' collective exhibition in New Delhi in the autumn of 1956. It was perhaps the first such exhibition since the 'Progressive Group' had organized one in 1949. It included, besides Husain and me, Krishen Khanna, K.S. Kulkarni, Mohan Samant and Ram Kumar.

Husain and I belonged to a small group of artists. Besides the two of us, there were Krishna Kulkarni, Kanwal Krishna, Dhan Raj Bhagat and

Ram Kumar. I do not know how Ram Kumar reacted to Husain; they had known each other for many years before Husain started visiting New Delhi. As far as the others were concerned, their observations about Husain were surprisingly similar. He impressed us with his modesty, which bordered on naivete. He was also a man of few words. Only a very perceptive mind could detect that behind the facade of unassuming reticence was an extremely calculating mind. If he felt it would serve his purpose, he would as happily go to a cocktail party as he would to a funeral. Neither his presence nor his absence from a function was accidental. He meticulously measured every step before taking it.

It took me a long time to understand this part of Husain's character, much longer than it took everyone else in the group. Kanwal Krishna and Kulkarni got his measure very quickly. They were wiser men than I and kept up appearances of friendship with Husain long after I had lost respect for him and ended our relationship. The responsibility for this break was entirely mine.

To start with, I found it easier to get on which Husain than Bhagat, Kulkarni or Kanwal Krishna. Husain had winning ways and charmed everyone he met. Even my wife, Kiran, who did not like going out with us because of Husain's outlandish clothes and appearance, was taken with him. We discovered in due course of time that he was very sensitive to criticism of his art. If any one of our circles commented on his work in even the friendliest manner, he would keep his distance from us for many days. When questioned, he would firmly deny he had been upset by anything we had said. I accepted Husain's explanations, but Kulkarni and Kanwal Krishna insisted that Husain could absorb any amount of praise but got acute indigestion with the mildest and smallest dose of criticism. Kanwal Krishna went out of his way to lambast him.

I recall a singularly acerbic exchange between the two at a show of Kanwal's paintings organized by Ebrahim Alkazi sometime in the 1980s. Kanwal was by then well past his prime, therefore Husain's question was intended to be hurtful. 'What happened to the Kanwal

Krishna of the forties?' he asked. Kanwal promptly retorted, 'He became Maqsood Fida Husain.' That was not enough. Kanwal continued, 'I spent the last twenty years wailing and beating my breast like they do at Muharram: *Ya Husain, Ya Maqsool.*' Kanwal turned to me to translate what he had said by writing on the palm of his hand with his index finger.

My break with Husain came sometime around 1965. I had become very critical of his work, largely because he had started to pander to popular taste to enhance his market value. As usual he gave me no indication that he resented what I said. But his disappearances became longer and longer. After a prolonged absence he showed up and invited us over for tea and kababs in his studio behind Jama Masjid. Bhubesh Sanyal, Kalkurni and Kanwal Krishna were also present. At this get-together Husain showed us his latest work. It took all of us by surprise. These paintings done on plywood appeared to be abstract play with gestural brush work. It was only after careful scrutiny that one discovered the trick. He had subdued his usual vibrant images with textures that gave the paintings a sublime air. The result was bewitching. It filled me with delight as much as with envy. He had managed to break out.

Later that night in my flat on Tilak Lane, I telephoned Husain and asked him to come over. When he did, I repeated with greater emphasis how much I had liked his new work. He sounded more self-assured and happier than he had been in the past. We parted with more warmth in our embraces than had been evident in the preceding months.

A week later, Kiran and I left for an extended tour abroad. We were away for more than six months. On our return we happened to visit the Kumar Gallery which was exhibiting, among others, Husain's paintings.

I had no difficulty in spotting his canvases because they were the kind of illustrative work he had been doing in the past. By sheer chance

I looked at one closely and noticed the date next to his signature. These were his latest.

Kumar confirmed that Husain had at first brought the paintings on plywood which I had seen in his studio. Despite the gallery owner's best efforts, he could not sell any of the works, because potential buyers could not identify these with Husain's style. Husain took them back and replaced these with works in his old style. They were sold out immediately, as was apparent from the red bindis on the side of each painting.

Our meeting following the visit to the Kumar Gallery turned out to be our last. I was rash enough to chastise him for succumbing to commercialization. He never forgave me for telling him the bitter truth.

Husain always had an eye on the art market and was willing to sell his talent for the highest bidder. I admired his commercial acumen but felt that the extent to which he compromised his gift and conceded to popular demand was unacceptable. It has to be admitted that there was no such thing as an art market till Husain created it. His mass-produced pictures of stallions were instant successes with the horse-racing fraternity, the richest and most elite section of Indian society. No one could deny that some of the hundreds of pictures he did of wild mustangs rearing or in full gallop had enormous animation, but quantity in which he churned them out not only made his motives suspect, they blocked his evolution as a genuine artist.

I had once recited to him an Urdu couplet that illustrated his plight.

Qafas main rehtey hee rehtey
Qafas say ho gayee ulfat
Main khud hee noch leta hoon
Jo mere par nikle hain

(My prolonged confinement in the cage
Made me fall in love with it
When I sprout new feathers
I pluck them out with my own claws)

Husain continued on the path of self-destruction. After having milked the theme of wild horses as much as he could, he turned to Hindu gods and goddess. Contemporary artists had long discarded the impulse to depict religious themes: these were left to calendar artists who continued to follow the approach initiated by Ravi Varma.

It is to Husain's credit that he found out why Indian society had become indifferent to art. He exploited his discovery to the fullest. It they wanted gods and goddesses, he would give them the entire Hindu pantheon—for a price. Husain embarked on his Hindu pilgrimage in the early sixties when he was asked to paint episodes from the *Ramayana* and the *Mahabharata* on the walls of a restaurant run by a hotelier in Hyderabad. I do not know whether Husain had read these epics prior to accepting the commission, but I do know that for psychological support he hired a pundit to recite the *Ramayana* to him every morning while he painted. He said this was to set the right mood in which he could create. He was well rewarded for his pains. The restaurant became the focal point for Hyderabad's art patrons, whose devotion to the Holy Scripture was as intense as their appetite for spicy food.

Husain knew he had struck gold. Like his horses, his Ganapatis poured out in profusion, and for a time seemed likely to overtake the elephant population of the subcontinent.

It took Husain a long time to realize that riding Durga's tiger had its hazards: he could not risk getting off the tiger's back for fear of being mauled.

Organized religions are like mafias. Once you join any even for the sake of appearance, you cannot escape from their clutches without putting your existence in peril. Husain soon realized that while he could get away with painting four-legged torsos with neither tails nor heads and describe these as horse, he could not take the same liberties depicting gods or goddesses. Each time he did so, he put his hand into the seething hive of Hindu fundamentalism. Hindu fanatics went for his jugular: for them, any talk of artistic freedom was nothing but a lot of irrelevant and iconoclastic garbage mouthed by long-haired deviants. It only proved the truth of the adage that one who lives by the sword must perish by the sword. Exploiting religious sentiments may initially pay dividends, but like revolutions, institutionalized religions are capable of devouring even their most fervent devotees.

The storm that engulfed the Indian art scene with Husain's depiction of the goddess Saraswati in the late 1990s proved that an artist must not flirt irresponsibly with religious sentiments. Although it cannot be denied that Hindu fanatics of the Bajrang Dal found Husain an easy target because he was Muslim, it has also to be conceded that it was precisely because Husain was Muslim that secular intellectuals rose as one to condemn the vandals who destroyed Husain's paintings in an art gallery in Ahmedabad. The secular and liberal community took our processions in all the major cities to defend Husain's right to paint what he liked. Had he taken the same kind of liberties with Islamic emblems and been similarly assaulted by Muslim fanatics, I doubt if many people would have bothered to raise their voices or lift a finger in his defence.

Ever since that night at my house on Tilak Marg in the mid-sixties, Husain and I have restricted our relations to exchanging pleasantries whenever we run into each other. Yet I never spare him whenever he indulges in histrionics to keep in the public eye. Once in a television interview Pritish Nandy asked me what I thought of Husain. I replied candidly, 'A remarkable talent entrapped in lust for publicity and money.'

I paid the price for my candour. Many self-styled secular intellectuals condemned me as a Hindu communalist and even threatened to ostracize me from their circles. I was indifferent to their vitriol. I abhor all institutionalized faiths, including the one into which I happened to have been born. Being branded a religious bigot did not disturb my sleep.

In 1968 I received an invitation to attend the World Crafts Meet at Lima in Peru. I decided to visit other countries en route, since I had a flexible ticket. My ceramics experiments had sharpened my desire to explore the potential of craft techniques in mural-making and sculpture. So on my way to South America I visited the Scandinavian countries, as well as Spain, Brazil, Argentina, and Mexico for the third time before going on to Peru. In Mexico I called at Siqueiros' home. He was in jail for trying to foment a revolution in his country the way Castro had in Cuba. Ironically, in spite of his being in prison, his birthdays continued to be officially celebrated on a national level. This was the last time I met him.

I returned home with a rich trove of foreign techniques. But ironically, it was in the back lanes of the locality I lived in that I discovered a mode which inspired the next phase of my work. The technique which attracted me was the one used by local craftsmen to make the kind of bells hung round the necks of buffaloes roaming about the roads and alleys. The metal used in making these became the base material for my art. I used it to make sculpture with tantric motifs which preoccupied me during these years. Finally I came to the use of burnt wood, which I started to exploit in the late seventies.

I began to encounter financial problems. With ceramics a part of the expenses could debited to Kiran; this could not be done with metal. I still needed the use of a kiln to melt and mould the metal into shapes I wanted, as well as assistance to chisel wood to be used as the base for this sculpture. At that time, few people were interested in mixed-media sculpture; I had to wait another ten years for my work to gain acceptance. And ten years is a long time to have to wait. The rapidity with which I changed techniques, materials and styles created piquant situations for me. My paper colleges found no buyers in India. I took them to the US where I sold my work and also received a fair amount of acclaim. In India, the only public acknowledgement and evidence of my success was a booklet an enterprising publisher brought out in 1968, based on ten collages and ten drawings.

The demand for paper collages was growing by the time I switched over from this medium to metal work. I had hardly any collages left to sell. The same thing happened when I made another switch. No sooner did I give up one technique for another than there was a demand for the one I had given up. As I look back, I wonder how I managed to preserve my faith in myself and in the eye of the beholder while continuing with my quest for new techniques and styles. I came to the conclusion that the urge to create is universal and overwhelming, but just as each catalysis requires specific chemicals to generate a particular reaction, individual creativity is also triggered by specific psychological and emotional forces.

I have never found any direct connection between my deafness and creativity. At best it probably brought out a hidden talent which might otherwise have remained dormant. The cathartic activities of painting and sculpture compensated for the absence of sound. Total silence could have reduced my life to eternal stagnation and ennui. I overcame the stillness around me by ceaseless activity, by constantly switching from one medium to another. Good or bad, individually styled or pastiche, original art or imitation—none of these were of the slightest concern to me. I used creativity as an instrument, as Rilke says, 'to live in haste, in pursuit, to possess all of life, right away, right here'.

My sense of isolation altered dramatically from the day Kiran came into my life. It reminded me of the story of Babar and his son Humayun. When Humayun was on the verge of death, Babar went round his son's bed chanting, *'Ya Allah!* Give me the sickness Thou hast inflicted on my son. Let him be restored to health and take my life instead.' The miracle occurred. Humayun regained his health; Babar died a few days later. Similarly, Kiran had taken the load of my isolation on her shoulders. She relieved me of my alienation, gave me a sense of being a part of society and stimulated me to produce my best. In my volatile creative life that was full of exhilarating heights and dizzying chasms of profound despair, Kiran's faith in me kept me going.

In the 1970s I went through a recurrence of those phases of depression—as a result of my feeling that I had reached a plateau in the style and the medium I had been working with. Taking into account the general apathy towards the plastic arts, I saw no future in further exploring that path.

I decided to try my hand at designing buildings. Even my close friends and admirers thought that I was making a serious and idiotic error. They tried to convince me that architecture was not a medium that permitted emotional expression, especially in the modern age when the demands of contemporary lifestyles had reduced the complex discipline of architecture to utilitarian structures—ugly, unwieldy and functionally problematic.

For others, the fact that I had never been to a school of architecture, had no degree or diploma, nor had worked in an architect's office, was itself proof of my having stupidly surrendered my aesthetic sense.

Of course I was not totally unfamiliar with the alphabet of planning. This had been a part of the curriculum of the Mayo School in Lahore. However, the credit for my jumping into this venture must be given to my Mexican pilgrimage, which had helped eliminate for me any doubts regarding the validity of changing the medium one worked in.

This was the logic behind my evolution as an artist. First it was my fascination with murals. In order to make them, I experimented with different materials. I found that simple paint was not good enough; I needed material that had volume and texture. I tried wood and ceramics, metal and stone. These took me automatically in the direction of sculpture. Having reached this point, I found that the buildings I was asked to paint murals on were essentially not suitable for them. Each time I was working on one it crossed my mind that I would have done a better job designing the building itself. I never dreamt of getting a chance to do so. Deviating, or rather transferring my skills, to the medium of architecture seemed a remote possibility, as I had spent all my artistic life immersed in the plastic arts.

The Embassy of Belgium in New Delhi was not the first building I was commissioned to design. It was the ensuing controversy which gave people the impression that it was my maiden attempt as an architect.

My experiments with architecture began when I started painting murals. In the early stages I could do no more than make alterations or additions to existing buildings. The first real assignment that came my way was to design a country house for the industrialist B.K. Modi, whom I had never met before. He asked me to design his residence that would adjoin the factory, Modi Rubber, which I was also subsequently commissioned to do.

The Modi site being outside Meerut, I was considerably less obstructed by regulatory laws and municipal limits. Bhupinder Modi, then a young man in his early thirties, was responsive to new ideas. This was why he had opted for an artist rather than an architect to design his house. While I was conceptualizing this project, I realized how easily and naturally the medium or architecture came to me.

My conviction was reinforced by my reading architectural history and the notable contribution of artists to its evolution as a discipline, especially in its earlier phases when no distinction existed between the artist and the architect. There was the example for Peter Behrens, an Austrian muralist who laid the foundations of modern architecture. Men like Le Corbusier, Walter Gropius, Nutra and Mies van der Rohe, who later dominated modern architecture, had served apprenticeships with Behrens. My association with Ted Bower in Shimla and later with Juan O'Gorman, the artist-architect of the University Library in Mexico, encouraged me to accept the challenge.

It is to the credit of Bhupinder Modi, who has since became a business tycoon, that he allowed me to work on his two-acre plot as if it were a canvas, and to let me freely exercise my imagination. I eagerly went ahead in the attempt to translate my concept of space, developed during the time I was working on rough textures and trying to visualize humans as an indivisible part of the space they lived in. Unlike painting on canvas, which offers only two-dimensional possibilities, I had the opportunity to freely manipulate fluid space in all directions.

Fortunately, Modi House was located at some distance from Delhi and escaped the notice of the capital's architects. They were not able to raise the furore they did later when I undertook to design the Belgian embassy in the heart of Delhi's diplomatic enclave, Chanakyapuri.

As I probed deeper into the problems of architectures, I grew more and more aware of the contradictions, ambiguities and paradoxes that seemed to be battling at the heart of modernism. This was further complicated by the problems of actually executing an architectural plan, and the question of the validity of experimental building in the Indian context.

Modernism had not arrived in India with Corbusier; he only gave it later respectability. There were others in pre-Independent India who had introduced modern concepts in the design of public and private buildings. Two of the best known were A.P. Kanvinde and Habib Rahman. Kanvinde and Rahman were products of Boston's Massachusetts Institute of Technology. Their style was dominated by the influence of Gropius, Nutra and van der Rohe. These early modernists were later overtaken by Corbusier and his colleagues who designed Chandigarh.

It was ironic that Corbusier's ascent in India peaked at a time when his influence in the West was on the decline. There the sixties generation, though not disrespectful of Corbusier, rejected his sustained practice of ignoring local traditions and regional and ethnic compulsions in the process of designing buildings.

Though Corbusier had his coterie of Indian admirers who continued to swear by him, their vocabulary underwent a complete change. They sang the praises of traditional architecture, Nehru's vision of an industrialized India, as well as Corbusier's utilitarian style, all in the same breath. In practical terms, it was the work of American-Jewish architect Moshe Safdie, who did the path-breaking Habitat 67 at the 1967 Montreal Expo, which became the ideal for these architects. Safdie's pyramidal buildings which inspired Indian architects were in fact conceived in the sixties as role models of heavy prefabrication. Though acclaimed as a triumph of technology, the heavy cost of Habitat '67 forestalled its acceptance in the West.

What was more ironic was the fact that in its method of construction Habitat' 67 subscribed to the concept of 'metabolism' which had originated in Japan in the early sixties, under the auspices of the Japanese chamber of commerce. This aimed at producing entire building units by methods of Industrial production, and exporting them for assemblage at their destined sites. Like all industrial production, the emphasis was on minimizing human input. Never before had there been an architectural concept that was so completely opposed to the concept of buildings as an extension of nature. It also opposed the idea of architecture being the embodiment of the cultural aspirations of a given community.

Moshe Safdie's notions worked into the Indian consciousness became overloaded with a lot of tantric motifs. His simple geometrical lines were rendered into *rasas* and *bindus* and *mandalas* and provided intellectual poseurs excuses to propound all kind of bizarre theories to justify this kind of architectural presence.

At about this time in 1974, I met the Shahbanu, the wife of the Shah-en-Shah of Iran. The meeting turned out to have far greater repercussions than I had anticipated. The Shahbanu's purpose in inviting me to Iran was to recruit me as a member of a panel she had instituted to bring back paintings of Iran's Kajar period, that were scattered in many countries around the globe, including India. Once I reached Iran she involved me in much else besides the recovery of Kajar paintings. My duties included cataloguing the architectural treasures of her kingdom and identifying buildings which could be categorized as classic examples of indigenous architecture.

The exposure to Iranian art and architecture rapidly stimulated concepts that had become dormant within me. More than anything else, the historical links between our two countries and their cultures fired my imagination to a degree I had not experienced before. Thereafter I visited Iran several times. And every visit excited and inspired me even further. Of all the Iranian cities I visited, Isfahan most captivated me.

I was lost in this Iranian haze when Ajit Haksar, Chairman of the Indian Tobacco Company (ITC), asked me to design a hotel on the island Jag Mandir in Udaipur's Pichola Lake. The invitation was made on the condition that the final approval was to come from the Maharana of Udaipur who owned the island. The Maharana had also offered the site to other hotel chains such as the Oberoi and the Taj groups, and had retained the right to veto designs he did not like.

Though ITC won the contract, the building I designed never rose above its plinth level. The Taj Group and the state bureaucracy effectively sabotaged the project. Nevertheless the exercise was worthwhile and I did not regret the experience. It taught me how the spirit of a location profoundly effects construction. It also taught me how to assimilate traditional aesthetic principles without blindly imitating or rejecting them.

The experience I gained in Udaipur proved profitable later. My Belgian friend Ronald Burny had been impressed by the scale model I had made of the Udaipur hotel and the Daryani House in New Delhi which I had renovated. He told me of the proposal to build the Belgian embassy in Chanakyapuri. He offered to have me included in the shortlist of Indian architects whose plans would be submitted to a committee for selection.

My initial response was not enthusiastic. No Western country had considered hiring an Indian architect to design its embassy. I submitted my plan more to please Burny than in any hope of getting the assignment. A few days later Burny rang me up from Brussels to say that my designs had been accepted as the best. I was elated, but a little stunned. Then I became increasingly anxious when I learnt what was expected of me. Besides the architectural responsibilities, I was to supervise the construction work as well: the project was to be handled on a turnkey basis.

I was daunted by the magnitude of the task. Kiran shared my misgivings. A couple of days after Burny's call, she rang him back and asked him to try and have the supervision of construction separated from the designing responsibilities. Burny told her that the jury's decision, which he had presumed was final, was actually being questioned. As was the practice, the jury had been provided only with the designs sent in by competing architects whose identities had been kept anonymous. This was to ensure an unbiased verdict.

As soon as the name and nationality of the designer of the winning entry was revealed, there was an uproar in the circles that mattered. Although Burny tried to reassure Kiran, his tone betrayed his doubts. He advised us not to raise the question of splitting responsibility as that would further prejudice my chances of getting the assignment. After this dialogue I became determined to take up the challenge. So did Kiran. We discussed the matter with Inder, who had long experience in the building industry. He reassured me that there were ways to divert and delegate this responsibility after I had officially accepted the commission.

Burny's next call came a fortnight later. The agonizing wait had worn my nerves to shreds. Our luck had prevailed. Later I learnt that it was not good fortune alone that had won us the deal, but that Burny had played the leading role in turning the tables in my favour.

It took the Belgian bureaucracy only a fortnight to shed its apprehensions about me. But Indian architects remained up in arms. They continued waging a losing battle against me till the building was completed, and even after that.

Prior to my forays into architecture, I had more friends among architects than I had in the artists' fraternity. After the Belgian embassy was assigned to me they began to cold-shoulder me. They had not resented my designing private houses, but regarded my getting the embassy assignment as an unqualified and unwanted encroachment into their domain. I had no academic qualifications nor a licence to practise as an architect. Though often beset with fears that their opposition to me might prevail, I carried on with dogged resolved till the time the Indian Institiute of Architecture recognized my contribution and admitted me in its fold.

While the construction of the Belgian embassy was going on, I designed another house for my friend B.K. Modi on Amrita Shergil Marg. During the construction of this house, about three months after the commencement of the building of the embassy, a makeshift bridge caved in under my feet during an inspection, sending me hurtling into a deep pit full of pointed steel bars. To avoid being impaled I jumped across to the other side and landed on my left foot—the same foot supporting the femur which had so tormented and ravaged my childhood. The brittle bone snapped like a piece of glass. Instantly I recalled Dr Ganesh Dass's warning: 'If broken, it will be impossible to put it together.' After a few surgical operations I was incarcerated in bed with a plaster cast from my hip to my ankle.

I had started work at the Belgian embassy with only two assistants at home and a supervising engineer named Kartar Singh at the site. This man was more interested in the poetry of Ghalib than in the construction work. Though I shared this passion with Kartar Singh, his aversion to prose, which led him to interpret every problem at the site in verse, made it increasingly difficult to discipline him or to get on with the project. The situation became worse as my injury showed no signs of healing. Finally Kiran had a palanquin made, and I was carried shoulder-high to the site every morning, and stayed there till sunset. It could have worked in my favour, but the succession of surgeries I had to undergo so that the fracture could heal continued to interrupt the effort. Every three or four months I was back on the operating table and unable to get to the site even on my palanquin.

I was in dire straits. Then my son Mohit came to our rescue.

Mohit had opted to study architecture. He had joined the architectural school at Ahmedabad three years before I started work on the Belgian embassy. He could not be of much help when I met my accident. But by the time the building was nearing completion and I was confined to bed, he decided to drop out of college and take charge of my work. He had only one year left to take his final exam. In six months at the site, he learnt more about architecture and building than he would have in ten years at the school. But for Mohit, I do not know how I would have been able to silence my critics. The international acclaim that the Belgian embassy received was largely due to the help my son gave me in the final stages of the building's construction.

I have no way of describing the inner contentment that the success of this project brought to me, but I can say with confidence that it greatly enhanced my emotional well-being and contributed immensely to putting me back on my feet once again. My preoccupation with the building kept me from brooding over my physical afflictions and the swarm of problems that threatened to devour me.

Four surgeries had failed to make my leg bones come together. At about the time the embassy project was almost finished, the doctors advised amputation of the whole leg up to the hip, as they feared a resurrection of my old malady if they left my leg in this condition any longer. The idea of being an amputee terrified me. A date for the amputation was fixed, a few days after the embassy building was completed. A fortnight before I was to be admitted for surgery, an examination revealed a glorious and entirely unexpected phenomenon: the bones had begun to fuse. Doctors still consider it the rarest of rare cases, significant enough to be recorded in medical journals.

I have little doubt that it was the completion of the assignment that prompted the miracle. I was cured of a disease which the doctors had pronounced incurable.

At the inaugural ceremony Mohit and I stood side by side, on our own feet. In my case though, full recovery was to take a few more months. But Mohit's feet were now firmly planted on the ground as an architect in his own right.

As time passed, controversy over the Belgian embassy faded into the background. What remained significant was its role in my evolution as an artist and an architect. Above all, it was crucial in the shaping of Mohit, both as an architect and as a loyal son.

Having Mohit by my side encouraged me to devote more time to painting and sculpture. I made another change in my medium. I turned from burnt wood to granite, confident that I could handle it as skilfully.

I would never have dared to switch to granite if Mohit had not eased the burden of architectural projects I had undertaken. His support also enabled me to resume painting on canvas with quite a fresh approach.

The success of the Belgian embassy project brought me a host of dream assignments. One was to design a large farmhouse in Saudi Arabia for the family of the late King Faisal. Another was to design the residence of the Prime Minister of Bahrain. I also designed the Ram Goolam Memorial and the Indian Culture Centre in Mauritius; the Indian Embassy in Kathmandu; the New University in Goa; the Research Centre for CMC in Hyderabad; and the Ambedkar Memorial in Lucknow. It is to Mohit's credit that he reduced my role in conceptualizing these projects to the minimum. We learnt to work as a team in absolute harmony. There was no dominance, no jealousy, no possessive dividing line to rigidly demarcate where the father's contribution ended and the son's began. This was amazing, because we are as different as any father and son can be.

Mohit's abilities cannot be ascribed to his having inherited my temperament. He took his good looks from his mother and his nature from my brother Inder whom he has idolized since his childhood. His other traits developed as a result of the atmosphere in our home and in the schools he was sent to.

He was first enrolled in English-medium boarding schools. He would have been thoroughly anglicized but for the thoroughly Indian atmosphere at home. He married Feroz, a charming and beautiful girl of Muslim and Christian parents, who won accolades as a fashion model as well as a designer of art objects. Though the couple were very westernized, they quickly adapted themselves to our more traditional way of living and thinking.

Like all fathers, I too had dreams for my children. I wished them to achieve what had remained beyond my reach. Above everything else, I wanted them to inherit and cultivate the gift I valued most—the gift of creativity. According to me, and uncreative life is a life gone to waste.

It was fortunate that though Mohit was completely different from me, he shared my commitment to creativity. He also had as big an ego as mine. I do not regard this as a shortcoming but as an asset. I believe that individual ego is the driving force behind all significant creativity.

It was Mohit's ego which later urged him to get out of my shadow and carve out his own professional niche. He resented being continually identified as my son. This hurt me initially, though later I was proud that he had struck out on his own. As a matter of fact, the older I get the more I become reconciled to seeing my contribution to the world in what I have created in painting, sculpture, architecture and writing, rather than through my children and their achievements.

Unlike Mohit, my daughters Alpana and Raseel inherited all my characteristics to the fullest degree. It was perhaps due to this that they also had more than their share of misfortune. Both married men of their choice. Both their marriages failed, despite the fact that the husbands they had chosen were absolute gentlemen. The one thing both men lacked was an interest in art, to which both girls were committed. Though neither Raseel nor Alpana had chosen a creative curriculum in school and college, the seed of creativity that they had suppressed or neglected, flowered within them later, when they found their marriage devoid of purpose or meaning. When they filed for divorce, both Kiran and I were very upset. Then we realized their compulsions and offered our unconditional support. We were proud of their resilience and determination to work towards independent goals. Raseel achieved renown as an interior designer and Alpana as a furniture designer. Like their father, neither has had formal training in their respective disciplines, yet they have, through hard work and the sustained effort of their strong imaginations, won acclaim and wide professional respect.

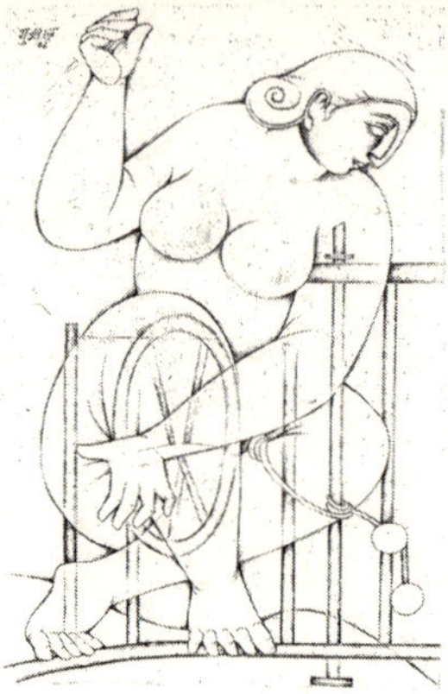

10

FRIEND AND BROTHER

THE TWO OUTSTANDING FIGURES IN INDIAN POLITICS I CAN LAY CLAIM to the pride are my brother Inder, India's current Prime Minister and Krishan Kant, India's former Vice-President.

My relations with Krishan Kant go back to the deep friendship between our fathers. Chacha Achint Ram, like my father had fallen under the spell of Lala Lajpat Rai during his college days. Having become an ardent admirer of Lalaji. Chacha Achint Ram had enrolled himself as a full-time active member of the Servants of the People Society—a position that demanded total devotion, and left no time for any other vocation or means of livelihood. Members of the society were provided an honorarium of Rs 100 a month and two rooms in a house called Lajpat Rai Bhavan that Lalaji had bequeathed to the society.

My own acquaintance with Krishan Kant started in the late thirties, when the society stationed Chacha Achint Ram at Jhelum and he moved there with his family. We were both about twelve years old.

Even at that age I was impressed by the simple and frugal way of living that Chacha Achint Ram had chosen for himself and his family. The house they rented was located just across the road from ours. It was a small building without even the luxury of a hand pump to draw water. Like many of our neighbours, Chacha Achint Ram made use of the tap in our house and carried buckets of water from our house to his own. He was often assisted by Krishan and other members of his family.

Chachi Satyawati, Krishnan's mother, spent hours washing her family's clothes at our tap—a chore that strengthened the bond between our mothers. My mother was four years older and had a commanding presence; Chachi Satyawati choose to address my mother as 'Bhuaji' (father's sister), a term of address that was commonly used by each member of the Achint Ram family, regardless of the generation they belonged to. My mother became Bhuaji to both Krishan and his parents. Chachi Satyawati courted arrest along with my mother, and Chacha Achint Ram and my father were imprisoned together.

Fortunately, the time my father chose for admitting me to the Mayo school at Lahore coincided with Chacha Achint Ram's shifting back to Lahore with his family. I openly criticize the authoritarian methods of Sanjay Gandhi and his hoodlums. Krishan was the one legislator who spoke up fearlessly in a parliament which in those days was mostly silent.

Mrs Gandhi's return to power in 1980 seemed to make men like Inder and Krishan rather irrelevant in the unpredictable game of Indian politics. When V.P. Singh was elected Prime Minister in 1989, he appointed Inder as his foreign minister. Inder in turn arranged for Krishan to be appointed the governor of Andhra Pradesh. Krishan carried out his duties with distinction during his tenure.

Krishan's parents had continued to live simply. The day he entered Raj Bhavan in Hyderabad was the first day that Chachi Satyawati did not have to perform domestic chores. One of the first trips that

Chachi and her son, the governor, made out of the Raj Bhavan was to the hospital where my daughter-in-law Feroz had delivered her first child, Arman.

Krishan Kant remained in the Raj Bhavan at Hyderabad while the Prime Ministership of India kept changing—V.P. Singh, Chandrashekhar, Rajiv Gandhi, Narasimha Rao, Deve Gowda and finally Inder. A month after Inder took office he asked me if I could think of any person better suited than Krishan Kant for the position of Vice-Presidentship. I did not answer, as I found myself struggling to think of a man of integrity and experience who would be acceptable to other political parties. My silence must have indicated to Inder that I completely agreed with him.

Krishan Kant, the man who carried buckets of water from our house to his family's house across the road, is unlikely to forget the toil and sweat of millions of people who have not been as fortunate as him. Especially since Chachi Satyawati still graces us with her presence, and is today as loving and compassionate as she was when she came to wash clothes with my mother at our tap, many decades ago.

Apart from Krishan Kant, the other luminary of Indian politics I would like to mention with pride and love is my brother Inder, who became Prime Minister of India in 1997. His journey to the Prime Ministership could be said to have begun when he became close to Indira Gandhi after the death of her father Jawaharlal Nehru. This was partly due to the fact that when other ambitious politicians began to desert her and switch their loyalties to Prime Minister Lal Bahadur Shastri, Inder stood by her. She sensed he was a man she could trust. When her father's body was being bathed prior to its cremation, she asked Inder to stand guard and prevent intruders from entering the room.

She knew that Inder's father and Lal Bahadur Shastri had been close friends, admirers of Lala Lajpat Rai and active members of his Servants of the People Society. Inder had not transferred his affiliation to Shastri's camp. He chose to stay with Indira, though the surest way of being blacklisted by Shastri's supporters was to be seen in the company of Indira Gandhi.

Shastriji had of course included Indira Gandhi in his cabinet as minister of information and broadcasting. But this, according to a local wit, was reminiscent of an American president who had explained why he had inducted an opponent of his government into his council: 'I would rather like the bastard to be inside the tent and piss out, than to stay out and piss in.' Indira Gandhi was well aware of this. She felt claustrophobic under the tension of working for a Prime Minister who wanted to keep his eye constantly on her lest she became too popular. At one time she seriously contemplated resigning and taking to art. On one of her visits to our house she consulted me about the aspects of painting as a vocation. The fact that she did not quit the cabinet was due to the persuasion of three friends in whom she confided: Dinesh Singh, Inder and Romesh Thapar. How long she could have remained part of the Shastri regime is difficult to gauge. Then came the news of Shastri's sudden death at Tashkent in the early hours of 11 January 1966.

Immediately after the shocking news was broadcast, Indira Gandhi rang up Inder, Romesh Thapar and Dinesh Singh and invited them over for breakfast next morning. Before the three went to her home, they spoke to each other on the phone and agreed that they should persuade her to contest the succession. By then it was common knowledge that several other contenders were working overtime to canvass support for themselves.

Indira Gandhi told her confidantes that Gulzari Lal Nanda, who had acted as caretaker Prime Minister after the death of her father, had already approached her for support in his bid for succession. She had avoided committing herself and changed the course of the conversation to harmless subjects. She tried the same tactics now with her three friends. She began by seeking their advice on domestic problems, such as her kitchen expenses. She launched into a long tirade against the ever-increasing prices of consumer items. The focus of her lengthy harangue was the wife of K.D. Malaviya who had been petroleum minister in Nehru's cabinet. Mrs Malaviya had a poultry farm from where Indira Gandhi got her supply of eggs. She was furious about Mrs Malaviya's exorbitant rates. Mrs Gandhi's three guests were flabbergasted. The future of the nation was at stake, and their hostess was wasting time talking about eggs! Surely the Prime Ministership of the world's largest democracy with one-fourth of the world's population was more important than the prices of poultry items! By the time Mrs Gandhi had finished venting her rage, it was almost 11 a.m. Then she quickly came to the subject uppermost in the minds of her visitors. She agreed to having her name put up for the next Prime Minister of India. She discussed her chances of winning and whether she could measure up to the incredibly complex, demanding and difficult job.

She asked Inder to draft a statement of condolence on Shastriji's death. In the same statement there was a clear indication that she considered herself a candidate for the Prime Minister's post.

Indira Gandhi's main adversary was the self-righteous Morarji Desai. He fought her to the last. But he had created too many enemies for himself. Indira had no enemies and was regarded as a pliable tool by the kingmakers of the day. In the final count she trounced Morarji Desai by a convincing margin.

I noticed the change that came over her following her victory. It could be seen in her face and in the way she walked. After her father's death she had a haunted look and nervous, distracted eyes. She moved unsteadily and often faltered in her gait. But after the election, almost overnight her face became radiant and she began to walk with a firm step. She regained her self-confidence at an astonishing pace. Inder accompanied her to the swearing-in ceremony. Before going to the Rashtrapati Bhavan she went to Teen Murti House where she had lived with her father during the years he was Prime Minister. She stood in front of her father's photograph and put a garland around its frame. Then she broke down. It was obvious that she realized she owed her elevation to the top post in the country to the reverence in which her father was held by her countrymen, rather than to any personal qualifications, charisma or achievements.

The night before the swearing-in she asked Inder, Dinesh and Uma Shankar Dikshit, an old family friend, to help her draw up a list of potential cabinet ministers. She had to accommodate most of Shastri's appointees. Regional and religious considerations had to be taken into account. Confabulations went on till midnight. Members of the conclave were asked to return early in the morning to accompany Indira Gandhi to Rashtrapati Bhavan.

Next morning, as expected, Inder arrived at Indira Gandhi's residence. He was in for a rude shock. An aide handed him the typed list of the proposed cabinet. It had all the names that Inder had helped to screen the previous night, with one single exception: Inder Kumar Gujral. His eyes went up and down the list looking for his name. It had been there the night before, it was not there in the morning. While Inder was still scanning the list in utter disbelief, Mrs Gandhi emerged in the hallway. She was dressed in her best and was all smiles.

Dinesh Singh and Dikshit were with her. She noticed Inder going over the list. For a fleeting moment they looked into each other's eyes—a moment that was to remain frozen in Inder's memory for years to come.

There was a chilling ruthlessness in her gaze. Such callous contempt for friends who had stood by her and had provided constant support through thick and thin was something he could not understand. She did not bother to explain. Inder realized that such disregard for others is manifested by people who suddenly breathe the intoxicating draughts of absolute power; they feel they owe no explanations to anyone.

Neither Dinesh nor Dikshit could provide a clue as to what had compelled her to eliminate Inder's name from the list.

Inder's acquaintance with Uma Shankar Dikshit and Dinesh Singh had begun after he got to know Mrs Gandhi. While Dikshit was an elderly, nondescript individual content to serve the Nehru family as a loyal retainer, Dinesh was an ambitious young man with aristocratic pretensions. He was a consummate *darbardar* (courtier). He was six years younger than Inder. His association with the Nehru family went back to the time his father had been Motilal's client and often consulted Jawaharlal Nehru as well. The family owned the zamindari of Kala Kankar in Uttar Pradesh and had adopted the style of minor rajas. Pandit Nehru had taken Dinesh into the ministry of external affairs. He served as private secretary to Krishna Menon in London and H.S. Malik in Paris. Panditji then inducted him into politics. He was elected to the Lok Sabha and made deputy minister of external affairs during the last months of Nehru's rule. He was quick to establish a personal rapport with Indira Gandhi. He pretended to be a socialist just as Indira Gandhi did. But she also felt more at ease with the social elite, the affluent and the land-owning circles. (In this she was quite the opposite of her father, who made no secret of his contempt for the rich.) Being dapper and aristocratic, Dinesh scored over both Dikshit and Inder.

No one else had seen Mrs Gandhi between the time the three men had parted and the next morning when they reassembled at her residence to go to Rashtrapati Bhavan. Inder had no reason to suspect that either Dikshit or Dinesh or anyone else had influenced Mrs Gandhi to drop his name from her list of ministers. He thought the decision was entirely hers. A few days later when she announced his name for inclusion in her cabinet, she admitted that dropping him from her first list was an exercise in statecraft. She acknowledged that she had every intention of including him and a few others in the cabinet but had decided to do it piecemeal to avoid criticism from veteran legislators who had helped her to come to power. She did not want them to feel that they had been overlooked to accommodate novices like Dinesh and Inder simply because they were her friends.

It took many years for Inder to understand the way Mrs Gandhi's mind worked. As her hands gripped the reins of power in an ever-tightening vice, she began to consult her favourites and ignore the old guard and other senior members of her government. This small coterie in which Dinesh and Inder were included came to be known as her 'kitchen cabinet'. Ironically, it was his closeness to Dinesh that later made Inder's loyalty suspect in Mrs Gandhi's eyes. Mrs Gandhi had her own reasons to start distrusting Dinesh and anyone who was friendly with him. Ultimately, she not only dropped Dinesh from her cabinet but also severed social relations with him. Dinesh was responsible for his own downfall. He had boasted foolishly that Mrs Gandhi could not function without him. She did not tolerate such arrogance from anybody, even her close confidantes. So out he went. Romesh Thapar met the same fate for the same reason.

Mrs Gandhi may have had good reason to cut her ministers and friends down to size if she felt they were overstepping the limits she had set for them. But she went beyond that. In public she belittled people she had herself befriended. She was forever suspecting her old allies of conspiring against her. After she had successfully humiliated Dinesh, she regarded everyone who went to meet him as her enemy.

Since Inder continued seeing Dinesh after the latter had incurred her displeasure, she convinced herself that Inder was part of Dinesh's conspiracy to topple her. She gave Inder a clear indication of her growing suspicions when she reshuffled her cabinet. She threw Dinesh out and took the important portfolio of information and broadcasting away from Inder, giving him the less glamorous housing ministry instead. This was followed by her insistence that Inder should ensure that Dinesh was evicted from the ministerial bungalow allotted to him. Inder's delay in complying with her wishes only confirmed her suspicions about his loyalty. Ever prone to lending her ears to gossip-mongers, she accepted whatever her yoga teacher, Dhirendra Brahmachari, told her. Though this man had been around since the twilight years of Nehru's regime, he had begun to make his presence felt only with the decline of the influence of Inder and Dinesh Singh. He found an ally in Mrs Gandhi's younger son Sanjay who had started interfering in politics.

The Brahmachari was a tall, handsome, bearded man who, like Rasputin, knew how to obtain the confidence of influential people. He went out of his way to befriend Sanjay because he knew Sanjay was Indira Gandhi's favourite son. Teaching yoga was his means of getting close to people who mattered, and amassing wealth and property worth crores of rupees. Later on he became involved in many ventures, including a film studio and the production of guns. He had his own private aircraft, imported cars and a herd of Jersey cows.

Before Inder assumed charge of the housing ministry, Mrs Gandhi had allotted the Brahmachari a government bungalow near Gurdwara Bangla Sahib, for running his yoga training institute. He wanted this bungalow facing the Gole Dak Khana to be transferred to his yoga institute for perpetuity. He had made all the arrangements with Inder's predecessor and only needed the minister's signature to finalize the deal. He did not visualize any difficulty in getting Inder to comply. He was well aware that Inder was no more as hot a favourite in the 'royal household' as he had been, and assumed that Inder would want to stage a comeback through doing the Brahmachari this favour.

But the yoga teacher was in for a nasty surprise. Inder, who knew why the Brahmachari had sought an appointment with him, sent for the relevant file. He was amazed at its contents. Here was a proposal to sell government property in a strictly residential area earmarked for government servants, to a private organization. And this while thousands of government servants were awaiting their turn to get accommodation.

The Brahmachari was in no mood to listen to Inder's objections. When Inder refused to budge from his position, the other man threatened him with dire consequences. It was not an auspicious start for Inder in the new ministry. He was aware that Mrs Gandhi had given him this portfolio because it reeked of corruption and had been a graveyard for the reputations of a string of previous ministers. Her game plan for Inder was the same as it had been for Dinesh Singh, whom she had shifted from external affairs to foreign trade—a ministry which had earned an unsavoury reputation under his predecessor, Lalit Narain Misra.

Inder was determined to prove to Mrs Gandhi that housing allotments could be made without resorting to corruption, and that urban decay could be significantly arrested. He worked out his priorities. The first thing he did was to form a committee under the chairmanship of Romesh Thapar to oversee compliance with the master plan of Lutyens' Delhi, and establish an urban arts commission to see that nothing unsightly was built in and around the city. He won worldwide acclaim for his efforts.

Mrs Gandhi and Inder were invited to be the key speakers at a global meet sponsored by the UN in Stockholm in 1972, on the subject of urban planning and design. While they were together in Stockholm Mrs Gandhi grudgingly admitted that Inder had done good work in the housing ministry. Since Dinesh was out of the way, her confidence in Inder was somewhat restored and she brought him back to head the ministry of information and broadcasting after her return to India.

Her image was taking a severe thrashing and she desperately wanted the official media to make up for what the privately owned newspapers were saying about her. The political tension in East Pakistan was also increasing and India's position needed to be explained to the world. Mrs Gandhi was not magnanimous or self-critical enough to admit she had made mistakes in judging people. The best she could do to make amends to Inder was to say to him, 'You are a problem for me:

wherever I put you, finding your replacement gives me a headache.' Even this compliment was paid without her looking him in the eye.

During his second term as head of the ministry of information and broadcasting, Inder finally discovered the real reason why he was dropped from the list of Mrs Gandhi's cabinet on the morning she was sworn in as Prime Minister.

Inder and Dinesh happened to be together in Ahmedabad during an election campaign. Everyone who was anyone in the Congress Party descended upon the city. All the hotels and rest houses were fully booked. Being a minister, Inder had a room allotted to him. Dinesh had nowhere to stay. Inder invited him to share his accommodation.

They talked late into the night, reminiscing about the past. Inevitably the conversation came to the first swearing-in ceremony. Dinesh confessed that it was he who had struck Inder's name from the list, fearing him as a rival for Indira Gandhi's favours. He had had to convince Mrs Gandhi that Inder's inclusion would invite dangerous criticism from old-timers whose support had been instrumental in her victory over Morarji Desai; none of these veterans were favourably inclined towards the younger candidates, including Dinesh. Since Dinesh had been a deputy minister in Nehru's government, he had justified his own inclusion and had Inder excluded. He broke down and cried while making this confession. Thereafter, the two remained close friends even after they were on the opposite sides of the political fence.

More turns and twists in Inder's relationship with Indira Gandhi were still in the offing. After the 1975 verdict of the Allahabad high court nullifying her election to parliament, she turned to Inder for solace and advice. She was willing to resign if she lost her appeal in the Supreme Court. The charges against her were flimsy, her popularity at its zenith; no matter what the Supreme Court decided, she was sure to return to power with an even greater mandate in the next elections.

The agitation against Indira Gandhi's government was spearheaded by Jayaprakash Narayan. There was no doubt that corruption in high places was touching its zenith. But Jayaprakash exhorting people to *gherao* legislative assemblies and the parliament, and urging the army and the police to revolt, was a dangerous sign. The 'total revolution' that he was preaching threatened to demolish the very foundations of the country's democratic institutions. Inder did his best to convince Mrs Gandhi that the anarchy which Jayaprakash had let loose would ultimately turn the scales in her favour.

She did not listen to sane advice or balanced logic. In the confusion and uncertainty about her political future she became a pawn in Sanjay Gandhi's hands. His failed Maruti car project had come in for a lot of parliamentary criticism and had been equally lambasted by the press. He knew that if his mother relinquished power for even a few days, he would be in dire trouble. He forced her into declaring a state of Emergency. The immediate outcome of the declaration was the near-banishment of all those who had had the temerity of advising her to resign from her darbar.

In the early hours of the morning of 26 June 1975, Mrs Gandhi sent for Inder to accompany her to a cabinet meeting. She informed her ministers that she had declared a state of national emergency and had ordered the arrests of all Opposition leaders the previous night.

As a supplementary she told Inder that she had imposed strict censorship on the media. This only added to Inder's bewilderment, as no ordinance to this effect had been issued. That fateful day had much more in store for him. As he left the cabinet room he was confronted by Sanjay Gandhi. The young man ordered Inder to forward all news bulletins to him for clearance, prior to their being broadcast. Inder politely replied that these bulletins were classified material till they were cleared for broadcasting, and hence not meant to be shown to any unauthorized person. Sanjay Gandhi immediately understood that Inder did not intend to acknowledge his authority. Before Sanjay could explode into one of his notorious rages, Indira Gandhi appeared, and fortunately intervened. After agreeing that Inder was correct, she ordered him to send all bulletins to the Prime Minister's residence before they went on the air. It was evident that she had abdicated authority and had consciously decided not to counter her son's arrogance.

When he returned home, Inder looked distraught and asked me if he should resign.

I had no information about these developments as no newspapers had been delivered that morning. (Later we learnt that on Sanjay Gandhi's orders, power supply to the printing presses of most newspapers on Bahadur Shah Zafar Marg had been cut.) Like most of my friends I had no sympathy with Jayaprakash's call for a 'total revolution'. As such, my reaction to the Emergency was not as hostile as Inder's. I advised him to wait and observe the situation before taking a decision. He was not wholly convinced by my argument but accepted my reasoning that the government had to take drastic measures to stem the lawlessness created by the insurgency Jayaprakash had successfully fomented.

Early the next morning Mrs Gandhi telephoned Inder. She was disturbed because a broadcast had not given full details of her speech in defence of the imposition of Emergency. She wanted to hear the complete recording of this broadcast. Procuring the recording took some time, and by the time Inder reached her residence, Mrs Gandhi had left for her office. Sanjay Gandhi confronted Inder. He was in an ugly mood and almost shouted at him for deliberately allowing the 'fragmentation' of Mrs Gandhi's speech. It so happened that the version of the speech that had been reported to Mrs Gandhi was broadcast not by All India Radio but by Radio Pakistan. But Sanjay's tone left no room for doubt that it was the Prime Minister's son and not the Prime Minister who was calling the shots.

Not one to be easily provoked, Inder calmly told Sanjay to control his abusive tongue. You are younger than my son. You ought to learn how to speak to your elders. And of course I am under no obligation to answer to you.' He turned his back on Sanjay, got into his car and drove away without handing over the AIR recording.

This time when Inder returned home he seemed quite determined to resign. Before he could go any further Mrs Gandhi again sent for him. Contrary to what we expected, it was not to apologize for Sanjay's behaviour. We were not even sure whether she had been told of the altercation that had taken place between Inder and her son.

Inder had never seen her more courteous and charming. It was the first time that she thanked him for all he had done for her and her government. She said she was fully aware of his reservations about the Emergency, and the censorship imposed on the press, and felt that it might be best if he were to be moved to a ministry which had nothing to do with the media. She almost pleaded with him to accept her proposition. She had never before spoken to Inder in this abject manner. It was difficult to gauge whether her humble tone was due to a growing fear of the devastating repercussions of Emergency rule, or a sense of guilt for arbitrarily removing a man who had stood by her.

She succeeded in touching Inder's heart. He compassionately agreed to abide by her decision. His giving in so tamely disturbed his conscience for many years to come. I had noticed that Inder's regard for Indira Gandhi was always tinged with emotion, which sometimes overwhelmed his normally clear and forthright logic. Indira Gandhi was aware of Inder's regard for her, and shrewdly assessed exactly how she could successfully appeal to him—both when she did something that hurt him, and when she went out of her way to favour him. She showered him with affection when she moved him to the planning ministry. She repeated this a few months later when she sent for him and told him that she was appointing him ambassador to Moscow. She pleaded with him to accept the position, saying that with the death of D.P. Dhar she could not think of anyone better suited than

Inder to represent her in the Soviet Union. She admitted that no one, including Inder, would regard the transfer as a promotion.

The Emergency ended. The election which followed proved disastrous for both Indira and Sanjay Gandhi. The failure of Morarji Desai and Charan Singh to successfully sustain the government brought Indira back to power. These turbulent fluctuations in her fortunes did not change Inder's affection and regard for her. Both of us admired her as an audacious woman of grace and sophistication who had played a significant role in the development of the country as well as in both our lives. It saddened us to see how the unscrupulous sycophants who came to surround her shamelessly exploited her position to their own advantage. Chief among these was an old family retainer, a former bureaucrat. The secret of his rise to eminence was his enthusiastic support for Sanjay Gandhi's dictatorial methods. This man evolved and sustained the practice of savagely harassing intellectuals and academics, whom he accused of conspiracy and treachery. He also harassed Mrs Gandhi's Kashmiri relations, whose influence in the Nehru-Gandhi household he envied. They in return never made a secret of their loathing for him.

This retainer had exploited the Emergency context to settle personal scores with reckless abandon, a pattern typical of totalitarian regimes. He was clever enough to pick on only a few who had been out of Mrs Gandhi's favour and thus create the impression that he was fighting her battles rather than his own.

One of his victims was Romesh Thapar, who had made no secret of calling him an 'executioner of the emergency'. Thapar preferred to close down his much-respected journal *Seminar* rather than submit to censorship.

The erstwhile retainer had always been suspicious of Inder. It was he who had given to Mrs Gandhi the garbled report of AIR having broadcast a 'fragmented' speech in defence of the imposition of

Emergency. Though Inder, as was typical of him, did not harbour a grudge against him, his name was never erased from the 'executioner's' list of potential victims.

A little before the end of the Emergency, Inder Malhotra, then resident editor of the *Times of India*, was bullied into writing a laudatory profile of this man. The night after the article was published, those present at a dinner at the house of senior journalist Prem Bhatia collectively castigated Malhotra for writing the piece. Poor Malhotra was having a hard time defending himself. By coincidence Inder and I happened to drop in and became embroiled in the argument.

The next morning the subject of Inder Malhotra's article met my brother. He was in a rage and told Inder that the Prime Minister had issued orders to arrest everyone who was present at the dinner party. He had, as we later learnt from Mrs Gandhi herself, reported to her that she had been the main target of criticism and that Inder Gujral had been the most vociferous in maligning her. Had it not been for Mrs Gandhi's timely guillotining of the retainer's sweeping powers, there is little doubt that he would have had all of us put behind bars. The night after Mrs Gandhi lost her election was a night to remember. Inder made it a point to be in New Delhi to watch the results as they came in. He had asked the information officer manning the teleprinter at the central newsroom to keep him informed minute by minute. The moment the news of Mrs Gandhi's losing her own seat come over the ticker, the officer on duty was so overcome with fear that he simply switched off the machine. When we finally heard the bitter truth I noticed a look of deep depression on Inder's face. He had prayed for this outcome, yet when it came he was unable to control his emotions.

The next morning we went to call on Mrs Gandhi. We found her curled up in an armchair, shrunken and crumpled and looking utterly desolate and defeated. As we sat down, she began to speak. 'I fear,' she said in almost a whisper, 'there will be a lot of witch-hunting.' A woman who had ruled a massive, chaotic nation with an iron hand for more than a decade, one who had withstood the bullying of global superpowers as easily as the pressures exerted upon her by her own partymen, seemed to have lost the will to fight. She looked pathetic and forlorn. The only gesture of consolation Inder could make was to hold her hand. He patted it once, twice. She kept staring into space. While leaving her house we saw Sanjay walking up and down the driveway. For a fleeting moment his eye met Inder's. Neither of them showed any inclination to talk to the other. In the car on our way back Inder told me of the letter Mrs Gandhi had written to him about a fortnight before declaring elections. I saw the letter afterwards; it was in her own handwriting. Each sentence betrayed the mood of despair that had overtaken her. She talked of the growing hostility to her regime, of her workers being beaten up, of one of her ministers having lost his mental equilibrium. What moved Inder was not so much the contents of the letter as the fact that she had thought of writing to him and no one else.

For the first time she addressed him as 'Dear Inder'. She ended her letter with the words, 'It is past midnight but I feel I must write to you.'

A day or two later Inder went to see Morarji Desai, the newly elected Prime Minister, and submitted his resignation.

While waiting in the ante room he ran into Atal Bihari Vajpayee, the newly appointed minister of external affairs. He expressed surprise when Inder told him why he was there. 'Morarji will not accept it,' he said.

Inder and Morarji had been adversaries from the day the news of Shastriji's death had reached New Delhi. The final contest between Mrs Gandhi and Morarji had been absolute and unforgiving, and Inder had emerged as a prominent and consistent supporter of Mrs Gandhi. No one had any doubts as to where his loyalties lay.

Though Mrs Gandhi had agreed to induct the implacable Desai as her deputy prime minister, her motives were the same as those of Shastri when he had included Indira Gandhi in his cabinet. The arrangement had not worked. Desai bore a bitter grudge against Indira Gandhi, and extended this ferocious hostility to Inder and Dinesh. That being so, Inder took Vajpayee's remark with a pinch of salt, but he was in for a surprise.

Vajpayee was right. As Inder handed Desai his letter of resignation, he said, 'No, you are going to stay. Your role in the Emergency is not unknown to me.'

Inder reminded him of the days preceding the Emergency. At no time had he been with Morarji, and he was not one to transfer loyalties. But Morarji finally succeeded in persuading Inder to join his government. That decision snapped my brother's links with Indira Gandhi. Thereafter they met only once—when she returned to power in 1980. Again Inder went to see her to submit his resignation. In contrast to Desai's dry manner, Indira radiated warmth and charm. It was only a facade. She accepted his resignation without demur. Like the Kennedys, the Nehrus and the Gandhis neither forgot nor forgave. Inder was a different kind of human being. His affection for Indira Gandhi remained constant, no matter how she felt about him. But he never again either wished or sought to re-establish the kind of close relationship that had once existed between them.

Not even after Sanjay Gandhi's tragic death did he make any attempt to get close to her. Inder was convinced that Sanjay had destroyed Mrs Gandhi's faith in her confidantes, and that he was largely responsible for his mother's downfall.

The Emergency swiftly became the favourite subject of scathing satire. Let me narrate a couple of jokes that did the rounds of artists' circles. They illustrate how the air had been fouled, and did not spare a community otherwise known for its loathing for the establishment. One such incident was related to me by an artist friend, the late Ghulam Rasool Santosh, the famed exponent of tantric motifs in contemporary Indian art. I liked and respected this man. On Republic

Day, 26 January 1976, when Emergency excesses had just reached their atrocious peak, I read in the morning paper that Santosh was among those awarded the Padma Shri. I asked Kiran to ring him up to congratulate him. Being unwell I was unable to talk to him directly. His phone was out of order. Just at the time we were trying to get Santosh on the line, Bishambar Khanna, another artist friend, came in and told us that he was on his way to Santosh's house to felicitate him. I requested him to convey my congratulations as well.

Bishambar was back within an hour. Santosh had not taken kindly to my message of good wishes. He knew how much I detested state honours. They had became symbols of sycophancy, like the titles conferred by the British on natives who were loyal to them. I had refused to accept honours from the government more than once.

When Bishambar conveyed my message, Santosh had given him a withering look. 'Well,' he blurted, 'tell Satish he should not brag too much about his refusal to accept this honour. After all, he has turned honours down in quite different circumstances. It is the Emergency, not the love of becoming a Padma Shri, that made me accept it. I was too scared of the consequences of my refusing.' It took me a long time to assuage Santosh's hurt feelings over my impulsive congratulations.

Then there was M.F. Husain. Immediately after the proclamation of the Emergency he had painted Mrs Gandhi as the goddess Durga astride a tiger. He glorified the Emergency as an act of political heroism. He was handsomely rewarded by commissions to paint murals for Congress Party sessions wherever they were held.

One such session took place in Chandigarh in 1976. It was to celebrate the 100th birth anniversary of the Indian National Congress. Husain portrayed it in his usual style, showing a horse in full gallop. He had even anointed different parts of the mustang's anatomy with twenty different colours symbolizing the *bees sootree* (Twenty Point) programme of the Emergency regime.

During the morning session Inder happened to be sitting next to Beant Singh, who later became Chief Minister of Punjab. Pointing to Husain's mural, Beant made no secret of his contempt: a multicoloured horse was a ridiculous image for the depiction of one hundred years of a party with a glorious past. Beant found this symbolism not only unacceptable but insulting.

The same evening Inder found himself again seated next to Beant Singh, He found Beant gazing at the mural with a thoughtful expression. Inder expected him to unleash some more earthy Punjabi invective. But the Sardar had completely changed his opinion. 'This mural,' he said to Inder, 'is a real work of art.'

You did not think so in the morning,' replied Inder. 'No,' admitted the Sardar in the same serious tone. 'I later learnt that this artist is a friend of the Prime Minister. Even Sanjayji has approved of this mural.

Once back from his diplomatic tenure in Moscow, Inder withdrew from active participation in politics. He devoted most of his time to travelling and studying international affairs. However, it was evident that he missed his favourite occupation—politics.

His 1989 appointment as minister of external affairs in Prime Minister V.P. Singh's government was uneventful. The family took his position in its stride. But his return to the same post in 1996 was very significant. This elevated him from being a minister in the Indian government to a world statesman. It brought him where he is today, the Prime Minister of India, at the age of seventy-seven.

Driving to Rashtrapati Bhavan for the swearing-in ceremony, we passed the secretariat building. I reminded Inder of the day, forty-five years ago, when we sat on the veranda of the North Block opposite what was later to be his office as Prime Minister. I was holding a canvas in each hand, waiting my turn to be interviewed for the scholarship to Mexico. Sitting there, Inder had kept on coaching me till I was summoned inside.

As the car approached the huge iron grille separating the Rashtrapati Bhavan complex from the secretariat blocks, we saw the place where we had sat after the interview, waiting for our stenographer friend to come and tell us of the outcome. The journey we had accomplished in the intervening decades had been arduous but miraculous. We looked at each other in silence. There was no need for words. We understood each other completely.

Kashf-o-kamal kun keh aziz-e-jahan shud
(Achieve excellence in your vocation
for that is the way to win the world)

This Persian saying that my father often used to repeat to us came to my mind. Never before had I felt its meaning as deeply as I did on that fateful and unforgettable day, 21 April 1997.

EPILOGUE

Mohit Gujral

EVERY CHILDHOOD IS SHAPED BY MEMORIES WE CARRY OF OUR PARENTS. Ours were shaped in a home full of art, energy and a sense of everyday extraordinariness. Though our father was deaf, the world my parents created never made us feel that anything was different. Disability wasn't part of the vocabulary of our lives. Conversations with him were fluid. He read our expressions, our gestures, our lips—and, often, our minds.

We knew, even as children, that he was famous. Our art teachers spoke of him with reverence. But to us, fame meant little. He was simply Papa—strong, creative, temperamental. My earliest memories are of his unpredictable moods, which often drew us towards our mother—the calm, intuitive centre of our home. She was the bridge between his intensity and our childhood.

But he was also playful—wildly so—and full of odd joys and eccentricities. He had a particular love for cars. I remember him once acquiring a vintage Adler sports car in exchange for a painting from his close friend, Patwant Singh. That car became our shared canvas—literally. He invited me to join him in painting it in vivid, wild colours. For a child, it was an unforgettable adventure: art, rebellion and machinery all at once.

Though he was deaf and technically didn't have a driver's licence, that never stopped him from driving—and driving fast. I often wonder how he managed, or how he got away with it. But that was him—fearless, instinctive, ahead, yet mindful of the rules. Never reckless enough to endanger lives, but always pushing the edge.

Because we spent much of our school years in boarding, our time at home was limited to vacations. Those middle years were filled with cousins, paternal family and festive gatherings—but we were somewhat distanced from our parents' daily lives. It was only in college that the dynamic truly evolved, when the relationship shifted from a traditional parent-child bond to an adult, interactive connection.

Our early years were spent in government accommodation allotted to my father at Tilak Marg. But my father felt the need to build a space that could fully express his vision—a house that was also a studio, a sculpture in itself. He believed art needed to be experienced in the context of space, and that clients and audiences should be invited into that world. He collaborated with a young Raj Rewal to design what would become our family home—a space he lived in from 1970 till the end of his life.

We also learned the art of being social from our parents. Beyond my mother's grace and charm and my father's sharp wit, they entertained a wide and varied circle—diplomats, bureaucrats, artists, writers, dancers, businessmen, politicians. No boundaries were drawn, no hierarchies enforced. Their friends appreciated this openness—a gathering of minds from different worlds, enjoying stimulating conversation without agenda. It was a home alive with ideas, humour and a shared passion for culture.

In the early years, my father's work found greater resonance abroad—particularly in Europe, America and Japan—where his art, bold and unflinching, was embraced precisely because it wasn't confined to decorative or drawing-room aesthetics. His visual language, rooted in struggle and raw form, spoke to a global post-war sensibility that valued authenticity over polish. This recognition led to frequent travel and exhibitions overseas, and as a result, large portions of our younger years were spent in the care of my uncle, Inder Gujral.

It was only later, as the Indian art world began to mature, that a more receptive audience emerged at home. Slowly, his stature within India caught up with his reputation abroad—and with it came a growing acknowledgement of the breadth and depth of his contribution to Indian modernism.

That evolution of our relationship deepened profoundly when I joined him in the world of architecture.

Though he had no formal training, his vision was fearless. He saw buildings not as structures, but as sculptural forms to be shaped by instinct and imagination. When I entered the picture in my twenties, it began as an apprenticeship. But over the next two decades, it became a true partnership. Together, we worked on the Belgian Embassy, Goa University, the Ambedkar Museum and many other projects in India and abroad.

He brought wild creativity; I brought precision, scale and pragmatism. He carved ideas in clay and wood; I translated them into drawings and building codes. Our collaboration was full of arguments and laughter—the kind of productive friction only deep trust makes possible. Architecture allowed us to build not just spaces, but a new bond. He treated me as an equal, a co-creator. It was one of the greatest privileges of my life.

His exposure to technology during that period fascinated him. He encountered new tools—digital modelling, rendering software—

which he later used in his artistic explorations. He saw technology not as a threat to the handmade, but as an extension of it—another ally in his endless pursuit of form and feeling.

He lived with a constant restlessness—a hunger to create and innovate that never left him. He had no weekends, no real holidays. For the last thirty years of his life, he worked with urgency—as if each year might be his last.

Architecture brought him recognition and satisfaction. Two of his projects were nominated for the Aga Khan Award. Though disappointed not to win, he took pride in being seen. The Indian Institute of Architects eventually bestowed a fellowship upon him—a formal recognition of what he had already proven through practice.

Recognition came from the state as well. He declined the Padma Shri in earlier years, believing it did not fully honour the scope of his work. But when the Padma Vibhushan was awarded, he received it with quiet pride.

One thing that stayed with me was something my father once said: 'Anything that can inspire you is worth having.'

I remember being in Europe in the early years of my architecture practice. I came across some very expensive books—well beyond my budget at that time. When I mentioned this to him, he said, 'Even if a book offers you just one idea that inspires you, it's worth it. The rest you'll still need your imagination for—how to translate that idea and make it your own.'

I bought the books on Carlo Scarpa, and I do believe they inspired us both. I think that staggered language of planes we later used in the Belgian Embassy was, in part, born from that moment of inspiration.'

Eventually, as all apprentices must, I stepped out on my own. He sensed that moment before I had to say it. 'I have other art forms to deal with,' he said. And just like that, he returned to his studio and gave me the gift of independence.

One of the most emotionally charged turning points in his life came when he decided to undergo cochlear implant surgery. He was childlike in his excitement—full of hope that he might once again hear the world he had lived in silence from for so long. He flew all the way to Australia to have the operation, despite doctors advising against it. He would be the oldest recipient they had operated on. They warned him gently: the brain must relearn how to hear, and in adults who have lived in silence, the experience of new sound could be overwhelming.

But he was determined. He had never allowed disability to define him, and he saw this as another frontier to conquer. The implant was done. And in time, sound returned—but not in the way he had imagined. It was fragmented, disorienting, almost alien. The world he had built in silence—his world of form and touch and shadow—began to feel violated. He could not bear the distortion.

In a remarkable act of self-possession, he chose to remove the implant. He returned to silence—not out of surrender, but because it was where he had found peace, purpose and mastery.

Yet that experience—painful as it was—did not go unexpressed. It ignited a new burst of creativity. In the years that followed, he created a striking series of paintings and sculptures celebrating sound and music. These works were filled with movement, rhythm and colour—visual compensations for what he had hoped to hear, and what he instead chose to imagine. In his hands, sound became image. Silence became song.

There were also two moments in his life when he came terrifyingly close to death. He later told us he had experienced something extraordinary—as though he had travelled through valleys bathed in surreal colours and radiant light, before life gently pulled him back. These were not dreams, he insisted, but journeys.

What followed was a remarkable period of creative output—a phase marked by new exuberance and intensified colour. It was as if he had returned with a vision of another realm and was now determined to paint its echoes.

Though he never belonged to an artistic clique, he was a regular presence at gallery openings. Many artists, especially younger ones, told me how much it meant when he came to see their work—his presence itself felt like encouragement.

In the latter part of his life, my father became increasingly family-oriented. His intensity softened. He was deeply proud of each of us. He adored his grandchildren and looked forward to laughing with them, sharing stories and quietly instilling his values.

Those who knew him closely often remarked on his sense of humour—sharp, disarming, always present. Perhaps it was also a shield, a way to keep sorrow at bay. I remember how moved he was while watching the television serial *Buniyaad*, tears welling up as memories of Partition returned. When he later visited his childhood home in Pakistan, the emotion overwhelmed him so deeply he suffered a heart attack and had to be flown back.

In his final years, long-term memory became a gentle companion. He often spoke of images from his childhood—objects, shadows and forms he had seen as a boy, now returning with unexpected clarity. Some of these resurfaced in his work, echoing the abstract forms of his earliest creative years. It was as if time had collapsed inward—and what remained was the distilled vision of a boy who had once looked at the world wide-eyed, now drawing it again with the wisdom of a life fully lived.

None of this journey would have been possible without my mother, Kiran—his voice, his protector and his constant anchor. She was more than a partner—she was his interpreter to the world, his emotional compass and often his first critic. What made her strength even more extraordinary was that she carried it all while dealing with her own health challenges. Through his deafness, surgeries, rejections and creative intensity, she remained unwavering. Her resilience gave him the freedom to pursue his art without distraction, and her quiet discipline held the family together. Ours was a house shaped as much by her dignity as by his genius. Without her, he may never have become who he was—and we, in turn, may never have found the grounding we now cherish.

In my view, his legacy must stand as a reminder to future generations that strife, disability, or hardship are not restraints for those who carry the courage to dream and the conviction to act. He showed us—through every chapter of his life—that it is possible to break through limitations, not by denying them, but by transcending them with grace, discipline and fire. He was, at heart, a true polymath—fearless, unbounded, led not by trends or schools or validation, but by what his spirit and heart demanded of him.

He lived not in silence, but in shape and shade—and with every brushstroke, he carved a life into art. Nothing would have pleased my father more than my ending this tribute with these words by Iqbal—words he lived, not just admired:

ख़ुदी को कर बुलंद इतना कि हर तक़दीर से पहले
ख़ुदा बन्दे से ख़ुद पूछे, बता तेरी रज़ा क्या है'

(Raise your selfhood to such heights
that even fate, before shaping your destiny,
must ask you what you desire.)
This is my father's legacy.
This is his brush with life.
And now, once again, it becomes yours.

New Delhi, August 2025

IMAGE CREDITS

1. My parents, Avtar Narain and Pushpa Gujral. Courtesy of Satish Gujral Archives, Gujral Foundation
2. At the Mayo School, Lahore, 1940. Courtesy of Satish Gujral Archives, Gujral Foundation
3. Gujral House at Pari Darwaza, Jhelum. Courtesy of Satish Gujral Archives, Gujral Foundation
4. My family in Jhelum, 1935. Standing: my father and Inder; seated: my mother and me; on the ground: my sister Uma. Courtesy of Satish Gujral Archives, Gujral Foundation
5. *Portrait of My Father*, 1957, oil on canvas. Courtesy of Naresh Gujral Collection
6. With my sisters, Niti and Uma. Courtesy of Satish Gujral Archives, Gujral Foundation
7. *Glory*, 1954, acrylic on board. Courtesy of Mohit and Feroze Gujral Collection
8. *Self-Portrait*, 1956, oil on board. Courtesy of Mohit and Feroze Gujral Collection

9. *Pilgrim*, 1953, acrylic on canvas. Courtesy of Satish Gujral Archives, Gujral Foundation
10. *Mourning En Masse*, 1952, casein on cardboard. Courtesy of Mohit and Feroze Gujral Collection
11. *Untitled*, 1952, oil on masonite board. Courtesy of Mohit and Feroze Gujral Collection
12. *Self-Portrait*, 1954, oil on hardboard. Courtesy of the National Gallery of Modern Art, New Delhi
13. In Mexico at an exhibition, 1954. Courtesy of Satish Gujral Archives, Gujral Foundation
14. In Mexico. Courtesy of Satish Gujral Archives, Gujral Foundation
15. Kiran at my show in New York. Courtesy of Satish Gujral Archives, Gujral Foundation
16. *Untitled*, 1960, mixed media on canvas. Courtesy of Mohit and Feroze Gujral Collection
17. *Adam and Eve*, 1960, mixed media on canvas. Courtesy of Mohit and Feroze Gujral Collection
18. Frida Kahlo painting. Archival image
19. With Diego Rivera, Mexico City, 1954. Courtesy of Satish Gujral Archives, Gujral Foundation
20. With Frida Kahlo, Mexico City, 1954. Courtesy of Satish Gujral Archives, Gujral Foundation
21. At Frida Kahlo's funeral—Diego Rivera (right) carrying the coffin, 1954. Courtesy of Satish Gujral Archives, Gujral Foundation
22. In Mexico, in front of my artwork. Archival Image
23. With Kiran at a show in Paris. Courtesy of Satish Gujral Archives, Gujral Foundation
24. Kiran with Shrimati Indira Gandhi at our wedding reception, 1957. Courtesy of Satish Gujral Archives, Gujral Foundation
25. Kiran with Pandit Nehru and me at our wedding reception. Courtesy of Satish Gujral Archives, Gujral Foundation

26. With my extended family and friends, 1958. Courtesy of Satish Gujral Archives, Gujral Foundation
27. With Kiran and her ceramics at Tilak Marg. Courtesy of Satish Gujral Archives, Gujral Foundation
28. With Pandit Nehru at the inspection of the portrait of Sardar Patelji. Courtesy of Satish Gujral Archives, Gujral Foundation
29. *Portrait of Nehru*, 1957. Courtesy of Mohit and Feroze Gujral Collection
30. With Shrimati Indira Gandhi, in front of her portrait. Courtesy of Satish Gujral Archives, Gujral Foundation
31. *Portrait of Indira Gandhi*, 1957. Private collection
32. Kiran at Tilak Marg with her ceramics. Courtesy of Satish Gujral Archives, Gujral Foundation
33. Kiran's ceramic installation at our home in New Delhi. Courtesy of Satish Gujral Archives, Gujral Foundation
34. Received the Lalit Kala Akademi award in 1956. Courtesy of Satish Gujral Archives, Gujral Foundation
35. Mural at the Punjab Agricultural University campus in Ludhiana, Punjab. Courtesy of Satish Gujral Archives, Gujral Foundation
36. *Untitled*, 1971, oil on canvas. Courtesy of Mohit and Feroze Gujral Collection
37. *Untitled*, 1971, paper collage. Courtesy of Mohit and Feroze Gujral Collection
38. With Kiran. Courtesy of Satish Gujral Archives, Gujral Foundation
39. With Inder in front of our father's portrait. Courtesy of Satish Gujral Archives, Gujral Foundation
40. Receiving the Padma Vibhushan from the honourable President, Shri K.R. Narayanan, in 1999. Courtesy of Satish Gujral Archives, Gujral Foundation
41. With Shri Krishan Kant, former Vice-President of India. Courtesy of Satish Gujral Archives, Gujral Foundation

42. With Dr Karan Singh. Courtesy of Satish Gujral Archives, Gujral Foundation
43. With Maharani Gayatri Devi at my show. Courtesy of Satish Gujral Archives, Gujral Foundation
44. With Her Excellency, Queen Elizabeth II, on her visit to Delhi, 1997. Courtesy of Satish Gujral Archives, Gujral Foundation
45. With Shrimati Sheila Dikshit, former chief minister of Delhi. Courtesy of Satish Gujral Archives, Gujral Foundation
46. With the honourable President, Shri K.R. Narayanan, 1997. Courtesy of Satish Gujral Archives, Gujral Foundation
47. Receiving the Lalit Kala Ratna Puraskar from the honourable President, Dr A.P.J. Abdul Kalam in 2004. Courtesy of Satish Gujral Archives, Gujral Foundation
48. At the Belgian Ambassador's residence, New Delhi. Courtesy of Satish Gujral Archives, Gujral Foundation
49. With Kiran, receiving the Order of the Crown from Prince Albert of Belgium, 1983. Courtesy of Satish Gujral Archives, Gujral Foundation
50. Central Stupa of the Ambedkar Sthal at Lucknow, Uttar Pradesh. Courtesy of Satish Gujral Archives, Gujral Foundation
51. Chancery at the Belgian Embassy, New Delhi 1980–84. Courtesy of Satish Gujral Archives, Gujral Foundation
52. The Al-Moughtara Farm in Riyadh, 2001. Courtesy of Satish Gujral Archives, Gujral Foundation
53. L–R: Pravina Mehta, Aditya Prakash, me, B.V. Doshi, Raj Rewal and Achyut Kanvinde. Courtesy of Charles Correa Foundation
54. L–R: Inder Gujral, Indrani with Ram, me, M.F. Hussain and Charles Fabri. Courtesy of Satish Gujral Archives, Gujral Foundation
55. With Charles Correa. Courtesy of Charles Correa Foundation
56. With Mohit. Courtesy of Satish Gujral Archives, Gujral Foundation

About the Author

Satish Gujral (1925–2020) was a pioneering Indian artist whose work spanned painting, sculpture, and architecture. His practice bridged disciplines and explored the texture of lived experience. He received the Padma Vibhushan in 1999.